Radicals in Australian Social Work:
Stories of Lifelong Activism

RADICALS IN AUSTRALIAN SOCIAL WORK:

STORIES OF LIFELONG ACTIVISM

Edited by

Carolyn Noble, Bob Pease and Jim Ife

Connor Court Publishing

Connor Court Publishing Pty Ltd

PO Box 7257
Redlands Bay Qld 4165
sales@connorcourt.com
www.connorcourt.com

ISBN: 9781925501711 (pbk.)

Cover design by Maria Giordano

Printed in Australia

CONTENTS

ACKNOWLEDGEMENT OF
TRADITIONAL LAND OWNERS

As white editors, we acknowledge the Aboriginal and Torres Strait Islander peoples, the First Australians, whose lands, winds and waters we all now share, and pay respect to their unique values, and their continuing and enduring cultures which deepen and enrich the life of our nation and communities. We pay our respects to the Elders past, present and emerging, for they hold the memories, the traditions, the culture and hopes of Aboriginal and Torres Strait Islander peoples across the nation. We commit to acknowledge and understand the historical and contemporary disadvantage experienced by Aboriginal and Torres Strait Islander peoples and other Indigenous peoples of the world and the implications of this for radical and critical social work practice.

CONTRIBUTORS

Mick Adams is a Senior Research Fellow in Australian Indigenous Health at Edith Cowan University. He is a respected Elder in the Aboriginal and Torres Strait Islander communities and a descendent of the Yadhiagana/Wuthathi peoples of Cape York Peninsula in Queensland and the Gurindji people of Central Western Northern Territory with extended family relationship with the people of the Torres Straits, Warlpiri (Yuendumu), and East Arnhem Land (Gurrumaru) communities. He is recognised and credited as one of the leading Aboriginal researchers on male health. He completed an Associate Diploma of Social Work in 1976 and graduated with a Bachelor of Social Work in 1995, Bachelor Applied Science 1997, Master of Arts 2001. His PhD research was published as *Men's Business: A Study into Aboriginal and Torres Strait Islander Men's Sexual and Reproductive Health.* His second book *My Journey through the Academic Mist* provides an insight into the trials and tribulations of academia.

Elder Jean Boladeras is a Balardong Nyungar woman from South Western Australia. She has a large family and is a great-grandmother to five. Jean has a Master's Degree in Indigenous Research and Development from Curtin University, and a BA from Murdoch University. Before retiring in 2009, Jean was a Lecturer in the Honours Program at the Centre for Aboriginal Studies at Curtin. In 2013, Jean was awarded the NAIDOC WA Senior Female of the Year. She was appointed as Mentor Support and Elder for the National Empowerment Project in 2014. Over many years, Jean has served on various committees, both Government and Community ventures, and is currently an active member of her local Aboriginal Community organisation, and a Director on the Board of Marr Mooditj Aboriginal Training College.

Jacques Boulet has studied, worked and lived in five continents, starting in his native Flemish Belgium, becoming a social worker in 1965. After three years of voluntary work in Africa, he obtained a Post Graduate Diploma in Community Development and Social Planning and started to teach in Social Work and community development in (West) Germany throughout the 1970s. From 1980 until 1985, he studied at the University of Michigan (US), graduating with an MSW and PhD (Social Work and Sociology). From 1985 until 1996, he was Senior Lecturer and Associate Professor at Melbourne and RMIT Universities, leaving academia in 1996 to help start several community initiatives, including the Borderlands Cooperative (learning and research/consultancy centre, in which he was involved with over 100 projects); and the accredited Graduate School, OASES. He is the Editor of the journal, *New Community*.

Linda Briskman is Professor of Social Work at Western Sydney University. She is a passionate advocate for Indigenous rights and asylum seeker rights and conducts research and publishes extensively in both areas. Linda is increasingly writing on the topic of emerging Islamophobia in Australia. Her latest book is *Social Work with Indigenous Communities: A Human Rights Approach* (Federation Press 2014). Linda's work on the social work initiated People's Inquiry into Detention, resulted in the Australian Human Rights Commission award for literature (non-fiction) in 2008 for the publication *Human Rights Overboard: Seeking Asylum in Australia* (with Susie Latham and Chris Goddard). In the same year, Linda was awarded the Eileen Younghusband Award of the International Association of Schools of Social Work. Ongoing advocacy includes as co-convenor of the Voices Against Bigotry Network and Social Workers Without Borders. She is also a regular media commentator and opinion piece writer.

Peter Camilleri was educated at University of Sydney in social work during the dynamic Whitlam period in which he focused on community development. He then worked in Tasmania as researcher on the evaluation of the Australian Assistance Plan and later for the then Department of Social Security on community projects. He moved to the UK and worked in a psychiatric hospital and completed a master's program in research methods. Returning to Tasmania, he worked in child and adolescent mental health. With a stint in the Northern Territory working in rehabilitation, he began an academic career. He completed a PhD through Flinders University, whilst working at the University of South Australia. He then moved to James Cook University and then Australian Catholic University where he became Professor of Social Work and Campus Dean. Peter was Professor of Social Work at Australian Catholic University where he held a variety of roles and recently finished at University of Wollongong Shoalhaven Campus.

Moira Carmody graduated from UNSW in 1976. Her early social work career involved working with adults and children with an intellectual disability, hospital patients and sexual assault survivors. She subsequently worked in a senior position in the NSW Health Commission, and then as a TAFE welfare teacher. In 1997 she became a university lecturer and subsequently Professor of gender and sexuality research at Western Sydney University. Since that time, her research has focussed on finding alternative approaches to preventing sexual violence against women and children. She has advised both state and federal governments on policy reform in this area and developed national standards for sexual assault education and designed sexual assault prevention programs for community and universities sectors. She has published widely intentionally on sexual assault prevention. Her most recent book *Sex & Ethics and Young People* was published in 2015 by Palgrave

Macmillan New York. She retired from fulltime university life in June 2016 and continues to work privately developing and running violence prevention training, providing social work supervision and critical reflection groups.

Bill De Maria graduated from the University of New South Wales in 1970 and was the first social planner in New South Wales, when he joined the Special Projects Team in the Town Planning Department at Bankstown Council. He was then the Director of Social Planning for the Riverina Council for Social Development under the Australian Assistance Plan. He joined the School of Social Work at the University of Queensland in 1978. He completed his Masters of Social Work there in 1980 and his PhD in 1988. He has an extensive national and international publishing record. His book, *Deadly Disclosures: Whistleblowing and the Ethical Meltdown in Australia* was published to wide acclaim in 1999. He was a member of the Commonwealth Administrative Appeals Tribunal from 1983-1993. He resumed his academic career in the University of Queensland Business School where he won acclaim for his work on African corruption, whistleblowing, and government corruption. He parted with UQ in 2012 and now operates a Belted Galloway stud.

Jo Dillon has taught for 35 years in social work in a number of Australian universities and most recently developed and taught new online units in community development for the Masters of International Community Development at Deakin University. Jo maintains her sense of outrage at increasing social injustice and remains passionate about social work as social change and education for social transformation as the core business of social work education. Her commitment to eco-feminism and treading lightly on the earth has seen her recently develop her interest in permaculture and organic gardening and she now spends the majority of her time on her small property in Tasmania and in working with her local community on projects focussed on social and environmental sustainability.

Christine Fejo-King is an Aboriginal woman from the Northern Territory and is an Elder of her clan and of social work in Australia. She is the Chairperson of the National Coalition of Aboriginal and Torres Strait Islander Social Workers Association (NCATSISWA), Foundation Fellow of the Australian College of Social Work and has written, edited and co-edited a number of books that focus on Aboriginal social work nationally and internationally, including her PhD thesis: Let's Talk Kinship: Innovating Australian Social Work Education, Theory, Research and Practice through Aboriginal Knowledge. She has been a social worker for over thirty years, during that time she has worked with the Australian Commonwealth, State and Territory Governments: in child protection, juvenile justice and in policy development, Aboriginal Mental Health and Social and Emotional Well-Being, Aged Care, Substance Abuse, Suicide Prevention and Palliative Care programs and as reviewer for all National Reconciliation Action Plans.

Jim Ife has been involved in social work education since the 1970s, and is currently Professor of Social Work at Western Sydney University. He was formerly Professor of Social Work and Social Policy at The University of Western Australia and at Curtin University, and was inaugural Handa Professor of Human Rights Education at Curtin from 2003 until 2006. He is Emeritus Professor at Curtin and has held honorary positions at Deakin University, Victoria University and The University of Queensland. He has been active in various community organisations concerned with human rights and social justice, including a period as President of Amnesty International Australia, and as Secretary of the Human Rights

Commission of the International Federation of Social Workers. He is the author of many articles and book chapters, and four books: *Community Development* (1995, 6th ed. 2016), *Rethinking Social Work* (1997), *Human Rights and Social Work* (2000, 3rd ed. 2013) and *Human Rights from Below* (2010). A fifth book, *Reimagining Social Work,* is in press at the time of writing.

Jude Irwin is Professor Emerita of Social Work and Social Justice in the Faculty of Education and Social Work at the University of Sydney. Jude worked at the University of Sydney for over three decades and her teaching, research, practice and policy interests span a number of areas including violence against women, children and young people, discrimination against gay men and lesbians, professional practice supervision, community development and learning in practice settings. Jude was a founding member and past Director of the Australian Centre for Lesbian and Gay Research.

Mary Lane was educated as a social worker and her involvement in community activism began in the 1960s. From 1974 through to 1982, she was employed as a community development worker in western Sydney. In 1983, she joined the staff of the Social Work Department at The University of Sydney, where her primary focus was community work and peace and conflict studies. Her research, particularly the documentation and analysis of community practice, has been widely published nationally and internationally. Mary's background includes terms on the National Women's Advisory Council and the Family Law Council of Australia. In 2012 the University of Sydney awarded her an Honorary Doctorate of Letters in Social Work.

Sharon Moore has been an activist and critical social worker since the 1970s. Contributing to Marxist Welfare education, working for the establishment of antisexist and antiracist practice theory and developing a curriculum informed by economic, social and political systems theory were part of her early experience. Appointment as a social planner/ action researcher employed by the Western Regional Council of Social Development in Melbourne was an early career highlight. Her inaugural leadership of the Carers Movement in Victoria and nationally also contributed to the establishment of the International Carers Movement promoting a political advocacy view of community care. She worked for a decade teaching critical management theory and social sustainability in MBA education for RMIT, and Western Sydney University as a Professor of Management. She returned to social work education in 2012 and joined Australian College of Applied Psychology in 2014 working on international development and community activism.

Carolyn Noble is Foundation Professor and Associate Dean (Social Work) at Australian College of Applied Psychology, as well as Professor Emerita at Victoria University, Melbourne. She has been an academic since 1984, and mental health and child protection practitioner before that in Sydney and London. She has taught and developed undergraduate and postgraduate programs in social work, counselling and psychotherapy, social science, mental health and professional supervision. She is active in Australian, Asia Pacific and International Schools of Social Work Associations and has held executive positions in each of these organisations. Her research interests include social work philosophy and ethics, work-based learning and professional supervision and theory and practice development in social work. Further areas of research include gender democracy and equal employment opportunity for women in higher education and human services. She has published widely in her areas of research and continues to present her work nationally and internationally. She is editor-in-chief of IASSW social dialogue online magazine www.socialdialogue.online

Bob Pease began teaching in social work education in the 1980s and until recently was Professor of Social Work at the University of Tasmania. He is currently Adjunct Professor in the Institute for the Study of Social Change at the University of Tasmania and Honorary Professor in the School of Humanities and Social Sciences at Deakin University. He has been involved in profeminist politics with men for many years, was a founding member of Men Against Sexual Assault in Melbourne and continues to be involved in community education and campaigns against men's violence against women. He has published extensively on masculinity politics and critical social work practice, including four books as single author and twelve books as co-editor, as well as numerous book chapters and journal articles. His most recent books are: *The Politics of Recognition and Social Justice: Transforming Subjectivities and New Forms of Resistance* (co-editor, Routledge 2014), *Doing Critical Social Work* (co-editor, Allen and Unwin, 2016), *Men, Masculinities and Disaster* (co-editor, Routledge 2016) and *Critical Ethics of Care in Social Work* (co-editor, Routledge, 2017).

Stuart Rees practised as a social worker in the UK, with the Department of Attorney General in British Columbia, in the War on Poverty programmes in the USA and with Save the Children in Sri Lanka. He has taught in universities in the UK, Canada and the USA. From 1978-2000 he was Professor of Social Work and Social Policy at the University of Sydney, inaugural Director of that university's Centre for Peace and Conflict Studies and, in 1997, the founder of the Sydney Peace Foundation. His books include *Achieving Power, Beyond the Market, The Human Costs of Managerialism, Passion for Peace* and three anthologies of poetry. His recent and widely acclaimed novel *A Lover's Country* tells the story of the Palestinian tragedy and identifies the courage required to insist on Palestinians' human rights in order to achieve peace with justice for all the Palestinian peoples and, by the same means, security for Israelis.

Ros Thorpe qualified as a social worker in the UK in 1967. Although her course was essentially conservative, she delved into critical sociology and became involved with neighbourhood community work. In her career, she has practised and researched in family and child welfare; worked in social work education in UK and Australian Universities, taught critical approaches in community work, women and welfare, family and child welfare, values and ethics; published several books, including *Murri Way, Aborigines and Torres Strait Islanders Reconstruct Social Welfare Practice.* and, for 30 years, has been part of a peer support and social action group called *Critical Edge*. In her retirement, she is engaged in empowerment community social work with the Family Inclusion Network Queensland in Townsville.

John Tomlinson studied Social Work at the University of Queensland. He has an honours degree in Anthropology and Sociology and a research Masters degree in Social Work involving community work with the Indigenous community of South Brisbane. His PhD dealt with the political obstacles to the introduction of a guaranteed minimum income in Australia. He has been a community and social work practitioner academic, writer and poet, and between 1987-1993 he was Director of the ACT Council of Social Service. His last paid employment was as Senior Lecturer in Community Work and Social Policy at the Queensland University of Technology 1993-2006.

Wendy Weeks became involved in the women's movement in Canada, where she lived and worked during the 1970s. Her involvement with women's services and organisations continued after her return to Australia in 1982. Wendy was previously Head of Social Work at RMIT University and later an Associate Professor of Social Work at the University of Melbourne. She has written many articles and research reports on women's services, women's issues and social policy. She is author of *Women Working Together: Lessons from Feminist Women's Services* (Longman 1994), co-author of *Making Social Policy in Australia* (Allen and Unwin 1996) and co-editor of *Issues Facing Australian Families: Human Services Respond* (Addison Wesley 1991, Longman 1995, Pearson Education 2000). She died in 2004.

PREFACE

Carolyn Noble

This genesis of this book emerged when Jim and I were together at the Asia-Pacific Schools of Social Work (APASWE) Regional Conference in beautiful Bangkok, Thailand in 2015 on a bus and on our way to the conference dinner. Listening to the many speakers and feeling somewhat disillusioned with the level of scholarship over the preceding days and uninspired with the conservative agenda of research and practice, I turned to Jim and said: "Where have all the good ideas, passionate speakers indeed the 'call to arms' gone from these conferences"? Move forward to the bi-annual International Association of Schools of Social Work (IASSW) global conference this time in Seoul, South Korea in 2016 we again found ourselves sitting together this time in the big auditorium sharing the same disillusionment about the state of social work politics and practice and its lack of a radical lens. I found myself reminding him of another shared experience in 1988, in Sweden, where many attendees were inspired by the tenacity of the Swedish social workers who boycotted the IASSW conference and withdrew their membership for accepting presentations from the South African schools. This was also time when Victor Frankl upset many with his stories of survival, saying if you had the will to live then you were more likely to survive. In Vienna, the same year I, along with Lena Dominelli, managed to have a Women's chair with voting rights established on the male dominated IASSW Board. In 1990, remembering when I was with Bob at the international social work conferences in Buenos Aires, Argentina and then Lima, Peru that the radical critique from our Latin American colleges positively lifted the roof with their idealism and Marxist critique. Social work was going to play a part in confronting capitalism, the imperialist West and inequality and rising levels of poverty and we were doing to do it through Freire's education as the practice of freedom and a return to a radical social work. In 2000 Jim's address at IASSW Montreal, Canada reminded us that human rights were paramount to a radical practice.

Since then, there has been many years of conference attendance where the talk was nowhere near as inspiring as those early days. Notwithstanding the occasional attendance by Ian Ferguson with his radical agenda! In 2004, as president of Australian Association of Social Work and Welfare Education (AASWWE), I was involved in co-hosting the IASSW conference in Adelaide, Australia where an attempt to present a radical and multicultural conference did achieve that inspiration to fight for a better, more inclusive world; but the enthusiasm was not captured in the following conferences. My disillusionment stemmed from the perception that each conference started as a blank page. It was as if there was no history or continuation of ideas that linked past struggles with current debates and there were no themes that linked our national and international colleagues together, despite the biannual meetings across the globe! Equally there were less and less activist voices appearing at these conferences; where were they? And how could they be captured if found?

In reflecting on this dilemma Jim and I reminded ourselves that Australian social work has a lineage of activism and campaigns, policy challenges and changes, and social movement success. Concentrating on human rights for women, migrants, Aboriginal and Torres Strait Islander peoples, this success has been captured and debated in several seminal books on radical social work by many of our contemporaries. But what was missing were the personal stories of the decades of activism that forged the way for a radical social work practice. Thinking of the many colleagues we knew who were long-term activists, we wondered about such things as; what was their motivation for sustaining a life-long activist practice? What were the obstacles, successes they encountered and the "maybe do it differently" reflections? And if they were to use their radical lens, how would they frame, explain and reflect on their years of crusading for social action?

Further questions emerged. Would individual stories frame a collective picture of our radical practice activities? Can we see a collective story in each individual's reflection? The answer to these questions would emerge if we asked our colleagues to write their stories of their activism. We were hatching a plan. Not only did Jim and I have a 40 plus year career behind us, we knew many of our colleagues who would be interested in preserving our activist past and would join us in the endeavour. We also felt there was an urgency to capture their stories, as retirement and withdrawal from their active practice was a likelihood given our age. We were also aware that we had already lost some inspirational colleagues too early.

Bob who likewise had attended many of the same international conferences and shared the disillusionment we described earlier welcomed the idea of a book of activist stories. In talking with him about this project, he quickly saw the value of gathering together stories from long term radical social workers. His authorship of critical social work books and earlier history of its radical past made him an ideal colleague to join with Jim and me to help make this project happen. An editorial team was formed.

In selecting contributors, we had in mind to cover as much of our radical past as we could from colleagues we knew, especially those colleagues that had been active in Australian social work for four decades or more. Stories of success and failures and attempts to change the status quo and develop a radical practice and research by policy and practice initiatives was our focus. Stories that attempted to shift the power from white Anglo men to women, from conservative to more progressive politics and enhance the welfare state project of protecting the most vulnerable people, especially Aboriginal and Torres Strait peoples, people with disabilities and refugees and people seeking asylum were key to our search. Activism to save the planet and nature from 'man-made' ecological destruction would also inform our search. We wanted to gather as many of these individuals who were a part of that story to give these events a personal voice. The stories would use a critical autobiographical approach.

We were ready. The book had its editors and its focus; we made a list of possible contributors and with abstracts that described the content, a publisher was engaged to help record these stories in print for future generations of social workers. Inspired by Bob's enthusiasm to make the project come alive and progress from our original idea, to production and finally fruition, we present a collection of radical stories from some of social work's ''elders' who were key to our radical past and, we would argue, its future success. These are the stories I was looking for.

Hooray and enjoy!

1

INTRODUCTION:

The Changing Socio-Political Context and Theoretical Frames of Radical Social Work in Australia

Bob Pease

The contributions to this book are from people who were involved, as academics, practitioners or both, in the radical and progressive movements in Australian social work. The book covers various time periods from the 1970s to the present day. Much of the activism described in the book focuses on the period of the 1970s to the 1990s as a foundational time for the development and consolidation of a more radical social and political agenda for social work, as it began to break away from its conservative and colonial heritage. However, the book also charts how contributors have weathered the challenges to social work's more progressive approach since 2000, as a conservative social and political agenda was re-established following this period of rapid social change. The aim of this introductory chapter is not to provide a detailed history of radical social work. Rather, it is to locate the emergence of radical social work in the changing social and political context in Australia and to outline the key theoretical debates at the time to situate the stories that make up the book.

Setting the stage: Whitlam, social movements and the Australian Assistance Plan

We locate the early radical social work movement in Australia in the context of the optimism of the Whitlam period which brought significant changes to welfare during three tumultuous years of government. Prior to 1970, the Liberal/National Party coalition had been in government for over twenty years. Many social policy writers have commented how during this time, the Australian welfare state was based on a residual system with narrowly targeted programs for specific population groups. With the election of the Whitlam Government in 1972, under the campaign slogan 'It's Time', there was a radical departure from this residual framing of welfare towards a more universalist approach to the delivery of social services. As many of our contributors note, this was a time of optimism and hope for social workers, community workers and others in the human services.

Most notable during this time was the introduction of the Australian Assistance Plan (AAP) which aimed to facilitate greater participation in decision making at the community and regional level. With an emphasis on social planning, bottom up policy formulation and community development, it provided the context in which innovative approaches to welfare were developed. Such projects challenged the dominant medical and psycho-social paradigms of social work that prevailed until that time.

The AAP developed in the context of new social movements arising in Australian society: the opposition to the Vietnam War, struggles for Indigenous rights, the women's movement and the gay liberation movement, student rebellion, the social wage campaigns and green bans in the trade union movement, environmental activism and the peace movement. Radical social work of the 1970s shared many of the aims, philosophy and social action strat-

2

egies characteristic of these social protest movements. The social worker as agitator was an important aspect of radical practice.[1]

There was only a short-lived period of radical reform within the government, as the blocking of supply in the budget by the Liberal opposition and concerns about overseas debt led to a constitutional crisis, which further led to the sacking of the Whitlam Government by the then Governor General in November 1975. Notwithstanding the anger and rage of large sectors of the population, a more conservative Government led by Malcolm Fraser was elected to office following the dismissal.

The emergence of radical social work in the 1970s

Within this governmental context of Whitlam and Fraser, the seventies saw the rise of what is now called the 'radical social work' movement. This movement was initially influenced by a Marxist critique of social work and welfare, primarily from the United Kingdom[2] but also from North America[3] and Australia.[4]

There were numerous dimensions to the radical critique of social work. However, the major elements of it were that: (i) social work is a social control mechanism that 'cools out' clients and keeps them submissive (ii) social work is a professional elitist activity that is more concerned with its own self-interest than with meeting client needs (iii) social work values foster conformity to middle-class

---

[1] C. Noble, 'Social Work, Collective Action and Social Movements'. In L. Dominelli (ed.) *Revitalising Communities in a Globalising World* (Ashgate, 2008).

[2] R. Bailey & M. Brake (eds.) *Radical Social Work* (Edward Arnold, 1975), P. Corrigan and P. Leonard, *Social Work Practice Under Capitalism: A Marxist Approach* (Macmillan Press, 1978).

[3] J. Galper, *The Politics of Social Services* (Prentice Hall, 1975), M. Moreau, 'A Structural Approach to Social Work Practice', *Canadian Journal of Social Work Education* (1979), 5(1), 78-94.

[4] H. Throssell, (ed.) *Social Work: Radical Essays* (University of Queensland Press, 1975), J. Tomlinson, *Is Band-aid Social Work Enough?*, (The Wobbly Press, 1977).

norms (iv) social work individualises and pathologises problems that are social and political in character and (v) social work operates in a theoretical vacuum, as it lacks an adequate knowledge base.[5]

It seemed at first that this radical critique had little to offer social workers who were 'caught up' in social agencies doing social work. The fact that there was little defence against the radical critique indicated some degree of sympathy from inside social work. However, what could social workers do about it?; there were still clients with immediate needs. The radical critique did not sweep away human misery. The critique was said to be too abstract, having little connection with the immediate problems of practice. In the words of one commentator from that time: "It's alright for you to talk.[6]

However, in response to this charge, some academics and practitioners in the 1970s attempted to develop approaches to radical practice in social work. Some of these approaches emphasised the role of social workers as moral witnesses who could document the failure of society to implement the ideals it already asserted in law or social policy.[7] Radical social workers could also challenge the standards of society by showing that they are irrelevant or have hurtful social consequences. They could aim to change oppressive social institutions and redefine social norms. Some radical social workers at the time talked about a new breed of profession; a profession more attuned to the strivings of the poor and alienated, and more able to influence social policy. Social workers could become institutional subversives and aim to bring about basic institutional reform. [8]

---

[5] J. Galper, op. cit., P. Corrigan and P. Leonard, op. cit. and J. Tomlinson, op. cit.

[6] S. Cohen, 'It's Alright for You to Talk: Social Work and Manifestos for Action'. In R. Bailey and R. Brake (eds.) *Radical Social Work* (Edward Arnold, 1975).

[7] M. Ryan, 'Social Work in Search of a Radical Profession'. In. M. Ryan, *Social Policy: Issues of Choice and Change* (Random House, 1970).

[8] A. Mendelson, 'The Case for Reform: The Emergence of a New Professionalism'. In. W. Richan & A. Mendelson (eds.) *Social Work: The Unloved Profession* (New Viewpoints, 1973).

Many of the models for radical practice in the 1970s emphasised the importance of adopting an educational role in relation to clients. Social workers could contribute to the development in clients of a critical consciousness of their oppression and of their potential with others to combat this oppression.[9] In this regard, Paulo Freire's writings on pedagogies for educating oppressed people in Latin America were very influential for many radical social workers.[10] Thus, in these models, the job of the front-line worker was to impart political consciousness to his or her clients. These early attempts to develop models for radical practice generated a range of different political responses from within the left.

Some radical critics argued that a radical practice in social work is impossible, if the structure of capitalist society continues to define the role of social workers. They emphasised the 'logic of place' which refers to the determining influence that the place one occupies in a social structure has on one's practice. For Skenridge and Lennie, for example, social work's place is as an ideological apparatus of the state. It reproduces domination-subordination relations through the worker-client relationship. Thus, the scope of social work is limited by social relations which are determined by the structure of the state. In this view, although the consciousness of social workers may become transformed, it is impossible for them to enact social change because of their position within the structure.[11]

In response to this structurally determinist view, other radical social work writers at the time argued that social work both reproduces and undermines class society. For example, Bolger et al. argued that all welfare state structures contain a series of contradic-

---

[9] R. Bailey & R. Brake, 'Introduction'. In R. Baily and R. Brake, op. cit., P. Leonard, 'Towards a Paradigm for Radical Practice'. In ibid.

[10] P. Freire, *Pedagogy of the Oppressed* (Continuum, 1970).

[11] P. Skenridge and I. Lennie, 'Social Work: The Wolf in Sheep's Clothing' (1978), *Arena*, No. 51, 47-91.

5

tions. These contradictions arise from the struggle between working people and monopoly capital.[12] In this view, the state does not simply reproduce the social relationships necessary for the interests of capital. Rather, the state is seen as an arena of class conflict, where struggles within and around the state take place. Thus, the structures of the state will reflect the balance of class forces at any point in time. It is these contradictions within the state that provide the potential for a radical practice. It is acknowledged that there are social forces that social workers cannot control. In contrast to earlier attempts to construct a radical practice, not everything is possible. However, in opposition to the structural determinist view, some specific forms of progressive practice are possible at specific times.

In this dialectical view of the state, social workers are positioned in a struggle against opposing sets of class forces and they are engaged in a continuous struggle against dominant definitions of the social world. Social workers are of and against the system because the state is not merely an institution; it is also a form of social relations.[13] As well as the potential to work on the contradictions within social work itself, there is also the potential for radicals to step outside the professional social work role.

At the organisational level, Inside Welfare, a group of socialist welfare workers, was formed in 1975 in Brisbane. They published a booklet of working papers, organised a conference on a Marxist critique of the Henderson Poverty Commission Report and produced an annotated bibliography of Marxist welfare literature.[14]

---

[12] S. Bolger, P. Corrigan, J. Docking & Nick Frost, *Towards Socialist Welfare Work: Working in the State* (Macmillan, 1981).

[13] An important publication at this time that theorised the state as a form of social relations was The London-Edinburgh Weekend Return Group, *In and Against the State* (Pluto Press, 1981).

[14] See Inside Welfare, *Working Papers No. 1*, (Inside Welfare, 1975), Inside Welfare, *First National Conference Proceedings* (Inside Welfare, 1976) and Inside Welfare, *An Annotated Bibliography for Marxist Welfare Workers* (Inside Welfare, 1979).

This was also the time when there was a breakaway group from the Australian Association of Social Workers, who formed the Australian Social Welfare Union (ASWU) to promote unionisation in contrast to professionalism in the welfare sector. The ASWU as a separate union dissolved in the late 1970s and the membership was incorporated into the Australian Services Union.

Hawke, Keating and new developments in radical social work in the 1980s and 1990s

The Hawke-Keating Labor governments (1983-1996) provided the back drop to the 1980s and the 1990s. The Hawke and Keating era heralded the experiment with corporatism and The Accord which facilitated new partnerships between Government, business, welfare groups and unions.[15] There was a renewed hopefulness in the welfare sector in the early stages of the Hawke government, after seven years of the Fraser Liberal Government and cuts to welfare. However, the Hawke consensus approach moved away from social democratic reform to a more corporatist approach to welfare. It was during this time, that neoliberalism and economic rationalism emerged and established dominance in Australian society. As the nineties wore on, Australian society was becoming more conservative, notwithstanding Labor governments in power until 1996. These changes in Australian society reflected wider global changes in the United States with Ronald Reagan's Presidency and with Margaret Thatcher's rule as Prime Minister in the United Kingdom.

In response to the perceived limitations of the Marxist critique at the time, feminism had a significant influence on social work during the 1980s. Key feminist texts from the UK[16] and North

---

[15] R. Mishra in *The Welfare State in Crisis* (Wheatsheaf Books, 1984) provided a detailed argument in favour of corporatism at the time.

[16] E. Brook and A. David, *Women, the Family and Social Work* (Tavistock, 1985), J. Hanmer & D. Statham, *Women and Social Work: Towards a Woman Centred Practice* (Macmillan, 1988), L. Dominelli & E. McCloud, *Feminist Social Work* (Macmillan, 1989).

America[17] heralded important feminist texts here.[18] Women in Welfare Education was formed in 1982 as part of the Australian Association of Social Work and Welfare Education.[19]

During the 1990s, postmodernism and poststructuralism began to influence radical social work. With Jan Fook, I co-edited one of the first books to explore what postmodern critical theory might offer a progressive social work practice.[20] As noted elsewhere, postmodern ideas were controversial in radical and critical social work because they could be used to support conservative policies and practices, obscure the material reality of oppression, and undermine the commitment to social justice and human rights by rejecting metanarratives.[21] There is an ongoing debate among radical and critical theorists in social work about the value of postmodern and post-structural ideas for progressive practice in the human services and these debates are considered by some of the contributors.

It was also during the 1990s that Green theory started to shape radical and critical forms of social work. The Australian Greens political party flourished and there was an increasing awareness among progressive social workers of the importance of ecological and environmental perspectives in promoting social change.

This was also a period which heralded the replacement of USA

---

[17] N. van Den Bergh & L. Cooper (eds.) *Feminist Visions for Social Work* (National Association of Social Workers, 1986); M. Bricker-Jenkins and N. Hooyman (eds.) *Not for Women Only: Social Work Practice for a Feminist Future* (National Association of Social Workers, 1986),

[18] H. Marchant & B. Wearing (eds.) *Gender Reclaimed: Women in Social Work* (Hale & Iremonger, 1986; J. Taylor, *Giving Women Voice: Feminism and Women's Services* (Brotherhood of St. Laurence, 1990).

[19] W. Weeks, 'Women: Developing Feminist Practice in Women's Services'. In J. Allan, B. Pease and L. Briskman (eds.) *Critical Social Work* (Allen and Unwin, 2003).

[20] B. Pease & J. Fook (eds.) *Transforming Social Work Practice: Postmodern, Critical Perspectives* (Allen & Unwin, 1999).

[21] B. Pease, 'A History of Critical and Radical Social Work'. In M. Gray & S. Webb (eds.) *The New Politics of Social Work* (Macmillan, 2013).

and UK conceptual social work frameworks with Australian perspectives. It was a time of challenge to the appointment of North American and UK social work professors in Australian universities and the widespread uncritical incorporation of American and UK social work text books in Australian social work courses.[22] Australian social work writings at this time also challenged the inappropriate imposition of North American and UK social work frameworks in non-Western countries. This marked the beginnings of anti-colonialist social work practice.[23]

These three decades marked a time of both debate and struggle within social work. The early Marxist critique of social work and feminist, postmodern, environmentalist and anti-colonialist debates that followed about the limitations and potential to develop a radical social work practice within the state became a focus of discussion within the profession. The proponents of the progressive critique saw themselves as radical academics and practitioners committed to lifelong activism for social change, human rights and social justice.

In this book, we follow these debates about radical and critical social work from the Whitlam years, through the context of the dismantling of reforms in the Fraser period, the corporatism of the 1980s under Hawke and later Keating and the rise of neoliberalism under Howard up until the most recent changes in government. These broader socio-political shifts provide the backdrop to the in-

[22] Beyond the Australian texts already cited, see also R. Thorpe & J. Petruchenia (eds.) *Social Change and Social Welfare Practice* (Hale & Iremonger, 1990); R. Batten, W. Weeks & J. Wilson (eds.) *Issues Facing Australian Families: Human Services Respond* (Longman Cheshire, 1991); J. Fook, *Radical Casework: A Theory of Practice* (Allen and Unwin, 1993); J. Ife, *Rethinking Social Work: Towards Critical Practice* (Longman, 1997).
[23] For an earlier Australian anti-colonialist critique, see W. Healy, J. Rimmer and J. Ife 'Cultural Imperialism and Social Work Education in Australia'. In R. Bereen, D. Grace and T. Vinson (eds.) *Advances in Social Work Education* (University of New South Wales, 1986).

9

dividual stories of activism and resistance enacted by radicals in social work who challenged the wider profession to live up to its espoused ideals of social justice and human rights.

Roadmap to the collection

The stories of activism begin with Ros Thorpe's account of her early experiences of radical social work in the UK and then, following her migration to Australia, her experiences at Sydney University in the late 1970s, where with colleagues she developed a radical social work curriculum. She later discusses her involvement with Aborigines and Torres Strait Islanders to reconstruct social welfare practice at James Cook University in the 1980s and her involvement with *Critical Edge,* a peer support and social action group. Since her retirement in 2010, she has established a service users' community organisation to encourage critical practice outside of the constraints of mainstream human service organisations.

In Chapter 3 Jacques Boulet reflects upon his early experiences in Belgium in the 1960s and later his community experiences in Africa in the context of critiques of international development. His education in neo-Marxism, psychoanalytic thinking and Critical Theory, provided a grounding to his integrative and trans-disciplinary approach to social work, community development and participatory action research. Disillusioned with universities, he left academia in 1997 to create alternative institutions, with the Borderlands Cooperative, the *New Community Quarterly* journal and the OASES Graduate School. He documents his attempts to reconstruct relational social systems to address the continuing crises of the global political-economy and their human ecological consequences.

Peter Camilleri in Chapter 4 locates his social work practice and social work academic journey through radical social work in the 1970s and beyond in the context of the Whitlam Government, and the Australian Assistance Plan which radically changed the discourse of community engagement through participatory democracy and community development. These developments provided a backdrop to his experience of grappling with the changing concepts in social work and how through his writings during this period, the contradictions and challenges at a personal level unfolded.

Jo Dillon charts her journey as an academic engaged in the teaching and practice of critical social work in Chapter 5. From discovering Marx and Freire in the late 1970s, through the personal and professional dilemmas posed by feminism and the diversion into corporatist welfare through the eighties, to the challenges posed by the neoliberal agenda into the nineties and beyond, she suggests that Social Work has lost its activist voice and sold its soul. In moving from a structural understanding of power to the more individualised understanding and notions of critical self reflection, she says that social work as a profession forfeited engagement with social justice agendas, and in the process lost much of its connection with emerging social movements.

In Chapter 6 Bill De Maria chronicles an audacious, but ultimately defeated effort to achieve a radical practice presence in the orthodox curriculum in the School of Social Work at the University of Queensland. He describes how, eventually, the subversive core of a brave pedagogic idea was too much for the conservative temperament reigning in a School of Social Work at that time. What is essentially a cautionary tale, is pitched at the next generation of social work students who upon graduation will have to figure out where they stand in the struggle against oppression in all its forms.

Jim Ife in Chapter 7 describes how he has been interested in Green politics and alternative Green philosophies since he first read *The Limits to Growth* in 1973. This convinced him that Western 'civilisation' was unsustainable and was living on borrowed time. He outlines how he became involved in the formation of The Greens (Western Australia) between 1989 and 1990, and in thinking about the truly radical alternatives that green political theory implied. He discusses his collaboration with politically engaged physical scientists in organising 'Pathways to the Future' conferences for senior high school students. He also outlines the ways that he sought to make sense of a Green analysis in social work and social policy, at a time when such ideas were seen as 'left field' and extreme.

In Chapter 8 Stuart Rees discusses his involvement in an alliance formed to oppose the powerful medical lobby in 1984 and 1985 who were insisting that even people with serious illness or injuries should only be treated if they were privately insured. Defend and Extend Medicare consisted of members of the Maritime Union of Australia (the MUA), nurses, a representative of the Doctors Reform Society (DRS) and himself as Professor Social Work at Sydney University. He outlines how radical social work perspectives influenced his motives and the success of the Defend Medicare campaign.

Carolyn Noble in Chapter 9 uses a feminist lens to take a retrospective and reflective view of her 'discovery' of feminism in the 1980s and how this lens provided a useful epistemology to review the issue of women and social work, especially women in leadership roles over the last 30 years. She explores through her beginning mental health practice and as a social work academic, what achievements and misadventures were encountered and addressed in trying to stay true to feminist principles. She concludes by exploring how social work today in the context of neoliberal / masculinist politics can mount new challenges as part of a broader emancipatory, social justice paradigm.

In Chapter 10, in this previously published chapter, Wendy Weeks charts her personal and political journey through social work, from being a student and practitioner in Melbourne in the

1960s, through her time in Canada in the 1970s, her involvement in social work education at Phillip Institute and later RMIT in the 1980s and to her final position at the University of Melbourne in the 1990s. She takes us through her discovery of feminism and her awakening to critical social theory. She reflects upon her early attempts to integrate feminist content throughout the social work curriculum and discusses her commitment to community development and community cooperation, with the ongoing support and mentorship of women in her life.

Moira Carmody in Chapter 11 reflects on her experiences of the political struggles to gain recognition of the needs of women and children affected by sexual violence and challenging the attitudes and behaviour that continue to result in sexual violence. She locates this discussion within a diversity of settings in which she has worked, including a hospital sexual assault service, a state health bureaucracy, the academy and within non-government organisations. She considers how this work has been strongly influenced by a critical social work perspective and how her approach has been strongly shaped by postmodern critiques of power and sexual ethics which has provided new hope in terms of preventing violence against women.

In Chapter 12 I chart the pathways to my involvement in profeminist practice with men, from the 1970s through to current times. I explore the impact of feminism on my theoretical understandings and practices and my involvement in anti-sexist men's groups. My postgraduate work led me into researching the pathways by which men became profeminist and how their politics were positioned in relation to feminism and the women's movement. While being situated as an academic in social work education for over 35 years, I discuss my involvement in activist politics throughout that time in relation to profeminist practice with men in promoting gender equality and prevention of men's violence against women.

Jude Irwin in Chapter 13 outlines the development of the gay and lesbian rights movement in the context of the social protest movements of the 1970s and the early radical social work movement. She describes how gay men and lesbians joined together to protest their second-class citizenship and fight for equality with heterosexuals. In the chapter, she focuses on the challenges that have confronted activists as they fought against the many forms of exclusion experienced by lesbians and gay men and as they struggled to understand the complex and multilayered causes and processes of inequality and oppression.

In Chapter 14 Christine Fejo-King discusses the context of social injustice and human rights violations perpetrated against Aboriginal and Torres Strait Islander individuals, families and communities. As an Aboriginal woman, who is an Elder of her clan and as an Elder of the social work profession in Australia, she reflects upon and critiques what is happening today with regard to two major issues that impacted on, and continue to impact on Aboriginal individuals, families and communities: the 'Royal Commission into Aboriginal Deaths in Custody' (1987-1991) and the 'Bringing Them Home Report' about the 'Stolen Children' (1997). She asks: "Has anyone been listening; have we learned nothing; and how do we move beyond this point?"

In the following chapter, Elders Mick Adams and Jean Boladeras point out how social work theories and practices are based on the principles of Western non-Indigenous principles and ideas. Consequently, social workers did not recognise or reference Aboriginal and Torres Strait Islander ways of knowing, being and doing within their scope of practice. In this chapter, the authors outline the ways in which, in Aboriginal and Torres Strait Islander's societies, the role of the Elders is paramount. They illustrate how they are respected for their narrative historical value, where testimonies about the Dreaming and daily community life help others to understand the practical aspects of life and society and how in telling the stories, the Elders make sense of people's everyday lives.

In her chapter, Linda Briskman reflects upon her early involvement as a rural social worker in country Victoria. While she knew something was wrong, particularly with social work practice with Aboriginal people, a critical and radical lexicon was not apparent to her at the time. This chapter narrates her journey from a practitioner struggling with complicity, bureaucracy and a modicum of subversion in the Aboriginal sphere. She describes how through critical social work, she was able to analyse the processes that shaped social work practice of the time. After traversing the murky field of practice, she examines how these early beginnings created an ardent social work activist and what lessons might arise from this for aspiring critical social workers of the present and future.

In Chapter 17, Mary Lane reflects upon her journey as a community development practitioner, researcher and teacher in the second half of the 20th century. She identifies contextual and theoretical influences, including the values and activism associated with the social movements of the 1960s and 1970s and the later impact of postmodern challenges to universalist blueprints for change. A particular focus for the telling of her story is the challenge for community development of the adage 'act local, think global'. The usefulness of this catchcry as a tool for analysis and evaluation is explored, keeping in mind critiques of localist work as well as those of 'global' explanations.

John Tomlinson in Chapter 18 describes how after graduating from the University of Queensland, he worked in Brisbane, where his clients were mainly single mothers, unemployed or homeless people. Later, after transferring to Darwin, many of the people he worked with were of Aboriginal descent. In the chapter, he charts how he became disillusioned by the bureaucratic obstructionism placed in the way of genuine improvements in the way people were treated. This was the background to his life-long determination to work towards ending poverty, homelessness, violence against vulnerable people, exploitation, war, racism, and alienation.

In the final chapter, Sharon Moore reflects upon her involvement in alternative professional groups such as the Australian Social Welfare Union, Women in Welfare Education and Inside Welfare. She outlines how the critique of charity models and the encouragement of client perspectives challenged traditional social work. She also considers the impact of Marxism and feminism, on her development as a radical social worker in the period and her participation in The Australian Carers' Movement and the People Together Movement.

This book has provided an opportunity for people who were actively engaged in radical and critical social work from the 1970s to tell their stories and to reflect on their achievements and struggles to promote progressive change in social work in Australia. In documenting these experiences, the book provides an important resource for students and practitioners about a critically important part of their professional and educational heritage. The book also outlines a platform of change strategies that can be useful for re-imaging a radical agenda, as social work responds to the impending environmental challenges facing future generations.

2

ACTION FOR SOCIAL JUSTICE –

Then and Now: A Memoir

Ros Thorpe

In this chapter I flesh out the changing contexts for my career as a 'radical' in social work, and especially the challenges and opportunities which in different eras affected the extent to which a more radical practice was – and is still – possible. I close with some reflections on the existential angst which is an inevitable constant companion in doing what is now known as critical social work for social justice.

My first thirty-two years in the United Kingdom (1945-1977)

I grew up in a family with a background in the east end of London and was well acquainted with the social issues stemming from poverty. My family's values flowed from a mixture of nonconformist religious beliefs and humanitarian political allegiances, with a commitment on my mother's side to both the cooperative movement and feminist ideals.

This family background influenced my involvement in oppositional politics while still at school in the early 1960s (for example, 'ban the bomb' marches), my decision to study the social sciences at university (1963-1966), and my subsequent choice of social work as a career. My values in support of progressive change for greater social justice stimulated my interest in exploring critical sociology

17

and, in turn, this exposed me to emerging structural analyses from the Community Development Projects in the United Kingdom.[1]

My social work education (1966-1967) was generic but I chose to specialise in family casework with a strong commitment to working supportively and preventively with families in order to keep their children out of the state care system. After two years practice in a well-regarded Children's Department, I returned to university, first as a research assistant on a social deprivation project,[2] and then as a PhD student (1970-1974) where I focused on the long term foster child's sense of identity, interviewing over 100 foster children and almost half of their natural parents. Looking back, I realise that this latter experience was the most powerful in my whole career, as I was exposed in depth to the chronic enduring sorrow of parents who have lost their children into care.[3] Thus, from early in my career, my radical commitments focussed at personal as well as political levels – a Radical Humanist position.[4]

During this time (1970-1977) *Case Con* – a revolutionary magazine for social workers[5] – appeared in the United Kingdom and its analyses of the state's controlling intervention into families were foundational for my career-long commitment to working in empowering ways with families. Thus, in 1974 I first established a support group for parents with children in care.[6] This group was criticised at a conference presentation I gave by some traditional social work-

[1] Community Development Project, *The National Community Development Project: Inter-Project Report, 1973*. (The Project, 1974).

[2] R. Holman, *Socially Deprived Families in Britain*. (National Council of Social Service, 1970).

[3] R. Thorpe, 'Mum and Mrs So-and-So' (1974), *Social Work Today* 4(22).

[4] D. Howe (1987), *An Introduction to Social Work Theory: Making Sense in Practice*. (Routledge, 1987).

[5] J. Weinstein, 'Case Con and Radical Social Work in the 1970s: The Impatient Revolutionaries.' In M. Lavalette (ed), *Radical Social Work Today: Social Work at the Crossroads*. (Policy Press, 2011).

[6] J. Gibbs and R. Thorpe, 'The Natural Parent Group' (1975) *Social Work Today* 6(13), 386-389.

ers for eschewing a directly therapeutic focus on parents' personal pathology. Instead, informed by my PhD research, I had used what later became known as strengths and empowerment approaches, supporting parents to navigate the child welfare system and claim a right to have continued contact with their child/ren in care and the possibility of reunification back home. Moreover, I found that working together with parents to challenge their powerlessness had in fact produced some 'therapeutic outcomes'. When parents began to feel respected and valued, some set about making changes in their families' lives. Looking back, I see this as 'radical' practice, in that parents were uplifted by a focus on their strengths in contrast to being ground down by child protection's more usual deficit focus.

The 1974 group was my initial first-hand experience of the value of more radical forms of social work, with a focus, not only on both the personal and the political, but also consciously breaking down the power imbalance between myself as a professional and fellow citizens on the receiving end of professional services.

I was thus heartened to find endorsement for my approach in the publication in 1975 of *Radical Social Work*,[7] and to learn about other ways of practising to counter oppression and facilitate empowerment of socially deprived fellow citizens. I was, however, naively flattered when a Professor of Sociology at Nottingham University took an interest in my work and I willingly lent him copies of *Case Con*, only to be mortified when he published a strident functionalist critique of emerging 'radical' theories in social work leading to political action. Conversely, at the same time, other sociologists in his department were fiercely critical of social work's primary attention to individual pain and urged social work to focus more closely on issues of structural injustice which give rise to much individual pain. Clearly the mid-1970s were a time of ferment in social theorising.

[7] R. Bailey and M. Brake eds., *Radical Social Work* (Edward Arnold, 1975).

My Sydney years (1978-1984)

In 1978, I migrated from the United Kingdom to Australia and a lectureship at Sydney University, where social work students had recently boycotted lectures for a term, protesting the conservatism of their course curriculum. In a history of social work education at Sydney University, Horsburgh[8] provides a negative view of this student activism, claiming it harmed the course for many years. This was certainly not my impression on arrival in May 1978. I was employed to teach community work to fourth year students and I was impressed with the depth and sophistication of the knowledge and wisdom they had gained from their experience the previous year in their boycott campaign.

As a consequence of this, I joined with colleagues, led by the newly appointed Professor Stuart Rees, to develop a radical social work curriculum in tune with students' demands. In support of this course redevelopment, two colleagues and I made a ground-breaking presentation at a social work educators' conference in Tasmania in 1985.[9] Subsequently, Judith Petruchenia (later Jude Irwin) and I edited three books on radical practice: (1) in community work; (2) across the social welfare field: and (3) with women experiencing violence.[10] [11] [12]

The first and third of these books were well received and my

---

[8] M. Horsburgh and University of Sydney, Faculty of Education and Social Work, *Doing Good Well: Social Work Education at the University of Sydney, 1940-2010.* (Faculty of Education and Social Work, University of Sydney, 2010).

[9] H. Marchant, J. Petruchenia and R. Thorpe (1985), 'A Radical Curriculum: Processes, Dilemmas and Directions'. *Issues in Social Work Education* 5(2), 103-116.

[10] R. Thorpe and J. Petruchenia (eds.), *Community Work or Social Change? An Australian Perspective.* (London: Routledge and Kegan Paul, 1985).

[11] J. Petruchenia and R. Thorpe, *Social Change and Social Welfare Practice.* (Hale and Iremonger, 1990).

[12] R. Thorpe and J. Irwin (1996), *Women and Violence: Working for Change.* (Hale and Iremonger, 1996).

chapter on community work and ideology[13] in the first has been – and is still – used in social work education across the country, while my chapter in the third on women, domestic violence and child abuse[14] has influenced many in this torrid area of practice where 'mother blaming' is rife. Although the second book is less well read, I personally consider the Introduction[15] is worth a second look, and the chapter by Jen Harrison[16] is of great value in stimulating critically reflexive practice.

Overall the publications with Jude Irwin were considered a great advance for women's scholarship in social work and our nurturing of practitioners to write about their practice for publication was, in our minds, a form of 'action for social justice'. This building of knowledge and capacity in others was something central throughout my career and over thirty years I encouraged and supported more than 40 students (mainly women) to enrol in research degrees and write for publication. This, I saw not simply as an integral part of practice as an academic but it was a means *to grow from the ground up our local Australian community of scholars in social work – and among them a few radical activists.*

One Sydney University curriculum innovation which I consider a valuable focus in the final year of a social work course, was the subject called *Resources and Constraints in Different Fields of Social Work*. If educators are to help students transition into the workforce with critical, counter oppressive values intact and operational

---

[13] R. Thorpe, 'Community Work and Ideology'. In R Thorpe and J Petruchenia, *Community Work or Social Change?* (Routledge and Kegan Paul, 1985) 11-27.

[14] R. Thorpe, 'High Expectations, Low Resources: Mothering, Violence and Child Abuse'. In R. Thorpe and J. Irwin, *Women and Violence: Working for Change* (Hale and Iremonger, 1996).

[15] R. Thorpe and J. Petruchenia, 'Introduction'. In J. Petruchenia and R. Thorpe, eds. *Social Change and Social Welfare Practice*. (Hale and Iremonger, 1990), 1-17.

[16] J. Harrison (1990), 'Confessions of a Competent Hoop Jumper: Becoming Aware of unconscious Conservative Values'. In J. Petruchenia and R. Thorpe, eds., *Social Change and Social Welfare Practice* (Hale and Iremonger, 1990), 114-125.

in practice, then there is a need to study in some depth the resources and constraints for and against this in different practice contexts, and the ways to work to optimise the expression of critical practice. Far too often I have seen students graduate with strong progressive values yet after only 6 months in a job become 'organisational functionaries' who seem oblivious to breaching the professional Code of Social Work Ethics[17] and practise in disempowering ways with 'clients', whom they come to see, not as fellow citizens but as the undeserving 'other'. A recent book edited by Bob Pease and colleagues would make an excellent text for a present-day version of this subject.[18]

Contrary to Horsburgh's view, I regard the Sydney University's social work students' strike of 1977 in positive terms not only as an action learning process in community work but also for its curriculum outcomes and the emergence of a collegial environment for students and staff to work together in power sharing ways. This latter outcome brought collective ways of working into the academy and gave students an alternative experience to the increasingly hierarchical bureaucratic human services which they were about to enter. First-hand experience of more 'radical' ways of operating is, in my view, fundamental to students being able to practise in similar ways in their careers.

There were, however, critics of the radical curriculum, most notably the then president of the Sydney University Students' Association, Tony Abbott who, decades later, became Prime Minister of Australia for a brief period. He wrote a strident piece published in *The Bulletin*,[19] alleging Marxist influences on the Sydney University social work course and criticising "the involvement of so-

---

[17] AASW (2010), *Code of Ethics.* Canberra: Australian Association of Social Workers.
[18] B. Pease, S. Goldingay, N. Hoskin and S. Nipperess eds., *Doing Critical Social Work: Transformative Practices for Social Justice* (Allen and Unwin, 2016).
[19] T. Abbott, 'Warfare Over Social Welfare' (1981), *The Bulletin.* 7 April, 34-40.

cial workers in overtly political activities such as holding protest meetings, defending homosexuals, promoting feminist views of domestic violence, and recommending the redistribution of private wealth". By contrast, he referred favourably to social workers who performed clearly defined casework or charity-type roles in hospitals and emergency relief.[20]

While Abbott's article posed a temporary challenge to the radical curriculum we were developing at Sydney University, we continued undeterred. A more difficult challenge awaited me when I moved to James Cook University (JCU) in 1985.

My North Queensland years (1985-2017)

I had barely arrived at JCU in Townsville in February 1985 when I was told I was seen by some as a dangerous Marxist, largely on account of the Tony Abbott 1981 *The Bulletin* article. By contrast, a year or so later someone else described me as 'a gentle feminist' rather than the pesky stereotype which, in my first year or so at JCU, had led to everything I did or said being perceived by some social work education colleagues as unacceptably 'revolutionary'.

Fortunately, there was a small group of progressive-minded colleagues teaching in the community welfare course. Welcoming my arrival in a senior position, we worked together to nudge the JCU curriculum in more progressive directions. One early initiative was to introduce a *Women and Welfare* elective into the undergraduate courses and a Women's Studies subject into the Master of Social Work (MSW) course. These subjects aroused opposition but we had a small 'l' liberal Head of Department who truly thought students should be exposed to a range of different world views. This leeway enabled me to decide to stay at JCU and I resolved to persevere with more progressive initiatives.

---

[20] P. Mendes, 'Public Attacks on Social Work in Australia: The Two Bulletin Affairs'. *Australian Social Work* (2001) 54(3), 55-62.

Thus, following the introduction of women's studies in social work and community welfare, I was able to use my position, as Dean of the Faculty of Arts to establish a Women's Studies Centre in the early 1990s. This Centre survived for over two decades and its work continues to this day, even though the title 'Centre' was lost in a recent round of university re-structuring.

Looking back, I regard these Women's Studies developments over several decades as one of my achievements as a 'radical' within an often hostile academy. Other colleagues have continued to carry the mantle for Women's Studies at JCU, despite setbacks which seem to have escalated with increasing managerialism in the University.

As an academic, part of my role was/is to do research and this provided an opportunity to explore areas of social deprivation where there had been little previous research. With Robyn Lynn, we obtained Australian Research Council funding in 1993 for a project to explore Aboriginal and Torres Strait Islander approaches to social welfare practice. With Aboriginal and Torres Strait Islander research assistants, we produced a ground breaking book, *Murri Way!*.[21] Aboriginal researchers have since developed and refined the *Murri Way!* findings and there are now emerging Australian Aboriginal and Torres Strait Islander culturally appropriate models for social work practice. Moreover, the inclusion of Indigenous Australian perspectives is now a required element in Australian social work. But the groundwork was laid during the 1990s, and I am told that *Murri Way!* made a significant contribution to this process.

During my last decade before retirement, I initiated a small study which has informed my transition into retirement from 'radical' academic to 'radical' practitioner. In first semester 2006, I su-

---

[21] R. Lynn, R. Thorpe and D. Miles, *Murri Way! Aborigines and Torres Strait Islanders Reconstruct Social Welfare Practice.* (1998), Centre for Social and Welfare Research, James Cook University.

pervised two third year students on a placement designed to explore the feasibility of involving social welfare service users, and carers of service users, in the social work and community welfare educational programs at JCU. The impetus for this project was a commitment to participation as a key aspect of promoting social justice,[22] coupled with awareness that, apart from community work, service user involvement is rare to non-existent in Australian social work education and practice. The aims of the Project were: (1) to enable service users and carers to have an influence on the content of the Bachelor of Community Welfare (BCW) and Bachelor of Social Work (BSW) degrees at JCU; (2) to ensure graduates were well informed about the experiences, needs and preferences of service users; and (3) to stimulate in future graduates an enduring commitment to facilitate service user participation in the human services.

The project led to a commitment within social work at JCU to have service user representation on the Advisory Committee, and a patchy commitment to include services users and carers in teaching programs. Involvement of service users in broader aspects of the course, including curriculum design and assessment, has not yet happened. Nor has greater service user participation occurred in local human service organisations. This less than full commitment to participation by academics, professionals, and HSO managers has led me to realise that bottom up pressure for participation from service user community organisations may be necessary for greater progress to be made. Accordingly, this has informed my retirement project, which I will outline shortly.

Meanwhile, in the context of increasing managerialism in universities, one achievement against the odds was my ability, while Professor and Head of the School of Social Work and Community Welfare (1966-2000), to build, maintain, and sustain a collegial

---

[22] R. Adams, *Empowerment, Participation, and Social Work* (Palgrave MacMillan, 2008).

culture within the school – an enclave of participatory democracy, while all around us the university was becoming increasingly hierarchical and a far less rewarding workplace for academics. In his book, *Whackademia,* Richard Hil[23] pays tribute to our work in the social work school at JCU as very different from what was happening at most other Australian universities. I see this as affirmation of the possibility of continuing to apply a vision of more progressive ways of practising despite an increasingly hostile environment. What is necessary, in my view, is vision, passion, commitment, an ability to reliably meet organisational goals while using different means, and the courage to speak out on the side of humanitarianism when the wider organisation is becoming ever more controlling. It helped that by this time I was a Professor so didn't need to worry about promotion, but even before I was a Professor, I had gained respect within the academy for acting with integrity, despite at times 'rocking the boat', and by 'delivering the goods'. Overall, I see sustaining a collegial culture as a 'pre-figurative' piece of radical practice, pioneering in our small part of the world the processes we would like to see in a transformed social order.[24]

One other highly valuable way to sustain a critical vision in a hostile environment, is the support to be gained from caucusing[25] with like-minded people. From 1988 until the present day I have been part of a small informal group in Townsville called *Critical Edge.* We meet monthly, often over dinner, and discuss the challenges in our workplaces and how we can maintain our 'critical edge' and act with professional and radical integrity, rather than succumbing to organisational edicts which are oppressive to those

[23] R. Hil, *Whackademia! An Insider's Account of The Troubled University.* Sydney, New South Publishing, 2012).

[24] S. Rowbotham, 'The Women's Movement and Organizing for Socialism'. In S. Rowbotham, L. Segal and H. Wainwright, *Beyond the Fragments: Feminism and the Making of Socialism.* (Merlin Press, 1979).

[25] B. Mullaly, *New Structural Social Work.* (Oxford University Press, 2006).

on the receiving end. For anyone wanting to maintain a critical approach to social work in the present day, I think that it is vital to draw together your own *Critical Edge* group and together nurture each other to sustain your collective vision and passion through everyday challenges.

Throughout my time at JCU, I had always remained involved with initiating and facilitating empowerment groups in the community for parents with children in care.[26] As I approached retirement at the end of 2010, I became dismayed by the way new graduates were less and less able to do empowering social work in the human services and I resolved to devote part of my retirement to demonstrating how 'critical' practice could be done, to provide social work students with a placement experience of critical practice, and to stimulate them to develop an ongoing commitment to critical practice, despite the constraints of their future employment. I also wanted to work with disempowered fellow citizens to claim a voice and achieve greater service user participation.

Providing a role model of critical practice (2008-present)

Following the creation of the Queensland Department of Child Safety in 2004, Jane Thomson and I (together with Karyn Walsh in Brisbane) approached the new Minister for Child Safety, Mike Reynolds. We requested funding to undertake exploratory research into how the new Department could better work with children's parents and families, and in late 2005 we received a grant which enabled us to run a number of focus groups in North Queensland and Brisbane with parents, grandparents, non-government organisation (NGO) workers, and Child Safety officers. We named the research team the Family Inclusion Network (FIN) and un-

---

[26] J. Thomson and R. Thorpe (2004), 'Powerful Partnerships in Social Work: Group Work with Parents of Children in Care'. *Australian Social Work.* 57(1), 46-56.

der this name a research report was launched in November 2007[27] at roundtable discussions in Brisbane. Inspired by these developments, several parents, supportive professionals, and I began meeting in Townsville in 2008 to form the self-funded Family Inclusion Network Queensland (Townsville) to: (1) assist parents, grandparents and significant others who are involved in the child protection system to achieve contact and, wherever possible, reunification home to family, community and culture; and (2) to add volume and credibility to families' voices in social advocacy. In 2010 FIN Townsville became incorporated as a community organisation and in 2011 registered as a charity in Queensland. Since then FIN Townsville has become a demonstration project working *with* parents and families at both personal and political/structural levels and in 2017 FIN Townsville has achieved national registration as a charity with the ACNC, and tax deductibility status with the Australian Tax Office.

Support volunteers in FIN Townsville are *Resourceful Friends,*[28] who offer information, individual and family crisis support, empowerment group support, advocacy, support for self-advocacy, and practical help. Additionally, as co-workers with families, we engage in fundraising and fun activities; we are co-creators of social work theory and we undertake systems advocacy by writing submissions, lobbying, creating educational DVDs and undertaking research for social change.

Importantly, in FIN Townsville, we also understand loss as experienced by all parents with children in care, and the trauma resulting from a sense of powerlessness and feeling judged when Child Safety

---

[27] Family Inclusion Network [M. Cary, C. Klease, J. Thomson, R. Thorpe and K. Walsh], *Family Inclusion in Child Protection Practice. Creating Hope: Recreating Families. Working with Parents to Ensure the Safety and Well-being of Children and Young People in the Queensland Child Protection System.* (Family Inclusion Network, 2007).

[28] B. Holman, *Resourceful Friends: Skills in Community Social Work.* (The Children's Society, 1983).

intervenes. We therefore have developed a model of working which synthesises Bob Holman's community social work, with Judith Herman's model of *Trauma and Recovery*,[29] and Judy Atkinson's *We Al Li* model for healing generational trauma for Aboriginal Australians.[30]

As of now, the FIN model of work follows a three stage trauma-informed community development process:

- **Forming Relationships in a Safe and Stable environment**. Being *with* and *alongside* parents and grandparents. Creating healing, empowering spaces.
- **Facilitating Remembrance and Mourning**: telling our stories; being heard and believed; working with anger, frustration, depression, and chronic sorrow; facilitating healing, hope, personal growth;.
- **Making Connections, claiming a voice**, and **taking action for change** – personally and (for some) collectively.

We have found in FIN Townsville that, as Herman asserts, activism is both a means for achieving social change and also, in itself, an additional powerful therapeutic tool, which can strengthen healing through the experience of dignity and a positive identity, and enhance empowerment.

As a self-funded community organisation which works *with* parents and families, FIN Townsville has some freedom to speak out without punitive repercussions (like funding cuts). It does, however, hear negative comments from some NGO workers – like, 'FIN rocks the boat' and 'no one who's been involved with FIN

[29] J. Herman, *Trauma and Recovery: The Aftermath of Violence from Domestic Abuse to Political Terror.* (Basic Books, 1997).
[30] J. Atkinson, *We Al Li: Healing Generational Trauma for Aboriginal Australians.* (We Al-li Pty. Ltd, 2012). http://fwtdp.org.au/wp-content/uploads/2013/08/Judy-Atkinson-Healing-From-Generational-Trauma-Workbook.pdf accessed 21/04/2017.

will get a job with us'. Of greater concern is the manipulative (mis) use of power by Child Safety Officers who sometimes advise parents 'things will work out better for you if you don't get involved with FIN', when experience shows us otherwise.

On the bright side though, in 2015 FIN parents were invited to work in partnership with Child Safety to create a DVD about good practice with parents and families under the new Practice Framework, *Strengthening Families, Protecting Children.*[31]

Other positive outcomes which FIN Townsville can report are:

- Effects on Practice, Programs, Policy
  - Greater justice in some individual cases
  - Some influence on the principles in the new practice framework
  - Invitations to join Advisory committees and/or to make presentations
  - Co-creation of social work theory.[32]

- Effects on many parents and grandparents themselves
  - Increased confidence, improved self-esteem, improved sense of hope, a greater sense of agency
  - Ability to help others
  - Motivation to pursue further personal growth, and take up 'new careers'
  - A greater sense of social injustice, leading to further activism.

---

[31] Department of Communities, Child Safety and Disability Services (2015), *Strengthening Families Protecting Children.* Queensland Government (21 April 2017) https://www.communities.qld.gov.au/childsafety/child-safety-practice-manual/framework-for-practice-and-maps

[32] R. Thorpe and K. Ramsden, 'Resourceful Friends: An Invaluable Dimension in Family Inclusive Child Protection Practice' (2014) *Children Australia* 39(2), 65-73.

- Effects on *Resourceful Friends*
  - FIN has had a powerful effect on our own learning. It gives us a *Critical Edge* in relation to personal and professional growth
  - We maintain hopefulness through practising in the way FIN does
  - We engage in critical reflection through active peer supervision and professional development
  - FIN facilitates us engaging in grounded critical research
  - There are significant joint achievements and reciprocity, acknowledging the expertise of fellow citizens in their own lives
  - FIN dissolves artificial boundaries/barriers to allow genuine working *with* others.
- Effects on social work students doing placements with FIN Townsville

  Being involved with FIN brings you to the crux of what true social work is ... to work with people and not against them. Supporting family members as equals is the true essence of achieving human rights and social justice. (Jane, July 2013).

  The most rewarding thing about working with FIN is learning about letting go of one's power over people. I like the fact that in FIN professionals and volunteers work alongside parents as equals. (Kay, July 2013).

  FIN gave me exposure to true social work values, 'nothing about us without us', and wherever I may roam within this profession, I will always have a piece of FIN at the back of my mind for every future engagement that I have with a human being who is utilising a service that I am involved with. FIN has given me the opportunity to keep my radical dream alive. (Pat, Sept 2015).

Summary Reflections

While much of my action as a 'radical' social worker throughout my career was in the context of social work education and research, I always kept in touch with radical practice through my involvement with empowerment groups with parents with children in care. I did the best that I could as an academic despite the growing constraints within universities since the 1990s. However, only in my retirement, without the need to earn an income, do I feel able to act with social justice goals absolutely central in my practice.

There is a great sense of accomplishment at the end of my career to be able at last to facilitate not only empowerment for parents with children in care, but also to demonstrate what social work values undiluted by managerialist edicts can look like, and to enable students on placement to practice progressively and develop an ongoing commitment to critical practice.

Way back in 1978 Daphne Statham[33] observed wisely that a radical cannot stay employed in social work without daily 'conscience compromise'. Nonetheless, Carole Satyamurti[34] found that radicals employed by Social Service Departments in London were less dis-satisfied with their jobs than others since their analyses of state power meant they didn't expect to be able to work in counter oppressive ways. They saved their radicalism largely for after-

---

[33] D. Statham, *Radicals in Social Work*. Routledge & Kegan Paul, 1978).
[34] C. Satyamurti, *Occupational Survival: Case of the Local Authority Social Worker.* (Blackwell, 1981).

hours commitments, for example as with The London Edinburgh Weekend Group.[35]

In my view, new graduates need to be able to do a number of things to maintain their commitment to social justice.

- Caucusing – creating a *Critical Edge* peer support group in order to gain support and optimise the ability to work critically in your current practice context
- Out of hours involvements and commitments to promote social justice at individual and/or structural/political levels
- Living everyday life as closely as possible to your social justice principles.[36]

And, as older graduates,

- Using some of your long service leave and/or retirement to work for social justice. According to Edgar and Edgar,[37] the new middle age extends now until about age 75. This provides a splendid opportunity for retired social workers, with an adequate retirement income for their needs, to: (1) work in (possibly establish) self-funded community organisations free from the constraints of an employer; and (2) actually practise in radical/critical ways, achieving greater social justice at least in some ways, and providing role models for the next generation.

Above all, in my view, it is crucial to always maintain your vision, scrutinise your values, and reflect critically on how, almost

[35] Edinburgh Weekend Return Group, *In and Against the State,* 2nd ed. (Pluto Press, 1980).
[36] B. Jordan, S*ocial Work in an Unjust Society.* London: (Harvester Wheatsheaf, 1990); B. Mullaly, *New Structural Social Work.* (Oxford University Press, 2006).
[37] P. and D. Edgar, *Peak: Reinventing Middle Age.* (Text Publishing Company, 2017).

inevitably, at some time in your employment you may breach the Code of Ethics and/or your framework for critical practice. Nonetheless, hold faith. And finally, keep reading radical, structural, critical, counter oppressive social work literature – it's inspiring!!

3

WHEN WE TRIED TO
'MEET THE UNIVERSE HALF WAY':[1]*

An All-Too-Brief Revolution in Social Work Education, Research and Practice

Jacques Boulet

Early stirrings

Whilst I'm[2]** a later (1985) entrant into *Australian* critical social work (education), formative years during the early- to mid-sixties laid the groundwork for being swept up in the political and practical tectonic shifts tearing through Social Work professional praxis in the end-sixties and seventies. The political-activist core of this shift gradually became grounded in epistemological and ontological transformations, the shape and import of which continue(d) to disturb the shreds of the veil of certainties wrapped around my early childhood upbringing in post-war, wall-to-wall (and floor-to-ceiling) catholic Belgium.

---

[1] *After Karen Barad's *Meeting the Universe Halfway: Quantum Physics and the Entanglement of Matter and Meaning* (Duke University Press 2007).

[2] **I wanted to replace the 'I' – the first personal pronoun – with a 'normal' 'i', except at the start of a sentence and in quotes; I (i) have come to resist the capitalisation of the *'perpendicular pronoun'* in recognition of the rather pretentious and simply wrong cultural assumption in western writing about the centrality of the speaking, writing or thinking author/subject – or more generally, of the individual person – in the entirety of the living and changing context and the complexity of the interconnections s-he reports on. However, I (i) was advised that this would most likely encounter the resistance of the publisher; so, with the understanding and support of the editors, I (i) have reverted to the capitalisation habit but have been invited to insert this footnote as a suggestion and invitation to move towards a more realistic ontological positioning of academic authors.

In the five years before graduating as a social worker in 1965, I had witnessed and absorbed three massive contextual changes demonstrating the futility of the inward-looking petty-bourgeois attitude I had grown up with and into:

- the violent end of Belgian colonial power in the Congo in 1960 (a quite personal affair, an uncle and aunt having worked for 15 years in the colonial administration – their return trips to and from their three-years 'terms' true and teary extended family events[3]);

- Pope John XXIII's *'aggiornamento'* (*'bringing up-to-date'*) internal shake-up of the Catholic Church from the late-fifties onwards,[4] urging us young people to take possession of 'our' church and fill it with life, thus inspiring deep transformations in the voluntary community and welfare sector (again, very personal during and after 14 years of serving as an 'altar boy' and chorister in my local parish church and a 'leader' in the local youth group);

- and the 1964-5 demonstrations against the Vietnam War in Leuven, the university town where I lived and studied in the first half of the sixties, urging me into pacifism and my refusal to serve the still obligatory 18-months' military service.[5]

Studying social work in a tertiary institute run by the activist Catholic Workers' Movement did assist in holding all of these contextual changes together (the course was imbued with the *Young Christian Workers'* philosophy inspired by Joseph Cardijn's '*See*

---

[3] T. Turner, *The Congo Wars: Conflict, Myth and Reality (2nd Ed.)*. London: Zed Books; Vanthemsche, Guy (2012). *Belgium and the Congo, 1885–1980.* (Cambridge University Press, 2007).

[4] https://en.wikipedia.org/wiki/Pope_John_XXIII

[5] https://www.timetoast.com/timelines/the-vietnam-anti-war-movement

– *Judge – Act'* approach, an early version of Participatory Action Research.[6]) My two placements occurred at the formation centre of the International Building Companions ('IBO'), a volunteer organisation established after WWII as one attempt to house the 17 million refugees from countries 'behind' the *'Iron Curtain'* separating the 'communist' East from the 'capitalist' West of Europe. From the mid-fifties, the IBO was involved in *'aid to underdeveloped countries'* (as they were then still unashamedly called), including Congo.

During three years of voluntary work in the Congo (1966-9 – as the alternative to military service) I encountered, practised and lived *'community development'* as it had become *'de rigueur'* in international development circles across United Nations and major non-governmental agencies. The working principles of *'self-help'*, *'felt needs'*, *'local leadership'* and *'participation'* when attempting to bring the 'masses' in formerly colonised territories into a modicum of self-determined *'progress'* felt right, even if soon emerging critiques of the 'development' mantra progressively took their shine.[7] Nevertheless, deep experiences in community immersion and the baffling encounter with a still *relationally saturated culture* did their job, even if it then took me twenty years to understand what they *really* meant and what their import could be for our dominant (gradually post-) modern individualist and self-centred culture.[8]

---

[6] R. Mathews, *Of Labour and Liberty: Distributism in Victoria 1891 – 1966.* (Monash University Publishing, 2017) (p. 18); http://jedo.perthcatholic.org.au/wp-content/uploads/ 2014/04/20140415-Reflection-Action-See-Judge-Act-booklet.pdf

[7] M. Max-Neef, *From the Outside Looking in: Experiences in 'Barefoot Economics'.* (Dag Hammarskjøld Foundation, 1982); M. Waring, *Counting for Nothing: what men value and what women are worth.* (Allen & Unwin, 1988); T. Trainer, *Developed to Death – Rethinking Third World Development.* (Merlin Press, 1989). For a 1956 UN definition: http://unesdoc.unesco.org/images/0017/001797/ 179726eb.pdf

[8] P. Verhaeghe, *What About Me? The Struggle for Identity in a Market-Based Society.* (Scribe, 2014).

Wading into the theory-practice gap... on the way to 'half way'?

Returning from Africa and living and studying (1969-70) with 120 post-graduate students from 80 mostly 'developing' countries at the *Institute for Social Studies* in The Hague (Netherlands) certainly helped ground, deepen and widen my understanding of (community) development; it also introduced me to radical critiques informed by (neo-) Marxism, feminism and initial ecological reflections of the 'development' hubris I had been part of. Those were also the heady days of Paulo Freire's *'consciousness raising'*[9] entering development debates and practices, the early translations of his *Pedagogy of the Oppressed* and the work of Ivan Illich,[10] unmasking and questioning the national and increasingly global institutional structures and processes maintaining inequality, the power of elites, the maldistribution of resources and benefits of technological and material advancement.

Landing a lecturer job at the Caritas School of Social Work in Freiburg (Germany) in 1970 introduced me to the vagaries of tertiary education, pedagogy, theory-practice integration and critical content in 'contextual' subjects. My struggle entailed the development of meaningful ways to conceptualise and introduce *'practice methods'* to social work students and doing so in a way which *integrated* their theoretical underpinnings and practical applications, avoiding undue 'specialisation' and the recipe-sets of successively emerging *'practice models'* with their technical and prescriptive rigidities. The ripple-effects of the movements of '68 and after were strongly felt in contemporary social work discourses in Europe, generating a myriad of activist involvements in areas like homelessness and housing, corrections, welfare and social security, (mental) health (deinstitutionalisation!) and work with children,

---

[9] P. Freire, *Pedagogy of the Oppressed*. (Continuum, 1970).
[10] I. Illich, *Celebration of Awareness. A Call for Institutional Revolution*. (Penguin, 1973).

youth and 'outsider' or disadvantaged groups (including Gypsies, refugees and migrants from Latin America, the Balkans, Middle East and North Africa).

These early attempts in social work education and later in curriculum innovation got me entangled for good into critical social work praxis; for five years (1974-9), I was involved in the development of a pilot social work curriculum at the Polytechnic University of Kassel.[11] The hallmarks of this new curriculum included the sustained attempt at *theory-practice integration*, the examination of the fundamental connections between *'personal troubles'* and *'social issues'* (as Mills[12] explicated the connections between 'structural' and 'personal' dimensions of everyday social and personal life and change), and the *generic* approach to practice (rather than the specialist 'model' disciplined into the three traditional *'methods'*, specific *'client'* groups or *'social problems'* or the typical institutional configurations *'dealing with'* them i.e. 'health', 'education', 'welfare', 'employment', etc.).

Project-oriented learning[13] was the pedagogical approach to teaching/learning we introduced in the curriculum; *'experiencing'* their theoretical-practical studies, students (guided and accompanied by lecturers/instructors) worked and learned for 2½ of their 4 years' social work studies in the project of their interest; they were encouraged and supported to

* make the connection between theoretical approaches

---

[11] http://www.uni-kassel.de/fb01/institute/sozialwesen/40-jahre-sozialwesen.html; J. Boulet, & D. Oelschlägel 'The Function of Social Work/Social Welfare as Society's Answer to Social Problems' in: *Eurosocial Reports #8 Current Problems in Training for Social Welfare*. (European Centre for Social Welfare Training and Research, 1976, 15-22); J. Boulet, *Action-Theoretical Reflections for Social- and Community Intervention*. (Unpublished Doctoral Dissertation, The University of Michigan, 1985).

[12] C. Wright Mills *The Sociological Imagination* (Oxford University Press, 1959).

[13] https://en.wikipedia.org/wiki/Project-based_learning

to understanding the 'workings' of the (capitalist) world in general and on different levels of explication (political-economic; institutional; every-day and personal/psychological);

- the specific application of those 'workings' to a particular 'field' of social work practice (e.g. homelessness; child care; social therapy; adult education);
- existing and change-oriented ways of (professionally and personally) dealing with the encountered structurally conditioned (inter-)personal and material realities;
- evaluating and reflecting on those practice conditions and processes and on their daily practice in the field;
- instigating – if deemed necessary – changes in the practice approach;
- simultaneously, learning to work in teams, reflecting on their own personal experiences and socialisation, dealing with the tensions and contradictions between politics, policies and practice and honing all ancillary skills necessary to function in professional and change-oriented social work.

Summarised, neo-Marxism with renewed psychoanalytic insights[14] merging into 'Critical Theory' (the 'Frankfurt School' and the many aligned and parallel theoretical, political and practical embodiments in Germany, Italy, France and elsewhere across Europe[15]), critical pedagogy and a growing focus on (everyday) action and the importance of understanding *process* and *relationship* informed the integrative and trans-disciplinary 'radical' directions

---

[14] e.g. J. Kovel, *The Age of Desire: Case Histories of a Radical Psychoanalyst.* (Pantheon, 1981); J. Kovel, *A Complete Guide to Therapy.* (Pantheon, 1976).
[15] http://www.iep.utm.edu/frankfur/

in social work and community development praxis (and education) of the time.[16]

Obviously, such excitement could not last... the mid-1970s '*oil-crisis*,'[17] the emerging '*tax-payer revolt*' in the US[18] and the return of conservative governments across Europe were symbolic and symptomatic of the turning tide, precipitating the trans-Atlantic Reagan-Thatcher head-lined economic-rationalist or neo-liberal version of voraciously globalising capitalism.

Five years of doctoral studies in the US (1980-5) allowed me to combine the structural critiques I had imbued during the seventies with action-theoretical approaches to social and community work (especially Giddens[19] and Bourdieu[20] were helpful). This connected closely with *Participatory Action Research* (PAR); with moving from '*community development*' (imbued with the idle pretences of 'development') to arguing about the need for '*the development of community*' (humbly admitting that 'we' have to re-learn everything about 'community'); the debates engendered by *post-structural* and *post-modern* approaches in the social sciences, especially the deepening of *phenomenological* and *realist* (constructivist) approaches;[21] and the resonance of *quantum-* and *ecological-influenced* epistemologies.[22]

[16] J. Boulet, D. Oelschlägel & J. Krauss, *Gemeinwesenarbeit als Arbeitsprinzip: Eine Grundlegung.* (AJZ Verlag, 1980); M. Brake & R. Bailey (eds.) *Radical Social Work and Practice.* (Edward Arnold, 1980).

[17] https://en.wikipedia.org/wiki/1973_oil_crisis

[18] https://www.nytimes.com/2016/10/17/us/the-california-ballot-measure-that-inspired-a-tax-revolt.html?_r=0

[19] A. Giddens, *Central Problems in Social Theory: Action, Structure and Contradiction in Social Analysis.* (University of California Press, 1979).

[20] P. Bourdieu, *Outline of a Theory of Practice.* (Cambridge University Press, 1977).

[21] R. Bhaskar, *A Realist Theory of Science.* (Verso, 1975); K. Gergen, and K. Davis (eds.), *The Social Construction of the Person.* (Springer-Verlag, 1985); K. Gergen, (2009). *Relational Being.* (Oxford University Press, 1985).

[22] D. Bohm, *Wholeness and the Implicate Order.* (Routledge & Kegan Paul, 1980); J. Boulet, *Action-Theoretical Reflections for Social- and Community Intervention.* (Un-

Back from trying to move 'half way'

Having witnessed during the years in the US the gradual neutralising (or collapse?) of many attempts at changing the world in directions more conducive to peace, equality and justice, wellbeing and the growing concern about ecological sustainability, I arrived in Australia in 1985. Here, the mid- to late-eighties remained resonant of the radical impetus generated throughout the seventies in this country.[23] The '*structural approach*' to social work practice, generated by the work of Maurice Moreau in Quebec, Canada[24] reflected strongly in the curriculum at Philip Institute of Technology ("PIT", amalgamating with RMIT University in 1992,[25] the second institution I taught at).

The PIT curriculum was dedicated to critical – if not radical – social work practice and education; enriched by consistent feminist approaches,[26] it remained faithful to the need for radical change and the importance of reflective practice. The curriculum also had

published Doctoral Dissertation, The University of Michigan 1985); J. Boulet, (1988). "'Action' as the core concept for social work epistemology, theory, and practice' in E. Chamberlain (ed.), *Change and Continuity in Australian Social Work*. Longman Cheshire, 1988, 56-68); D. Haraway, 'Manifesto for Cyborgs: Science, Technology, and Socialist Feminism in the 1980s' in *Socialist Review* 80, 1985, 65-108. D. Haraway, *Staying with the Trouble* (Duke University Press, 2106); K. Barad, (2007). *Meeting the Universe Halfway: quantum physics and the entanglement of matter and meaning*. (Duke University Press, 2007).

[23] E. Chamberlain, *Change and Continuity in Australian Social Work*. (Longman Cheshire, 1988); J. Ife, S. Leitmann & P. Murphy (eds.) (1994). *Advances in Social Work and Welfare Education*. (School of Social Work, University of Western Australia, 1994); J. Fook, (1993). *Radical Casework, A Theory of Practice*. (Allen & Unwin, 1993).

[24] M. Moureau, & L. Leonard (1989). *Empowerment Through a Structural Approach to Social Work*. (Carleton University School of Social Work, 1989); R. Mullaly, *Structural Social Work: Ideology, Theory, and Practice*. (McClelland & Stewart 1993).

[25] https://en.wikipedia.org/wiki/Phillip_Institute_of_Technology)

[26] H. Marchant & B. Wearing (eds.), *Gender Reclaimed: Women in Social Work*. (Hale & Iremonger, 1986); W. Weeks, 'Towards Non-sexist Social Work Education: A Personal Professional Point of View' in *Contemporary Social Work Education*, 3(2) 144-157, 1980.

a strong and consistent focus on research, featuring progressive introductions into the philosophical, methodological and practical aspects of social research, culminating into a final research project during the fourth year, taking on the character of PAR-informed engagement with a social or community issue. Indeed, PAR was the preferred research approach, based on the seminal work of Yoland Wadsworth[27] and informed by exposure to Action Research networks in Australia and beyond.[28]

Many of those efforts and approaches were rather rudely and savagely interrupted, undermined and rendered impossible by the impositions occasioned by economic rationalism (or neo-liberalism) in all facets of societal reproduction, especially in education (increasingly transfiguring into 'training') and welfare (increasingly moving to *'control and marketised adaptation'*, often erroneously referred to as *'mutual obligation'*). The adoption of neo-liberalism by the Labor government in the early nineties – presumably preventing Australia's descent into becoming a banana republic, as Paul Keating memorably declared – in my view, utterly rendered impossible what we had come to understand as enlightened and progressive social praxis, especially (tertiary) educational praxis.

A few years later, Paul James[29] had this to say:

> Universities today are in deep trouble... [they] are steadily being hollowed out, left to the mercy of both state and

---

[27] Y. Wadsworth, (2011). *Do it Yourself Social Research (3ʳᵈ edition)*. (Allen & Unwin, 2011); Y. Wadsworth, *Everyday Evaluation on the Run (3ʳᵈ edition)*. (Allen & Unwin, 2011); Y. Wadsworth, *Building in Research and Evaluation*. (Allen & Unwin, 2010).

[28] P. Reason, (ed.) *Human Inquiry in Action: Developments in new paradigm research*. (Sage Publications 1988); P. Reason (ed.), *Participation in Human Inquiry*. (Sage Publications 1994); O. Fals-Borda, 'The Challenge of Action Research' in *Development: Seeds of Change, no. 1*, 1981, 55–61; and local networks ARIA www.action-research.net.au/; ALARA https://www.alarassociation.org/?q=networks/around-the-world/australia_nz)

[29] P. James (ed.), *Burning down the house: The bonfire of the universities*. North Carlton: (Arena Publications & Association for the Public University, 2000) 6.

market. The ALP under John Dawkins began the process. The Coalition government has by thousand slow cuts set the context for a new stage. Despite the continuing commitment of many of its staff to the dual purpose of learning and research, the universities are now setting fire to their old selves. Out of the ashes they are making themselves into big, prefabricated, empty corporations. Education is business, classroom-time is money; progress is measured in terms of performance indicators; the vice-chancellor is a chief executive officer.

... rather than a sense of vindication, this statement still leaves a bitter taste, especially when the universities' *'deep trouble'* has spread and deepened globally.[30]

Just one example of the ir-rationalities occasioned by economic 'rationalism'; around 1995, my university decided that all curricula were to be adjusted to a uniform number of weekly credit-hours. This was to facilitate transfers between universities and improve 'flexibility' for students; by 1996, weekly contact-hours in our social work curriculum were reduced to twelve hours from a previous average of twenty-two in all campus-based study semesters. This necessitated the 'contracting' of several critically important subjects into an 'omnibus' *Theory-Practice* sequence across the three years; it eliminated intensive small-group reflection opportunities; increased the number and size of large-theatre lectures and decreased the number of tutorials whilst vastly increasing their sizes.

So farewell to pedagogical attempts at bringing integrative theory-practice reflection into the classroom; farewell to much of the research sequence; gone the possibility of project-oriented learning. Much of the load of theory-practice learning was delegated

---

[30] A few recent accounts are in *The Political Economy of the University INC* http://wer.worldeconomicsassociation.org/files/WEA-WSER-8.pdf; C. Pattanayak, (2017). 'The Dumbing of Indian Education' in *Centurion Journal for Multidisciplinary Research 2(1)* 2017, pp. 124-139.

to the learning sites of the two placements, counting on the voluntary commitment and expertise of supervisors and their already stretched agencies (also suffering the consequences of imposed economic 'rationalism' through spending cuts).

After over 25 years, I found that what I had come to understand as the necessary institutional integrity for appropriate educational and community praxis – including support for rich and transformative teaching-learning relationships and processes – could not be assured anymore because of the imposed and institutionalised economic ir-rationalities of the university, and so I decided to leave academia.

I will never forget the casual remark made by a colleague teaching a 'theoretical' social science subject in our course at that time: 'Never mind, you were '*over-teaching*' social work students anyway…!' – and I am still not sure whether that remark can be credited to pedagogical indifference, ignorance about the specific requirements of teaching/learning social work (or any other 'professional' practice) or to the trickling-down plausibility of economic-rationalism into their thinking. Probably it is a potent combination of all these, aided and abetted by the growing '*on-line*' enthusiasm in educational circles, relegating learning to students' spare hours between the obligatory several part-time jobs necessary to pay for the privilege and away from the relational and interactional-participatory learning modalities we had come to believe in in the seventies.

Trying (yet another) 'half way'… this time at arms' length of institutions

So there I was, together with a number of friends and members from several networks, wondering about how to resist and live with the gradually more severe consequences of growing conservatism and the neo-liberal inspired regressive re-invention of the political-

45

economy of capitalism. Our concerns converged on the demise of community and education funding, the gradual undermining and increasingly punitive nature of the Australian welfare system, the worsening ecological conditions and its persistently ignored causes.

The 1992 arrival of the Kennett Coalition government started the rot in Victoria, soon followed by the Howard Coalition government coming to power federally in 1996, comfortable with the economic-rationalist ideology and governance infrastructure already in principle and practice established by the Keating ALP government and exploiting it to the hilt. In Victoria, in half a decade, we witnessed the demise of thousands of small local and interest-based community organisations and action groups as the 'divide and rule' strategy (masked as *competitive tendering*') employed by those in power worked its way into the hearts and souls of the diverse movements and the mere struggle for survival by organisations and individuals alike did the rest.

The rapid demise of programs, funding and infrastructure for and of CD-inspired approaches, some still faintly reminiscent of their Whitlamite *Australian Assistance Plan* origins[31] – together with the constant '*restructurings*' devised by managers, CEOs and government department heads – created a great deal of despair. Particularly in Victoria, where CD was a generic ingredient in many established practice, policy and institutional contexts, this slash-and-burn demise hit hard. CD was present in community (mental) health,[32] education, neighbourhood houses, public housing and homelessness, bushfire and other disaster areas, in advocacy work with people with disabilities and other forms of disadvantage, as documented in the *Community Quarterly* journal and discussed in

---

[31] R. Davis, 'Community Involvement in Government Resource Allocation Decisions' in *Proceedings Social Change in the 21st Century Conference*, (QUT Carseldine, 2005). http://eprints.qut.edu.au/3538/1/3538.pdf (accessed 20/05/2017).

[32] e.g. https://www.cohealth.org.au/about/our-history/brief-history-community-health-australia/

regular conferences. Similar to ideas we developed in Germany and without being named as such, CD had become a '*working principle*' across many modes of social and community practice and in many areas of social engagement, referring to some of its core principles (e.g. 'empowerment', 'inclusion', 'participation', etc.). Numerous position and program descriptions included reference to relevant CD skills – even if often quite perfunctorily.

Of course, such 'incorporation' also led to a degree of 'assimilation' of CD, gradually distancing it from its foundational and principled activist origins, the '*corporatization of activism*'[33] and social media-based '*clicktivism*'[34] doing the rest. Meanwhile, vulnerability to the threat of regulation, cuts to funding and resourcing, the loss of amenities, the privatisation and commercialisation of previously public places and programs, the imposition of a new '*production*' and '*consumption*' vocabulary both brutally and subtly changed our ways of thinking and talking about citizenship, rights, welfare and social programs ... indeed, of life in general.

In the next section, I briefly share some of the things we tried as a response, and keep trying.

The Borderlands Cooperative, the OASES Graduate School and *New Community*

The Borderlands Cooperative[35]

Before and after leaving university at the end of 1996 and in conversation with many friends, colleagues and members of the various

---

[33] An early warning was L. Bryson & M. Mowbray, "Community': The Spray-on Solution' in *Australian Journal of Social Issues Vol. 16(4)*. 1981, 255-267, and re-stated and updated in L. Bryson & M. Mowbray, "More spray on solution: Community, social capital and evidence based policy" in *Australian Journal of Social Issues vol. 40(1)* 2005, 91-106; and globally confirmed by P. Dauvergne & G. Lebaron (2014). *Protest Inc. The corporatization of Activism*. (Polity Press, 2004).

[34] https://www.micahmwhite.com/clicktivism/

[35] www.borderlands.org.au

networks I was part of (participatory action research, eco-philoso-
phy, international and community development, academia, social
work), the idea to create a 'place' where CD could be supported
and kept alive started to take shape. It was to become a *collectively-
run community-based 'learning- and action place'*; a place where
people could talk with and learn from one another; from where action and resistance to the powers that be would emanate and where
new forms of collaboration could be experimented with. It was to
be a place in the suburbs (where the majority of Australians live)
and we started to *'pre-figure'* it as a *'sub-urban university'*, cheek-
ily abbreviated to *'sub-versity'*. *'Borderlands'* – the title of Gloria
Anzaldua's magnificent book[36] – seemed an appropriate name for
the place we dreamed of and – by November 1997, having found a
suitable place through coincidence, serendipity and network connections in premises of Camberwell's Anglican church – I wrote a
long letter to everyone in my address book and networks, inviting
them to be part of the launch of *'Borderlands'* and the creation of

> ... a place where people can meet, talk, reflect, learn and
> teach, read and study, do 'cultured' things together, organ-
> ise, administer and manage their networks or activities in
> and from, where consultation, consulting and counselling
> can happen, where a broad spectrum of basic resources
> are made available and accessible and which thus would
> become a 'node' of various intersecting local, national and
> international networks concerned about any, more or all of
> the issues discussed in more detail below. In short, a place
> where people can develop other ways of doing things to-
> gether and have fun in the process of doing them.[37]

[36] G. Anzaldua, (*Borderlands – La Frontera*. (Aunt Lute Book Company, 1987).
[37] J. Boulet, 'Borderlands sub-versity: a neighbourhood place for local-global reflection and action' in *Community Quarterly No. 44/45*, 1997, 3-10; J. Boulet, (2003).
'Borderlands: Developing a Cooperative' in W. Weeks, L. Hoatson & J. Dixon (eds.)
Community Development in Australia. (Pearson Education 2003, 121-126); J. Boulet,
(2015). 'The Borderlands Cooperative: a place of inclusion and co-production' in M.

The goals of the to-be-evolved organisation were 'dreamt' as varied and multi-facetted but necessary responses to the need

- ... for a profound re-development of our local communities;
- ... for ecologically sustainable local (suburban) living;
- ... for international and inter-cultural learning, exchange and awareness;
- ... for critical (self-)reflection and for action oriented and participatory research and respect for people's knowledge;
- ... and for a (re)new(ed) spirituality, based on a newer-older understanding of 'spirit', as that

> ... which stitches the parts into the whole; ... as that which connects; ... acknowledging the ravages undue divisions of labour and 'expert' specialism have done and are doing to us and to the world ... Borderlands should be about all-at-once.

We launched Borderlands (or its dream) on the 21 December 1997 (a hot-humid last shopping Sunday before Christmas); about 100 people participated and a call was made to join and together develop the place, the organisation and its resources. As my university had decided to 'downsize', I had applied for one of the 150 'voluntary leave' packages on offer and – to my own surprise – was accorded one, allowing me/us to pay the rent for our premises for the following two years – a true stroke of luck.

The first months of 1998 saw us organise workshops, invite speakers and networks to hold their regular meetings in our prem-

Epstein, M. & J. Boulet (eds.) *Doing it Together: A Collection of Approaches, Experiences and Purposes of and in Groups, Committees, Organisations, Networks and Movements*. (Our Community, 2015, 143-115).

ises, whilst developing Borderlands' organisational framework, its vision, mission and objectives, 'rules' and strategies to become and remain sustainable. Various organisational formats – association, incorporated business, co-operative, for-profit or not-for-profit – were considered, our early sympathies being for the *co-operative* form, given its historical origins and philosophical foundations which resonated with the vision we had for Borderlands.[38]

Borderlands espouses an ideology of *sharing* and *partnership*; previously private books and journals found a place in our library (meanwhile about 16,000 catalogued volumes); previously private furniture and equipment evolved into collective offices, kitchen and 'lounge' areas; we were proud possessors of a 're-socialised' laptop and soon joint projects started to 'happen', whilst other community-based action groups came to share the premises and lessen the burden of rent and maintenance costs whilst complementing our own goals and purposes.

As a not-for-profit co-operative, Borderlands has over 120 shareholders and a changing number of annually subscribing members; after 20 years, a core of 20 to 30 people are regularly present and 'do' things at and through Borderlands and its associated organisations. Over the years, hundreds have attended and participated in events, activities or actions; they include a number of 'birds of passage': people come to rest or cooperate for a while and then move on; others stay for many years and there's a number of founding members still taking part in activities. More than 90 students in Social Work, Community and International Development, Welfare Studies and other courses did their placements with us. Via our quarterly newsletter, website, flyers and word of mouth, we stay in touch with thousands of people and we are regularly approached to

---

[38] R. Mathews, *Jobs of Our Own: Building a Stakeholder Society.* (Pluto Press, 1999); https://en.wikipedia.org/wiki/Cooperative; https://www.consumer.vic.gov.au/businesses/registered.../co.../what-is-a-co-operative

present and tell people *'what we're on about...'* We're rather flexible and pragmatic about 'membership' and rejoice when we see the place being used and resources are being put to work to achieve the ends of those who – like us – want to change the world a bit for the better.

One of our founding ideas was to evolve other ways of 'valuing' work and 'making a living', both to sustain the co-operative itself and to secure a personal income for those who do the work. After the disappointments with the growing size and internal transformations of the institutions and agencies we worked for and in and reluctant to join the growing armies of 'self-employed' – and competing – individuals, we hoped for collaborative income generation through the cooperative and to distribute it according to the *needs* of co-operators, rather than on the basis of the assumed intrinsic value of their work. We also were – and are – wary of joining the many NGOs chasing the 'grants' or 'philanthropic' dollar because of the strings attached; so we decided to use the research, evaluation and consultancy experience and capacities of several of our early members and looked for tenders for projects. Waxing and waning groups and teams of ex-academics and students-on-placement have together worked in over 110 small to medium projects during the 20 years of Borderlands' existence, the first few ones almost 'falling into our laps' because of existing relationships and connections. We have developed experience in researching and evaluating in the areas of problem gambling, violence against women and children, volunteering, community and international development, Indigenous issues and an array of welfare and social work issues like health, housing, work and employment, disability, etc..

Financially, the co-operative has developed a loose formula for distributing the income from project and other work: about 20% of the income remains with the co-operative and 80% is distributed amongst those who do the work and who decide about the way it is

distributed amongst team members. There have been some dona-
tions and we try to create 'overlaps' with other small organisations,
capitalising on our joint human and material resources.

In addition to Borderlands' 'distributive' practice, we experiment with mixing and matching paid work, voluntary work, 'apprentice' work (e.g. the students on placement) and 'bartering'
work. Early on, we established a 'Local Exchange Trading System'
(LETS)[39] which at its peak had more than 100 members and then
slowly faded after our move to new premises. Like cooperatives,
LETS is one Borderlands' interests as part of the 'social economy',
with a focus on working and living relationships between members of (local) communities, helping to regain degrees of control
over the means through which local people sustain themselves.
That strongly evolving interest certainly has to do with the growing signs of a collapsing global capitalist economy, of the demise
of democracy and the destruction of Mother Earth, the basis of our
very survival.[40]

Many formal processes set up in the 'regular' economy and work
settings are part of the problem we want to address and, where
possible, alter; existing and surviving in this 'in-between' space
of complying with certain formalities about workplace regulation,
accounting and taxes whilst also wanting to change them demands
a pragmatic approach – dealing with issues as they come and not
letting formalities defeat the purpose. The friendship and love we
have for one another and the commonality of purpose will carry us
more safely than setting up rigid structures and process aiming to

[39] https://en.wikipedia.org/wiki/Local_exchange_trading_system; B. Lietaer, (2001) *The Future of Money: A New Way to Create Wealth, Work, and a Wiser World.* (Century/Random, 2001); D. Boyle, *Funny Money: in search of alternative cash.* (Harper Collins, 1999).

[40] T. Scholz, *Uberworked and Underpaid: How Workers Are Disrupting the Digital Economy.* (Polity Press, 2016); T. Scholz, *Platform Cooperativism: Challenging the Corporate Sharing Economy.* (Rosa Luxemburg Stiftung, 2016); W. Streeck, *How will Capitalism End?* (Verso, 2016).

cover all eventualities and vagaries of unfolding human relationships. Embracing *precariousness* as 'normal' for human and earth-
ly existence helps in not even trying to find security and certainty
where there are none.

The OASES Graduate School[41]

Moving to Augustine Centre[42] in 2002 gave Borderlands a welcome
shot in the arm; from the onset, there was a great convergence of
interest in education, awareness and consciousness building work
and soon we together organised events, conferences and learning
opportunities in cross-disciplinary and wholistic philosophies and
practices. By 2004, Paul Sanders, then Augustine Minister, and I –
gradually joined by members of the Augustine Centre, Borderlands
and several present and former PhD students I had continued to supervise – developed the idea to together offer a formal educational
program, which eventually became an accredited Graduate School
offering a *Master's Degree in Integrative and Transformative Studies.*

It would take an entire book to describe properly the educational
program we envisaged; a section of our Accreditation document
submitted to the then relevant State educational authority, the Victorian Qualification and Registration Authority, will have to do:

> Using current academic terminology, the *oases*' postgradu-
> ate program in Integrative and Transformative Studies is a
> four-year part-time Master's program, with nested leaving
> points after one year (Graduate Certificate) and two years
> (Graduate Diploma). It is structured as a ***Master's by Proj-
> ect***, much of the '*contact time*' being '*guided research,*'
> experienced through active participation in a combination
> of seminars/workshops, small group gatherings and con-

---

versations with academic staff. The pedagogical 'spine' of the program is an *Integrative Seminar*, continuing across the whole of the program. In the first year, the learning is supported by four '*entry units*' – focusing on each of the four facets of *oases* (the *A*esthetic, the *S*ocial, the *E*cological and the *S*piritual – words which, together with the *O* for '*O*rganic integration,' make up the acronym *oases*). The *entry units* are designed to 'enter' each facet theoretically and experientially and the Integrative Seminar in the first year established links and connections between these. In subsequent years the integrative seminar is the home 'strand' from/through which specific content emerges and is 'called for'; this is accompanied by a set of electives sometimes run as specific experiential workshops or theory seminars or meditative retreats or expeditions into the bush or any other 'unit' of theory-practice-praxis entry-points offered recurrently.

From the third year onwards, supported by a '*co-visor*', participants undertake research projects that are both action-oriented and reflective. Learning is conversationally experienced throughout the whole program and participants offer an '*account of their learning*' (our term for 'assessment') to the entire learning community at the end of each year before the three aforementioned leaving points.

There was a great deal of interest for this course; we graduated about 40 Graduate Certificate, Diploma and Master's students over the 10 years of its existence. Unfortunately, the shift of Tertiary Education regulation from State to Federal level introduced a host of new legal and financial regulations and expectations; in typical neo-liberal fashion, we were expected to 'grow' in the three years after our re-accreditation in 2012, after which we would be given access to '*fee-help*'; but as we didn't grow, we were not able to obtain fee-help and so didn't grow.

With a group of OASES graduates, we are now considering where next to take our educational efforts ... and I wish I could say 'watch this space'.

New Community[43]

The only CD journal in Australia, the *Community Quarterly*, having originated in the early eighties as part of the early Hawke ALP government's efforts at creating local employment, ran out of steam in 2000. A number of us engaged in discussions about reviving it and in 2002, thanks to a donation from the Social Developers Network,[44] we were able to bring it out again as the '*New Community Quarterly*.' After fifteen years, the journal (now '*New Community*') has persisted in keeping the idea of CD alive, linking it with the many new developments in alternative organising and with new forms of and efforts at sustainable local living.

The journal continues to give a voice to the many groups and individuals attempting to change the world for the better, one community at a time.

Concluding

As for most activists who will regularly wake up with a cold, nightmarish fright, wondering whether their attempts at changing things have indeed done what they hoped they would achieve, that has been my experience for most of the years this brief account has documented. Asked to offer the now fashionable '*evidence*' for anything I would have changed for the better, I must remain silent but heartened by a subtitle in a recent report: '*absence of evidence*

---

[43] http://community.borderlands.org.au/
[44] http://sdn.ned.org.au/

55

is not evidence of absence'.[45] Based on what people we worked
with and for told us, we probably have made and continue to make
a positive difference even if it's only in the daily lives and feelings
of those who have found solace and purpose in the relationships we
tried to cultivate at Borderlands and in the deeply-reflective learning processes we attempted to generate here and in OASES and
the New Community; parenthetically, good work rarely starts with
'*going for funding*' but with *relational energy.*

Indeed, I have had the privilege of moving into a deeper/broader
understanding of my/our human entanglement in a much larger story than the one I grew up with[46]... a story which has re-emplaced
me in the responsibility of helping to maintain a *larger-than-human
commons* and for which my ability-to-respond is feeble and full of
hesitations. I have come to know that I/we need to move from the
ancient Greeks' '*gnothi seauton*' (*know thyself*) I learned in High
School as the Western ideal of humanness, to Haraway's *sympoesis*
mode of relating, which she so forcefully describes:

> Finally, and not a moment too soon, sympoesis enlarges
> and displaces autopoesis and all other self-forming and
> self-sustaining system fantasies. Sympoesis is a carrier
> bag for ongoingness, a yoke for becoming-with, for stay-
> ing with the trouble of inheriting the damages and achieve-
> ments of colonial and postcolonial naturalcultural histories
> in telling the tale of still possible recuperations.[47]

And it seems to me that this should be programmatic for 'work'
that continues to refer to itself as 'social'.

---

[45] A. Detges, *Climate and Conflict: Reviewing the Statistical Evidence.* Adelphi and German Federal Foreign Office, Berlin 2017).
[46] K. Raworth, *Doughnut Economics: 7 Ways to Think Like a 21st Century Economist* (Chelsea Green Press, 2017).
[47] D. Haraway, *Staying with the Trouble.* (Duke University Press, 2016) 125.

4

WITHIN/WITHOUT:

Conversations on the Journey of Critical Social Work

Peter Camilleri

Introduction

With apologies to The Beatles for bastardising their song *Within You Without You*:[1] the concept of space between us all that The Beatles song represents, for many, is also space between social work academics and the world of practice and practitioners. In engaging with this chapter, I was concerned that it not be a nostalgic trip through my working life but a reflective and analytical discussion of the major changes that have affected social work theory and practice.

How do I approach this? In looking at authors struggling with representing their life and experiences but in a reflective space, the concept of auto-ethnography became a lifeline for me.[2] Tsolidi[3] noted that this approach is contested, and the question of whether it can do more than provide 'self-referential life narratives' is problematic. Yet it can be a focus for engaging one's life experiences within an analytical framework to distill knowledge and theory.

In this chapter I explore how class, culture and gender have

---

[1] G. Harrison, J. Lennon, and P. McCartney. *Within You Without You*. (Northern Songs limited, 1967).

[2] G. Tsolidis, 'Is there Anything Better than Working-Class?' In D. Mitchell, J. Wilson and V. Archer (eds.) *Bread and Roses*. (Sense Publishers, 2015, 119-125).

[3] Ibid., 119.

shaped my experience as a social work academic. It was about being within and without, and it provides a sense of discomfort. Class is a significant shaper of identity. What does it mean to be *working class* as an academic? Ethnicity and culture – and privilege in our society for those who are white – are also shapers of identity. Gender has been important for understanding social work, and what it means to be a man in social work is explored. The notion of 'radical practice' seems to be problematic in teaching in the contemporary university, yet that is where my practice is located. The challenge and excitement of social work education is the 'space' many of us occupy and how we remain critical theorists and practitioners in that environment.

Auto-ethnography is also about locating yourself in time, culture, class and gender. This needs to be explored. As Tsolidis[4] noted, 'it sheds light on various power relations that shape work and education spaces because experience is connected to social processes that mediate identification'. As a social work academic (white and male), the reality of privilege cannot be overlooked.

Class, culture and gender

'Within/without' is about not only place in social work but also place in class, culture and gender. The book *Bread and Roses*, edited by Dee Mitchell, Jacqueline Wilson and Verity Archer[5] a collection of narratives by academics from the working-class in which the working-class location is central to their identity, uncertainty and radical politics, provides an opportunity to engage the sameness and differences of experiences. In that collection and in this book, the starting point for many is the opening up of higher education opportunities and the movement of working-class people into

---

[4] Ibid., 119.
[5] D. Mitchell, J, Wilson and V. Archer, editors. *Bread and Roses* (Sense Publishers, 2015).

universities. The narratives are similar for many who were educated in the 1970s. The Whitlam government reforms in higher education meant that universities were no longer just for the elite and privileged but were open to others, as 'no fees' meant that barriers to participation were less restrictive. The entry of the working class was perhaps more of a trickle than a flood, but many were the first in their family to attend university. It was entry into 'sandstones' that provided a clear sense of difference in class.

My identity is itself within the metaphor of within/without: I was not first in my family to attend university, but I was the first to complete university studies. I come from a working-class family. Our father worked as a storeman and packer. He had six children, so resources were very stretched. My elder brother started at university in the early 1960s, but, even with a scholarship, he was unable to attend full-time; rather, he worked and studied part-time. At one point, he stopped studying but then re-started many years later and completed a teaching degree.

I was at university age in the last few years of Commonwealth scholarships, and I was able to get one. The alternative was the teaching scholarship, which was less attractive. You were 'bonded' to the education department for a number of years (to be so fortunate again!). The Commonwealth scholarship paid the fees and there was a government grant to live on. You could choose from a range of courses depending on your final mark in the Higher School Certificate, but you had choices.

In attending university, the inescapable issue of identity of class faces working-class students. Vocabulary, dress and other class markers set working-class students apart. Pease[6] (2015) noted the importance of 'vocabulary'. The language resources available to working-class students are distinct from those of middle-class stu-

---

[6] B. Pease, 'Injuries and Privileges'. In *Bread and Roses.* (Sense Publishers, 2015. 85-93).

dents. As Pease[7] noted, 'my general vocabulary was more limited and this would become evident in relation to use and pronunciation of certain words. When I spoke, my class markers were often openly displayed'.

Very few academics from working-class backgrounds acknowledge this, yet it is central to the discomfort that many experience. In my situation, it was not just 'vocabulary' but language itself. With undiagnosed dyslexia, I still struggle to put words on paper, irrespective of how many publications I produce. Like many, I am more comfortable in the oral tradition. Of course, this is highly problematic in universities, where written output is the main measure of academic credibility.

This is the first time I have ever put this to paper and, consequently, it makes me feel vulnerable. Writers such as Pease,[8] Tsolidis[9] and Karger[10] note that this sense of vulnerability is part of the conscious and unconscious aspect of having a working-class background as an academic. Am I going to be 'unmasked', am I really a fraud and what becomes of my identity? Brown et al.[11] describe it as the 'imposter syndrome'. How important is my identity as an academic and how does that shape my world view? These are questions that need to be addressed.

Holding onto a 'working-class' identity is problematic. While many academics (see chapters from Mitchell et al.,[12] 2015) claim that the reality of the academic lifestyle, in which privilege is accorded and financial resources are accrued that are beyond the ex-

---

[7] Ibid., 88.

[8] Ibid.

[9] Tsolidis, op. cit.

[10] H. Karger, 'From the Shtetl to the Academy' In *Bread and Roses*. (Sense Publishers, 2015. 163-170).

[11] G. Brown, M. Petrakis, B Flynn, Saunders, P. Mendes and M. Dragic, 'Social Justice, Respect and Professional Integrity. in *Bread and Roses*. (Sense Publishers, 2015).

[12] D. Mitchell, J. Wilson and V. Archer, Verity. Editors, op. cit.

pectations of working-class people, can 'blind' academics to current realities of the lived experience of working-class people. There
is no doubt that a sense of 'otherness' is experienced, and it reflects
what I termed 'within/without' – not being part of the middle class
from upbringing and no longer being working class. However, as
Pease[13] notes, that does not mean that one abandons connection to
class injustices and recognition of many other societal injustices.

My family moved from an inner-city, working-class suburb
(Woolloomooloo – though now costly beyond even an academic's
salary) to the suburbs, where blocks of land were all the same and
families built their houses. There was a mix of working-class war
veterans, middle-class families and veterans moving out of the inner city. These suburbs did not have a working-class identity. The
only distinguishing aspect was that working-class people had vegetable gardens, fruit trees and chickens – not for a 'healthy lifestyle'
but to feed the family. I came from a working-class family background but grew up in a middle-class environment, neither working
class conscious nor middle class.

While there did not appear to be an identity marker of class in
these suburbs – in a sense, the new middle class was to include everyone – there was, of course, culture. These new suburbs, as new
greenfield sites, saw many flock from the inner city to the spaces of
the new suburbs. Many of those people moved out to the southern
areas of Sydney in particular, and these became spaces for mainly
Anglo-Celtic families: everyone in the suburb had an Anglo name
and saw themselves as Australians, and that meant Anglo white
Australians.

As the narratives in *Bread and Roses*[14] identify, culture was an
import marker for many working-class academics. Those academics were not just working class in origin but migrant as well, and

[13] B. Pease, op. cit.
[14] D. Mitchell, J. Wilson and V. Archer. Editors, op. cit.

they experienced not only a sense of dislocation but also unease of culture, which included language, food and dress.

For me, this was less problematic: while my family was Maltese, I was third generation. My grandfather migrated to Australia between the two waves of large-scale Maltese migration (in the 1890s to Queensland for the sugar cane industry and post Second World War – see York[15] for history of Maltese migration). My father was born in Australia and did not retain the language. Our move from the inner city to the south meant less contact with an extended Maltese family and created more 'distance' in terms of being Maltese. Identity of culture was missing: I had a 'wog' name but I was not a wog. Again, within/without provides a powerful metaphor for being part of Australian identity but not quite.

The inescapable privilege of being male in a female-majority profession cannot be ignored. It permeates what social work and being in university is all about. Pease[16] (2015) outlines how the working-class background was embodied with a sense of masculinity ('"Real men" worked on the factory floor': p. 85). Paul Willis's[17] classic study on *working class* notes the importance of masculinity to the identity of working-class boys. Not all working-class males were in traditional 'hard' jobs; many, particularly from migrant backgrounds, were cleaners in factories or had other 'dirty' though not 'masculine' jobs.

Gender is an integral part of identity. Yet, for many males in social work, there is little awareness of this. The focus of gender in social work tends to be on the 'other' – the client, service user or 'case'. There is no doubt that male social work students are challenged in their views, attitudes and practice towards their potential

---

[15] B. York, *The Maltese in Australia.* (AE Press, 1986).

[16] Pease, op. cit.

[17] P. Willis, *Learning to Labor: How Working Class Kids Get Working Class Jobs.* (Columbia University Press, 1977).

clients. Yet the issue of gender *in* social work is often not directly addressed. That is, social work as a gendered activity is rarely unpacked. Do males *do* social work differently, and how?

For many males, this is uncomfortable. The status of social work itself is relatively low and, for many men, this sense of low status and the issue of privilege seem contradictory. Gender just is, and it seems unproblematic, as social workers work with many high-status professionals – doctors, lawyers et cetera. As Pease[18] wrote, 'Although men may not feel privileged in social work, this experience flies in the face of men's continued dominance in management and high-status specialisms in the profession'.

Few male social work academics challenge this paradigm, although a core of writers from UK, US and Australia[19] are challenging this. For social work students, both male and female, the issues of gender and privilege are intertwined throughout their lives. It is about how their careers are constructed and what they see as their identity in being a social worker. It is about an understanding of one's own privilege and space and needing to work through the discomfort and at times searing personal challenge.

It is important that male social workers not only recognise their inherent privilege but also take responsibility to challenge or disrupt gender inequality in social work.[20, 21] This is acknowledged as difficult and confronting. For many men who have experienced

[18] B. Pease, 'Men in Social Work: Challenging or Reproducing an Unequal Gender Regime?' *Affilia* 26.4 (2011): 406.
[19] See M. Kimmel and J. Hearn. *Handbook of Studies on Men and Masculinities*. (Sage, 2005). B. Pease, 'Engaging Men in Feminist Social Work.' In S. Wendt and N. Moulding (eds.) *Contemporary Feminisms in Social Work Practice* (Routledge, 2016): 287 and K. Pringle, 'Doing (Oppressive) Gender Via Men's Relations with Children.' *Critical Perspectives on Masculinities and Relationalities*. (Springer International Publishing, 2016, 23-34).
[20] C. Noble and B. Pease. 'Interrogating Male Privilege in the Human Services and Social Work Education'. *Women in Welfare Education* 10 (2011), 29.
[21] Pease, op. cit.

disadvantage because of class, ablism, sexuality and ethnicity, the concept and experience of privilege is problematic.

Those who have it do not recognise status and privilege – it simply is.[22] As Marston[23] argues, gender is a form of what Bourdieu[24] referred to as 'habitus'. It is our daily lives through which this is expressed. The recognition of privilege of gender can be 'conscious', but how that is lived is more contentious. It is in 'everyday life'[25] where gender is played out; it is through our daily interactions that 'privilege' occurs. As Giddens[26] notes, while men say they want equality, the reality is very different. It is 'how' we do our relationships every day that allows privilege to be 'unpacked'. It has to be a constant struggle for men who engage in what Pease termed profeminist practice.

In my own private life, I have constantly saw my relationship with my partner as equal, in which we have shared as much as possible the mundane aspects of life – cooking, cleaning and child raising. This has not always been easy as we both worked full-time in demanding professions – she as a lawyer and I as an academic. This is a constant negotiation of everyday life that De Certeau talks about.

These theoretical constructs that shaped our understanding of class, ethnicity and gender are the 'stuff' of sociological theorising. The trinity of Marx, Durkheim and Weber still provide the framework for the debate of the 'dualism' of agency and structure.[27] This

---

[22] Noble and Pease, op. cit.

[23] G. Marston, 'From Being a Fish Out of Water to Swimming with the School'. In *Bread and Roses.* Sense Publishers (2015).

[24] P. Bourdieu, 'Habitus'. *Habitus: A Sense of Place 2* (2005, 43-52).

[25] M. De Certeau, 'The Practice of Everyday life' (1980), translated by Steven Rendell (Berkeley, 1984).

[26] A. Giddens, Anthony. 'The Transformation of Intimacy: Sexuality, Love and Intimacy in Modern Societies.' (*Polity*, 1992).

[27] A. Giddens, *Capitalism and Modern Social Theory: An Analysis of the Writings of Marx, Durkheim and Max Weber.* (Cambridge University Press. 1971).

is important for social work, as it locates itself in the space between the individual and society. It argues that social work is more than the 'poor person's psychologist'; it is about locating the person in their social and environmental context. Most importantly, social work is about 'practice'. It is not about theorising; it is about using theories to make sense of and work with people.

Starting the social work journey

Most of the contributors to this collection would have started their journey into social work in the late 1960s or 1970s. While it is important not to look back with nostalgia, the ferment of the 1960s caused social work to shift its gaze from the individual to structures. Social work did not do this itself but became influenced by the debates occurring in cognate disciplines, particularly sociology and political science.

I studied social work in the early to mid 1970s. It was an exciting time at two levels: the Whitlam Labor government had been elected in late 1972 and more radical social theories were being discussed in university. Policies were changing rapidly in terms of social infrastructure. The role of government was to assist the individual in developing their full potential. The Commonwealth led in providing social benefits for the disadvantaged, extending health insurance to all citizens and seeing the citizenry as partners in a changing society (see Mendes[28]).

At a second level, radicalism in sociology, political science and educational philosophy saw new influential ideas challenge the status quo. Social work was still very insular; its intellectual resources were dominated by US and UK texts. While more radical texts influenced by Marxian concepts slowly started to be published, they

---

[28] P. Mendes, *The Australian Welfare Wars Revisited* (UNSW Press, Third Edition, 2017).

were not widely disseminated. The classic texts of the US were still being prescribed for study. The texts that were influential for me were from the philosophy of education – the work of Bowels & Gintis,[29] Paulo Freire[30] and Ivan Illich.[31]

Like many social workers, my early career was more determined by where I could get a job than necessarily by an ideological commitment. I worked in a variety of places and practice situations. I learned all the time, mainly from my clients, who tended to be very generous with young and inexperienced social workers. As many young social workers did, I travelled to the UK and worked as a social worker. I moved from seeing myself as a community worker to ending up working in psychiatric hospital. This may seem like a move from a societal-level concern to individualistic practice.

The challenge for social work is how we see the individual in their context and what that implies for practice. The chance to undertake further study in the UK was both opportune and exciting. Being situated in sociology, the Master's program I undertook, allowed me the freedom to wrestle with the work of the major social theorists as well as to become exposed to emerging new theories that were challenging understanding of everyday life.

The space that social work occupies is 'everyday life': it is where the state 'intervenes' in what is the ordinary and mundane but where things fall apart. The work of Mead,[32] Becker[33] and Goffman[34] provided an insight into the everyday world and its problematics.

---

[29] S. Bowels and H. Gintis. *Schooling in Capitalist America.* (Basic Books, 1976).

[30] P. Freire, *Pedagogy of the Oppressed.* (Penguin Books, 1971).

[31] I. Illich, Ivan. *Deschooling Society.* (Harmondsworth, 1973).

[32] G. H. Mead, *Mind, Self and Society.* (University of Chicago Press, 1934).

[33] H. Becker, Howard. *Outsiders.* (The Free Press. 1963).

[34] E. Goffman. *Asylums: Essays on the Social Situation of Mental Patients and Other Inmates.* (Aldine Transaction, 1968).

Most importantly, it affirmed the agency of people. Garfinkel[35] and the ethnomethodologists,[36] who challenged our notions of how the 'everyday' is done, brought a new perspective to understanding the agency/structure problem.

This provided me with abundance of intellectual ideas that I explored in both my Master's dissertation and PhD thesis. In my dissertation I explored how people who had non- accidentally over-dosed on a variety of medications, including over the counter, made sense of this. The complexity of their relationships and how they accounted for the overdose as an eventuality of that was a sophisti-cated analysis of wanting to see it as a consequence of relationship breakdown. There was agency in their actions as well as structure of relationships – how do women deal with relationship breakdown in the context of patriarchy. My PhD was more focused on how social workers made sense of their practices. The powerful voices of gender and agency came through.[37]

Giddens[38] argues that 'social structures are both constituted by human agency, and yet at the same time are the very medium of this constitution'. This duality of structure[39] sees structure as enabling human agency. Structure is produced though human agency and at the same time allows for human agency. By examining our practice critically, we can analyse the structural constraints as they are or-ganised and also see how our clients reflexively make sense of their world. The location of power within this social interaction provides for the discursiveness of it. Our clients are not powerless, though their opportunities and choices are limited.

[35] H. Garfinkel, *Studies in Ethnomethodology.* 1967.
[36] See K. Leiter. *A Primer on Ethnomethodology.* (Oxford University Press, 1980).
[37] P. Camilleri, *(Re)Constructing Social Work: Exploring Social Work Through Text and Talk.* (Avebury, 1996).
[38] Giddens, op. cit., 121.
[39] C. Bryant and D. Jary, eds. *The Contemporary Giddens: Social Theory in a Glo-balising Age.* (Palgrave, 2001).

From practice to academia: Critical social work in neoliberal institutions

The opportunity to work in higher education came after eight years of working as a social worker in Hobart, Darwin and England. While I enjoyed practice, the idea of working in higher education was very seductive. Being able to read all the time and get paid for it seemed to be the height of luxury and indulgence. Little did I know I was entering a new world where reading itself was a luxury. Staying one step ahead of the students was the name of the game. The pressure to undertake further study (a doctorate started to become the new norm) and balancing teaching with being actively involved in local community stretched every social work academic.

How do you make sense of practice within academia as a social worker? What is my practice in this context? How does critical theory makes sense of that practice? Few social work academics have turned inwards and critically analysed their place of work. A few (Noble & Pease,[40] Hill[41] and Fraser & Taylor[42]) provide for at times grim reading. The transformation of higher education in Australia has seen academics become detached from their colleagues and focused on increasing their 'productivity'. The notion of collegial decision-making has disappeared from universities; they have become increasingly market-oriented and they focus on seeing each academic unit as a 'business unit'. Many universities have cut departments because they are no longer 'viable' – that is, they are uneconomic. Their value is no longer in their intrinsic worth as repositories of knowledge.

---

[40] Noble & Pease op. cit.
[41] R. Hill, *Whackademia: An Insider's Account of the Troubled University.* (New South, 2012).
[42] H. Fraser, and N. Taylor. *Neoliberalisation, Universities and the Public Intellectual.* (Palgrave Macmillan, 2016).

The complexities of teaching as a practice and educating social workers, in which you prepare people for a contested, confused and problematic 'world', has both challenged and excited me. As a social work academic since 1986, my understanding of and contribution to social work education has been in curriculum design and peer assessment of social work programs across Australia, Hong Kong and New Zealand.

Teaching social work has for me been a commitment to ensuring that graduates have the beginning skills, knowledge and values that will lead them to work effectively with the most vulnerable and disadvantaged in our community. At the forefront of my mind is the recognition that they will be working with people and making decisions with and sometimes for them, which can be life changing. This is both sobering and at the heart of professional practice.

How do you that? How do get students to think, feel, empathise and critically reflect? How do you get students to challenge their own values, examine them and integrate them within a professional value scheme? How do you get students to recognise when the 'goodness of fit' between their values and professional values is problematic? Social work is not 'rocket science', but it is damned hard work.

Social work is a practice. It involves getting students to *think, feel, plan, do and reflect*. This is an integration of Bloom's[43] taxonomy of cognitive, affective and psychomotor domains and Kolb's[44] learning styles. For me as an academic, social work has to challenge, support and nurture students. Importantly, it has to provide students with the skills to work effectively within a frame of lifelong learning. Their journey in social work has just begun.

---

[43] See M. Forehand, 'Bloom's Taxonomy'. *Emerging Perspectives on Learning, Teaching, and Technology* 41 (2011, 47).

[44] A. Kolb and D. Kolb. 'Kolb's Learning Styles'. *Encyclopedia of the Sciences of Learning. (*Springer, 2012), 1698-1703.

The work of Schon[45] on reflective practice has been seminal for understanding how to educate professionals. While there has been a criticism of his approach (see Eraut[46]) – in particular, in regard to classroom teaching – for social work, this recognition of experienced practitioners' engagement with clients as 'reflection-in-action' provides the frame for learning.

For social work, it is the 'doing' where learning occurs. The challenge has always been to determine what content knowledge is needed, and how students process that knowledge, so they can 'do'. Curriculum designs for professional programs are restrained by accreditation requirements and employer demands. Creativity and radical teaching and learning strategies have to be managed within the tension of accreditation and needs of employers. The focus of higher education is on reductionism in teaching, in which 'marking rubrics', learning outcomes and constant monitoring of teaching, with subsequent loss of control, are barriers to a critical stance. Critical theory is not just what we teach but also what we do in the classroom.

This is the arena in which I have had to develop my individual teaching philosophy. These are the questions I have had to address at a very personal level. The challenge for all social work academics is the integration of personal and professional values. The core social work values of personal integrity, respect for the individual, social justice and human rights are not abstract values but are demonstrated in the very way we approach and deal with students. It is important to both mirror and demonstrate these values so that students can see and experience the values in action. These values are demonstrated in the classroom, in interactions with other students and in their field education practicums. The challenge is always to

---

[45] D. Schon, *Educating the Reflective Practitioner: Toward a New Design for Teaching and Learning in the Professions.* (Jossey-Bass, 1987).

[46] M. Eraut, 'Schon Shock: A Case for Reframing Reflection-in-Action?' *Teachers and Teaching* 1.1 1995, 9-22.

confront students where these values are not being displayed and to work with them on the barriers to their adoption.

Social work as a practice is about engaging students in doing in order to reflect as much of the 'real world' as possible. The crucial question asked of educators, 'What effect am I having on students and on their learning?' (see Brookfield)[47] p. 16, is one that continually haunts me. Are we developing the skills that will make students effective and, most importantly, how will I know?

Where to now?

As I enter the 'backend' of my career, I face the confronting examination of how I have managed to live my values within my work life. I am struck when I read biographies of people such Nelson Mandela and Joan Baez, who withstood enormous challenges (from jail to personal vulnerability) to be consistent in their commitments to justice and working for the most vulnerable. Universities, while they are places of corporate neo-liberalism, still have 'space' for critical enquiry where we can engage our students in social justice activities.[48]

The experience of being a social work academic has been a personally rewarding one, though it has not been without its tensions. I am aware that my career would be very different if I were not male and white. I cannot escape the privileges that they provide, nor would I want to argue otherwise, as it is a starting point from which to question critically the structures that allow for that. Through my teaching more than anything, I have striven to provide a critical framework for students. Critical pedagogy as Fraser and Taylor[49] note, is about 'activism and caring'.

---

[47] S. Brookfield, 'Authenticity and Power'. *New Directions for Adult and Continuing Education.* 111 (2006), 5-16.
[48] Fraser & Taylor, op. cit.
[49] Ibid.

We are talking about the space between us all
And the people who hide themselves behind a wall of illusion
Never glimpse the truth, then it's far too late ...[50]

---

[50] Harrison, George, John Lennon, and Paul McCartney, op. cit.

5

FROM RADICAL SOCIAL WORK TO CRITICAL REFLECTIVE PRACTICE:

On Selling the Soul of Social Work

Jo Dillon

The 1970s and 1980s were arguably a golden age for social work in Australia. The shift to the populist right in recent local and international political events might suggest that as a profession we have been caught somewhat 'off guard' in our collective understanding of the political processes which shape the policy context social workers inhabit. In contrast to the po-faced and heartless austerity we have been witnessing for the last three decades, the 1970s was a time when the collectivist ideals characteristic of post World War II political systems in most industrialised countries came to the fore in Australia. This was accompanied in this context by an increased global engagement and a more generous and expansive view in political culture that extended well into the 1980s. Against this backdrop, this chapter narrates my personal, theoretical and professional journey as a critical feminist social work academic through that period. From radical social work in the 1970s to the narrowing range of theoretical understandings known as critical reflective practice in the late 1980s, this snapshot of a halcyon time shows that another way forward is possible.

1970s: From Greer, Gough and gremlins with razors: Into the mix where the personal meets the political

The 1970s were an exciting time to be at university and I just loved it. Among other sweeping changes, the incoming Whitlam Labor government had abolished tertiary fees and brought in the National Employment and Training Scheme (NEAT), an initiative of the Whitlam Labor government, enabling a broader range of people who would otherwise have not envisioned tertiary study to attend university. I was one of those people and university for me was a remarkable journey into the world of ideas and of self-discovery wherein the realisation of the interconnection of the personal with the political slowly but surely dawned.

For me, that realisation played out in many ways throughout the 1970s. As a 'baby boomer', I had spent five years in the 1960s in a Catholic boarding school and my feelings about that experience are mixed. On one hand, the loss of the freedom I had experienced as a child on a farm in the country and the restrictions of boarding school were at best a serious test to my resilience and at worst a form of trauma. On the other, the opportunity to be educated by nuns, many of whom were inspirational role models in terms of the potential of women for academic high achievement and educational leadership, alongside the commitment to social justice and community service which underpinned the ethic of that particular school has had a lasting impact. I had married in the late 1960s. Sung by the school choir, I had been a part of such a short time before in the cathedral attached to the school I had left barely two years earlier, at all of 18 years of age and still needing parental consent for this imprudence, I stood before the god I then believed in and swore everlasting love and fidelity to a man I had known only six months, just two years older – and definitely no wiser than me. What was I thinking? At the time that I was engaged in this folly, radical feminist writers such as Firestone, Greer and Millet were

74

formulating their various treatises on heterosexual 'love' as the foundation of women's oppression and the family as the ultimate source of ongoing inequality between men and women. And thus, it could be argued, it remains.

I entered the 1970s as a refugee from an increasingly unhappy marriage largely to do with the fact that my then husband had been drafted into the army and was being trained along with other 'Nashos' to fight in Vietnam. In this we were saved by the incoming Whitlam government, which recalled all servicemen and women from Vietnam and ended conscription. The damage had been done, however, as the fallout from enforced army training rang the death knell for an already faltering relationship.

So it was that I had my first encounter with a social worker in the early seventies. In those days, there was a six month gap between separation and eligibility for Commonwealth benefits – the 'Widow's pension' as it was then called. There was no single parent benefit at the time, one needed to actually have been married to be seen as deserving. In urgent need of financial assistance, I approached the state welfare department and was referred for assessment to a social worker. While in hindsight, she was simply doing her job in implementing policy as she understood it, I will never forget the patronising attitude nor the judgemental and intrusive approach she took to her determination of my eligibility for a small amount of money euphemistically called 'relief'. Feeling totally demeaned, I resolved never to go back and at the end of my six months as a 'deserted wife,' became eligible for a Commonwealth pension, which I continued to receive as I commenced university education until the implementation of Whitlam's NEAT scheme. That experience, a valuable lesson in how *not* to treat people, has stuck with me through my career in social work and social work education.

In providing those on low income with a basic wage to retrain in a chosen trade or profession, the NEAT scheme enabled me to study Arts and then a social work degree. At university in the 1970s, the intellectual stimuli of grappling with philosophy, politics, international relations, sociology and ecology opened doors to a labyrinth of hitherto unexplored regions of my consciousness and awareness. I was instantly drawn to the macro and excited by the conviction that this study was my route to making a difference – and I was but one of many students in the 1970s who believed that we were on the threshold of creating great change. My developing passion for social justice was further reinforced by moving into social work study in a newly established social work course headed by Adam Jamrozik with a strong emphasis on social work and social policy as activism. Although the context has changed significantly, the intellectual grounding I received at that time equipped me with an ongoing critical and structural analysis that has served me well over the intervening years and firmly pointed me in the direction of social work and social work education as a basis for social transformation. By the end of the seventies, that commitment to activism was increasingly informed by feminist understandings.

I came to social work study with an awareness and indignation about social injustice inherited from my schooling and upbringing in a politically activist family. Through the social work degree however, I became much more aware of the nature of disadvantage of specific groups and the impact that social work and social policy had on either improving or exacerbating the situation. Indeed, more often than not, the effects of our 'interventions' were contradictory. Such contradictions inherent in the welfare state were seen in Marxist analysis to be a key to bringing about a transformation to socialism, that idealised state of equality, the elusive end point of campaigns for social justice. The vision of radical social work was to work towards structural change alongside oppressed groups and through making links with unions and other social movements.

The latter half of the seventies was also a time when the notion of professionalism was under challenge as being elitist and benefitting from the status quo.[1] At this point, many newly graduated social workers, myself included, were taking up positions in areas that had not previously been the province of social work, such as work with unions, tenant associations and in advocacy organisations loosely allied with broader social movements.

As an explanation for social disadvantage, for me, Marx's theory of historical materialism had no equal, despite its clear limitations for late Western industrialised economies. I was concerned that Marxism ignored power relationships other than class, as even in the 1970s, I felt the concept of class was becoming increasingly complex and no longer fitted the intricate and multifaceted lives of workers and the socially disadvantaged of late 20th century capitalism. There seemed to me to be a certain amount of romanticism and selective blindness within Marxist critique to the potential collusion and incorporation of the 'working classes' of late capitalism and some implied magical process in the transformation of 'false consciousness'. This simply did not fit with my emerging understanding of the complex nature of disadvantage, nor indeed the power of identity in co-option of those 'upwardly mobile'. In practice, to me, Marxism was vague on alternatives to capitalism and indeed history had shown that in those societies where revolution among the working classes had resulted in state socialism, the resultant 'equality' was maintained under very repressive regimes. While for me, the experience in those contexts did (still does) not negate arguments for socialism per se as potentially the most equitable social system yet devised, I thought that there needed to be a stronger explanation grounded in the politics of identity that explained the lack of progress towards the 'necessary' revolution

[1] I. Illich *Disabling Professions* (Boyars, 1977); H. Throssell, ed. *Social Work: Radical Essays* (University of Qld Press, 1975).

and which also provided the key to social transformation. I also felt that Marx and Engels could not have predicted the 20th century rise of consumerism and sport, which appears to me to have gradually replaced religion as the 'opiate(s) of the people'. The power of these new hegemonies to ensure a new kind of subjugation among the general populous, in my view ensures the demise of Marx's predicted 'necessary revolution'. It was at this point that I discovered the writings of the Brazilian educator Paulo Freire[2] and the neo-Marxist leader of the communist party in Italy in the 1920s, Antonio Gramsci.[3]

The world of liberation and the role of intellectuals in creating an alternative hegemony that Freire and Gramsci painted in their writings was attractive to the somewhat naïve idealism of this newly graduated social worker at the end of the 1970s. Freire's ideas about the liberating potential of education and the use of dialogue as a tool for raising consciousness and the role of intellectuals in the process simply sang to me as the basis for a way of working with people, especially at the community level. In the research dissertation required to complete my social work degree, I utilised ethnographic and participant observation research methods to determine if a Freirian approach to community development could result in galvanisation of a disadvantaged group in southern Tasmania over issues that affected their local community. In concluding that building relationships within marginalised communities through the use of a Freirian dialogical approach was an effective form of practice at the community level, I developed a framework for a critically reflexive praxis that has continued to ground and guide my approach to social work practice and education ever since. The song still plays, refined but the same basic tune.

Importantly, I was becoming aware of the gender blindness of

[2] P. Freire *Pedagogy of the Oppressed* (Penguin, 1970).
[3] A. Gramsci cited in J. Femia, *Gramsci's Patrimony* Pol Sc 13. (1980).

major theories informing social work practice. This had been brought home to me very clearly in my social work placement in the local women's hospital. Here, I saw women consistently belittled and vulnerable to the patriarchal and blatantly sexist attitudes of male medical students with whom I had shared first year science subjects at university some five years previously. Somewhere in their training, these young men – and indeed some young women – had taken on as part of their developing professional identity that particular brand of hubris that exemplifies at one and the same time their capacity for 'power over' and their comparatively lowly status in the medical hierarchy. At that stage, my feminist consciousness was just beginning to evolve and while this experience of gender injustice galvanised me into an advocacy role, it also set me on a quest for a satisfactory explanation of what I was witnessing and more importantly, how I could make a difference. I was familiar with feminist literature but still intellectualised the world primarily through a neo-Marxist lens. As such, I continued to individualise my experience of gender even after having my second child when my live in relationship had become emphatically unequal, in that it took me the same amount of years to complete one degree as it took my partner to complete two. Through the social work course, we had been acquainted with C. Wright Mills'[4] notion of the indivisibility of private troubles and public issues. As far as I was concerned personally, the private and public spheres remained quite separate. As I later gleaned from my reading of Dorothy Smith[5] (1991), the spheres of my existence and hence my consciousness remained categorically 'bifurcated', characterised by 'double days' running between the set of the public stage and the joys and demands of the private

---

[4] C. Wright Mills *The Sociological Imagination* (Penguin, 1970).
[5] D. Smith *The Conceptual Practices of Power: A Feminist Sociology of Knowledge* (North Eastern University Press, 1991).

sphere.[6] Despite my tertiary education, I had uncritically and of necessity adopted dual roles in a system whose boundaries and time frame were clearly set by patriarchal understandings. My consciousness had started to shift, however, and as I entered the eighties as a newly graduated social worker, I was equipped with a complex, albeit somewhat chaotic academic awareness of the relative disadvantage of women. Through my readings of Elizabeth Wilson's landmark book, *Women and the Welfare State*,[7] and shaped by my contact with disadvantaged women through my placements and ongoing conversations with other women students/graduates, I had the tools to cautiously identify my sense of injustice at the way women were treated and perceived as socialist feminism.

Armani suites, shoulder pads and big hair: Challenges and revelations in my journey through the 80s

As a newly graduated social worker, for me the eighties was a busy and rich decade. At every turn, the points where the personal intersected with the political, with the professional, with policy and with the theoretical, became abundantly clear. The 1980s were such an exciting time that it is difficult to choose points to highlight but I have chosen a couple of examples that tell a tale, not just about my positioning in terms of theoretical development, but also to convey the complexity of the time, especially in relation to social justice and gender awareness.

Early practice

In 1980 I discovered non-violence. I had previously been vaguely aware of a Ghandian philosophy and was acquainted intellectu-

---

[6] D. Smith op. cit.

[7] E. Wilson *Women and the Welfare State* (Tavistock, 1977).

ally with various non-violent campaigns for social change. Contact with the (late) Sugata Dasgupta[8] and workshops that he and his colleagues were running on challenging structural violence through community development were, however, to have a profound and lasting impact on my life and social work practice. The inextricable links between the personal and the political were brought home to me very clearly through non-violence. The principles of starting with the weakest; that there is no enemy (only potential allies), and of non-cooperation with unjust systems[9] were as inspiring as they were potentially profoundly challenging to my personal and intellectual privilege. Those workshops of discovery had been well attended by my work colleagues and were ultimately adopted as guiding principles for my workplace at the time. The subsequent actions of a number of my male colleagues, however, made me re-alise that Ghandian non-violence had no words for the subtleties of gendered injustice and as such an important dimension of structural violence was missing from the analysis.

After the mid 70s, social work skills were increasingly in de-mand in community development, in administration and in policy and project development. Such it was that I found myself employed in the Youth Support Unit in Hobart, an innovative specialist ad-visory unit on youth affairs attached to the Premier's Department and with a direct line to the Minister. The existence and form of this unit alone speaks to the halcyon days of the late 70s and early 80s for the welfare sector. While the primary focus of my position was research and policy development, it also involved work with individuals in crisis and various community groups around youth issues.

The varied nature of the work at the YSU consistently brought

---

[8] S. Dasgupta *Philosophical Assumptions for Training in Non-Violence* (University of Queensland, 1977).
[9] Ibid.

home to me the complexity of ethics while raising the question of the importance of context in ethical considerations. Working with groups such as the transsexuals to whom the centre provided support confronted me with challenges about professional boundaries, the vexed question of what it means to 'work with' and the limiting nature of gender identity. There was a serious research and policy development aspect to the job too, and in this environment, I found the nexus between community development and social policy that continues to guide my practice. One of the projects that my team undertook was to make recommendations for future employment possibilities for young people in Tasmania and part of this involved the possibility of establishing worker cooperatives as a socially just way of creating employment. In this we drew on information and the philosophical traditions associated with the Mondragon Cooperatives in the Basque region of Spain, wherein true to the Marxist perspective, social justice was equated with collective ownership of the means of production. Alongside social sustainability, we were concerned about ecological sustainability and in this sense were somewhat ahead of our time.

My time at the Youth Support Unit expanded my view that to be an effective social worker is to work at a multitude of levels. For me, then as now, social work is about working *with* people to cultivate socially sustainable relationships and systems. In order to achieve this, it is often necessary to develop and create community-based alternatives that are economically and socially just and environmentally and ecologically sustainable. It is also a solid base from which to influence, lobby and create social policy that challenges social disadvantage. At that time, the broad range of knowledge and multiple skills that made up social work degree programs in Australia meant that social workers were uniquely equipped to do this. I also learnt the value of teamwork with other professionals and the importance of making links with broader movements for change. It was an inspiring time in retrospect because all of us who worked in the Youth Support Unit were dedicated to social change and had a lot of autonomy to work with people in developing their creative potential. I felt, even in the short time that I was there, that in working at varying levels as a team we were able to make a difference to many people's lives.

Moving into social work education

In the early 1980s, I was appointed to a position which involved part-time tutoring at the Western Australia Institute of Technology (now Curtin University) in newly developed units in Radical Social Work and Community Development and supervising students on job creation projects in a partnership between the School of Social Work and Anglicare. Initially a one year contract, this was to be the start of a 30 year career in teaching social work.

There was so much going on in Western Australia at the time and I felt I had landed right in the thick of a buzz of resistance to an ultra-conservative political climate with a state government concerned primarily with law and order and supporting mining interests. In this climate, progressive social workers met in secret and on first name basis only to discuss how they may collectively contribute to policy change in the knowledge that identification could result in instant dismissal or relocation to the nether regions of their respective bureaucracies. At the time, just a few social work staff and students were taking leadership roles in certain campaigns, most notably working alongside Aboriginal groups at Noonkanbah[10] and in the campaign with local unions for the rights of workers who worked the mines at Wittenoom.[11]

---

[10] Noonkanbah, a campaign for land rights by aboriginal groups in the North West of Western Australia in 1980/81.
[11] This refers to the claims against the Hardy Group by unions supporting workers who contracted Asbestosis through their work in the mining town of Wittenoom, Western Australia.

In that environment, teaching was a lively business with much critical debate on current campaigns and policies in workshops and tutorials. Over that first year, the students and I were instrumental in getting a number of innovative projects off the ground. I was initially involved in coordinating the establishment of a recycling project with unemployed young people with the support of one of the Anglican parishes and a local council in Perth. In doing so, I was building on the experiences I had at the Youth Support Unit in the development of cooperatives and ecologically sustainable practice. Bayswater Recycling ran for five years and was a prototype for re-cycling programs now run by other municipalities across Australia, except that it was organised as a cooperative of unemployed young people rather than as a fund raising venture by local councils, an important difference in terms of socially just objectives.

By the early 1980s, I had joined a small number of women colleagues in incorporating feminist theory into the curriculum. In 1982 I attended my first Women in Welfare Education meeting and through membership of this group was able to start reflecting upon and linking my Freirian educational practice with a feminist approach to teaching. To this end, I introduced an option on Women and Social Policy into the curriculum. This unit quickly turned into a de-facto consciousness raising group where we came together to discuss each week the impact of gender and sexism on our lives. These sessions were semi-structured around themes which participants themselves chose as a topic for the week. They were highly emotive sessions and there was much anger directed at men in general. We all learnt so much and it provided space for us as women to articulate in a safe environment that which we felt, but hitherto may not have been able to find words to say. Most of the time, the groups consisted solely of women but the unit was also open to men. On the occasions that men joined the group, they were usually very quiet and often seemed to feel uncomfortable in the group

84

for simply being a man. Whether or not the group should include men was a constant source of tension for me as an educator and also a dilemma for women participants. Certainly, the dynamics were different when men were present. Women were not as forthcoming and when they were there, I felt sometimes the men were protected and often 'rescued' to some degree by some unnamed code of discretion. It always seemed that different dynamics, often unconscious, came into play when men were present.

These gatherings provided an outlet for pent up anger at the oppressive practices we had allowed ourselves to be subject to in our everyday lives and relationships. For me as woman and as teacher, the collective experiences of women shared in this way provided more fodder for critical reflection than the reading of feminist texts alone. While this experience certainly echoed the Freirian notion of 'conscientisation',[12] my role as academic and assessor did raise ethical questions about power that were difficult to resolve within the theoretical framework.

In the late 1980s, my colleague and I changed the title of the unit 'Radical Social Work' to 'Critical Reflexive Praxis'. At the time, we thought this new title reflected the critical content of the unit more effectively, especially the emphasis on the Freirian approach to empowerment and other critiques which drew breath from the critical school. We were also concerned at the time that the title 'radical' may set up an artificial binary between traditional social work theory and the message about structural social work we were trying to get across. We also felt that the word 'radical' might not capture the complexity of critical reflection which we believed needed to be incorporated across *all* units. The title of the unit was very quickly simplified to 'Critical Reflective Practice' and it caught on elsewhere. Given the latter-day co-option of the term for a rather more conservative approach of critical *self* reflec-

---

[12] Freire, op. cit.

tion in social work, not necessarily informed by structuralist understandings of social justice, I wonder in hindsight if we had not opened the doors for the conservatising trend we were to witness in the nineties.

In many ways, the eighties for me was the time when feminism and the linking of the personal with the political came to the fore. Feminism in the early 1980s seemed like a rather fixed ideal and I can certainly identify in some ways with those who saw feminism as overly militant and politically correct. It was only in the mid to late 80s that I became aware of the many different expressions of feminism, largely as a result of reading Marchant and Wearing's 1986 book.[13] Equipped with this knowledge, I continued to wear the hat of socialist feminist for the remainder of the 80s as it allowed for heterosexuality, class and culture to be a legitimate part of the juggling act I increasingly considered my feminism to be.

Working in the university sector brought benefits. While on study leave in the late 80s, I attended an international social work conference in Stockholm where I was privileged to hear Paulo Freire speak just before he died. This was as inspirational for me personally as visiting Sweden was enlightening from a social justice and policy perspective. The assumption of social democracy, which permeated all aspects of Swedish culture, alongside ideas of social justice and fairness as integrated and visible aspects of social policy, were like a breath of fresh air. Although political and economic culture may have shifted to the right of the political spectrum in the decades since, at the time, the ideals embedded in the political culture of Sweden provided a beacon of light as to how the economic and social could happily co-exist with minimal tension. This revived my faith that socially just societies are possible with collective will and understanding. Unfortunately, the experience

---

[13] H. Marchant and B. Wearing eds. *Gender Reclaimed: Women in Social Work* (Hale & Iremonger, 1986).

left me rather disillusioned about the possibilities for a similarly collective understanding in Australia and my faith in this possibility declined even further throughout the late 80s and 90s as Australian social policy along with political culture moved increasingly to the right of the political spectrum.

Overall the 80s were an opportunity to enact in practice the ideals with which we were inculcated as students in the 70s. Here I have mentioned only a few key highlights from practice and teaching, but in general, despite an increasingly austere economic and political context, there were ample opportunities to reflect and incorporate the theories of community development and transformative educational practice that I had written about in my undergraduate degree. My work with unemployed young people had initially been influenced by the radical possibilities of the cooperative movement which emanated from the United Kingdom as far back as the 1880s, but emulated in Mondragon in the Basque Region of Spain in the mid 20th century. I believed that if we were to talk socialism as a vehicle towards social change, then basically we had to live it. This sense was reinforced through exploring the radical possibilities of Ghandian non-violence[14] and applying it more specifically to the practice of community development. My earlier reading of Tonnies[15] had given me a theoretical base to the practice of community development with the simple idea that the more industrialised society became, the more atomised, individualised and instrumental our relationships would become. The shift from 'gemeinshcaft' to 'gesellschaft'[16] seemed to me to be as prophetic as Marx and Engel's historical materialism and perhaps even more so with the benefit of hindsight. In Australia in the 1980s, I did not feel that revolution was anything like an inevitable outcome of the

---

[14] Dasgupta op. cit.
[15] F. Tonnies *Community and Association* (Routledge, 1955).
[16] Ibid.

alienation associated with industrialisation. Rather, it seemed to me that with rampant individualist consumerism increasingly creating an alternative dominant hegemony, revolution remained a long way off and the concept of alienation somehow did not capture the complexity of the late 80s industrialised soul. In addressing the issue of structural violence and positing non-cooperation with the system as a realistic alternative, the Ghandian view, alongside an understanding of the radical potential of the concept of gemeinshaft, allowed for a reclaiming of the human spirit through non-violent process as an indispensible part of any desired outcomes. To me therefore, for individuals engaged in the process of 'regaining collective spirit', building community was a necessary starting point for change to occur. At the beginning of the 1980s, my views on the role of social work in social change were idealistic, and perhaps even naïve. I became increasingly disillusioned with my profession as the eighties wore on as the professional voice of social work became subdued; less occupied with issues of social justice and social disadvantage, (let alone advocacy for social change) and increasingly marginalised from decision making at policy or administrative levels. As the 80s drew to a close, optimism for the future began to wane in social work as social change theory began to be challenged by the discourse of individualism that heralded a move to the right in political culture. In the welfare academy, those of us committed to social justice ideals began to experience a general sense of weariness.[17] In some instances, in a number of universities, women social work academics reported incidents of backlash, specifically against feminism but also against the collectivist ideals which informed the social change agenda of social work.[18]

These, however, were only the early days of economic rational-

[17] J. Dillon, *Thirty Years of Feminist Activism: Women in Welfare Education Reflect* (unpublished PhD thesis, 2007).
[18] Ibid.

ism and it was to be the precipitous swing to the right that accompanied the globalisation project of the 90s and noughties that was to sow the seeds of dissatisfaction among those most affected that would create the conditions for the 'revolutions' inspired by the right of the political spectrum that we are witnessing today.

Conclusion

The picture that I have painted here is of my journey and engagement with radical social work through the 1970s and 1980s to a broad understanding of what it meant to be a critically reflexive practitioner. Each part of the narrative charts how the personal intersected with the political and the theoretical and as such, is located within and is at one and the same time an allegory of a rapidly changing context. In the intervening years, economic globalisation has taken its toll and the outlook for those most affected is grim. The task ahead is not easy.

Capitalism has always had globalising tendencies. When we look at how economic globalisation has played out since the 1990s and the relentless neo-liberal political agenda that has accompanied it in varying degrees worldwide, it is no accident that moves to the right in populist discourse support increasing individualism, a reemphasis on personal responsibility and a move away from structural explanations of social disadvantage. While the rhetoric from policy makers may be about 'diversity', there are clear boundaries and contradictions which beg questions about social sustainability. Increasing complexity at the social level is juxtaposed against the rhetorical search for simplicity that the cultural turn to the right brings. Of note is a rise in calls for traditional 'family' values and a resurgence of fundamentalist religion while notions of social justice and redistribution of wealth disappear as part and parcel of increasingly outmoded ideas of collectivity. Some commentators

89

have written of the 'politics of hate' resulting in rising xenophobia in a time of increasing diversity and the widening of gaps world wide between the haves and have nots. Increasingly the search for simplicity results in polarisation between disparate groups, increased social division and conflict alongside increasing poverty.

In response, social work in the Australian context has seen a shift from a proactive and broadly engaged, independent profession in the 1970s and early 80s to a narrowing of focus and has now become by and large a reactive, inward looking and parochial quasi profession with little power to influence policy decisions in anything more than a tokenistic way. The professional body remains preoccupied with localised and micro issues such as professional registration. In the increasingly globalised context, Social Work has indeed lost its soul and it is no wonder. The neoliberal agenda of politicians both left and right, keen on maintaining competitiveness in a global market has seen decreases to funding in universities that have led to cuts in funding to social work schools, resulting in decreasing class time against higher numbers of students. This combined with market-led demands has resulted in an educational culture in universities such that concern with mechanics and process has increasingly overtaken critical debate, especially on social issues. While Social Work academics in universities struggle to keep critical debate alive, the reality is a narrow focussing of the curriculum, as the local market for social work graduates largely emphasises the economic rationalist agenda.

While there are exceptions and while the rhetoric informing social work is about change, by and large social work students no longer see themselves as activists and are inclined to question engagement with the macro. In my view, this may reflect the dominant individualist discourse, but may also reflect the increasingly limited access to higher education that mature age activists experience. Once again, social work graduates are becoming the 'soft cops' of a parochial social system whose task it is to ensure the conformity of those 'deviants' who are ultimately the losers in the globalised economic climate. Once again, it is social workers who administer tightened eligibility for income and services, and the increased surveillance that now accompanies claims on welfare systems. While the International Federation of Social Workers (IFSW) engages with the rhetoric of international activism and human rights at the local level, social work graduates increasingly have little room for professional autonomy or the exercise of political voice that challenges the system on issues of concern. Where there is radical activism, it is likely to be in the area of international development and in global campaigns for human rights rather than localised campaigns. All this I suggest is compounded by a culture within the social work profession that identifies social work as casework or working with individuals. At the same time, the profession has conceded ground in community development to other specialist and non-social work courses and in research and social policy to economists. The narrowing of focus and of activity has left us less broadly skilled, less critically reflective and arguably co-opted into the parochial neoliberal agenda where an uncritical concern with free market economics has become the arbiter of all that is 'professional'.

This change is precisely at a time when social work needs to be more positively engaged within communities and more broadly concerned and active with/in both local and international movements for change. In order to do, this we need to encourage curriculum development that reengages structural theories and which reemphasise skills in understanding, researching and developing policy in both local and international settings. In addition, we need to revisit the notion of professionalism in a more critical way. If 'radical' means responding to the fundamental or root cause, then in our work with disadvantaged people our knowledge and skills need to consistently locate the causes of social disadvantage in the structures of late capitalism so that we can more effectively work with individuals, groups and communities with a clearer understanding of what empowerment actually means. I suggest that a reinvigorated social work curriculum with its broad base of knowledge, skills and the understanding that critical theory brings, still has a capacity to make a difference. Certainly, in the challenging climate of the globalised economy and the swing to the right exemplified in Brexit and the recent election of Trump, it will need a large dose of creativity and innovation to progress. The lessons from the past are there for those who are willing to heed.

6

FROM THE LIMP HAND TO THE CLENCHED FIST:

Framework Firestorms in a School of Social Work

Bill De Maria

On 19 August 2016 the cream of Queensland social work met at historic Customs House on the Brisbane River to "celebrate" 60 years of social work education at the University of Queensland. Social workers, past and present, mingled and reminisced. It must have been a jolly night. The collective memory, however, did not flow quite as easily as the expensive wine. What was missing is the subject of this chapter; an event that so confronts the public image of the School of Social Work as an ethical workplace, that it has, until now, been weeded out from the carefully manicured historical record.

Introduction

1 July 1998 was one of the coldest days of the year in Brisbane. Things were about to hot up. Around 11.00am, I was called by the personal assistant to the University of Queensland Vice Chancellor, John Hays. "Dr. De Maria, the Vice Chancellor has an important letter for you. Where are you"? I took the call half way up a ladder in an ex-brothel I was renovating in Woolloongabba.

Flash back twelve months; night time 8 July 1997. Fresh from giving a day seminar to the Northern Rivers Special Interest group of the Australian Association of Social Workers on radical social work in non-radical settings, I was summoned before the Head of School, a young person whose ambition sat poorly with his inexperience. With the Head of School was the reliably pugnacious Director of Personnel. This man (a former Christian Brother) took over what was to be my summary professional execution Seething with rage, he told me, with the Head of School in mute concurrence, that I was suspended from the University, was not to enter its precincts, not to have contact with any staff, and prepare myself for a misconduct tribunal. He bellowed: "By the way, your nomination for the UQ Teaching Excellence Award will not be processed now".

My academic social work career ended that night. I recall the last thing I said to them both; "You cannot reprise me like this, I carry the full protection of parliamentary privilege". They scoffed at this claim. As future events would so clearly show, the University had just made the first of many blunders it was to make in its attempt to bring me down. In fact, I owe a weird sort of debt to the people in senior management at the University. Their arrogant incompetence in the prosecution of the case against me gave some neutral observers the impression that these managers had just strolled off the set of *Dad's Army*.

It was 8.00pm when I reached my car in the Social Work parking lot after that life changing meeting. The night offered itself as a silent witness as recollections zipped through my mind. One gained prominence; the silence, the complete silence of my Head of School. It was obvious that my suspension from the University, after 19 years in Social Work, was a result wanted that night. The Head of School offered no peace overtures nor expressed regret that it had come to this. Nothing, just silence; like the night.

Twelve months later, and 12 minutes after the call from the Vice

Chancellor's PA, a black limousine quietly glides up to my broken-down bordello. Out stepped the Vice Chancellor's chauffer in black suit and driving cap. Walking carefully between scattered tools and wall sheeting he handed me a letter from the Senior Deputy Vice Chancellor, Ted Brown. The letter, opened with dusty work-worn hands said, in paraphrase; Dr. De Maria…Ah sorry! Everything is forgiven. Your year-long suspension is lifted and the allegations of serious misconduct against you are unilaterally withdrawn. Why don't you come in for a little chat as to your future at the University? And don't go near the Social Work School until we have spoken.

From my persecutor to my new best friend. What had triggered the University's dramatic *volte face*? The previous night, the powerful Senate Privileges Committee of the Commonwealth Parliament, under the chairmanship of the Victorian ALP's Robert Ray, had tabled its 72nd report, *Possible Improper Action Against a Person (Dr. William De Maria)*. Its unanimous finding, so momentarily devastating for the University of Queensland, was one of contempt of the Senate for taking disciplinary action against me for exercising a right that goes back to Charles II. The University of Queensland had illegally punished me for drawing Parliament's attention to the decade long harassment. I was subjected to in the Social Work School. What a victory! I thought. The first time ever in the legal history of any Commonwealth law country that a university has been found guilty of contempt of parliament. Other than imprisonment, this is the greatest punishment parliaments can impose, and it was being imposed on my university.

This massive back step and forced peace overture by the University made me feel triumphant and vindicated. The University was very shaken by this turn of events which they very definitely were not expecting. My so-called misconduct tribunal was set up, the noose ready and swinging in the breeze; they were rearing to go. The lights burned into the night in the Brian Wilson Chancellery Building as shocked senior management processed the Senate findings and plotted their next course. I gave myself a few minutes to savour a fallen University Goliath at my feet. But make no mistake, this was a Pyrrhic victory. A little battle won in a huge, never-ending war between outspokenness and obedience that I would so utterly fail in.

After my forced re-instatement, I elected not to go back to the School of Social Work. Being out of action for a year with no classes or students had dried me up. Much to the satisfaction of my former social work colleagues, radical social work had vaporised from the curriculum. While my writings in the area ceased and I never returned to this important area of scholarship, I did enjoy an intellectual renaissance. The University very reluctantly brokered an arranged marriage between me and the UQ Business School. My location in this gaudy shrine to capitalism is a delicious, comedic irony. But that's a story for another time.

Self-doubt taps me on the shoulder every now and again and whispers: "Given the enormous consequences of your action in going public about the goings on in the UQ Social Work School, could you have not found a better way"? After all these years, my answer is the same: "Probably not." Hidden in the folds of that response is a remorseless self-critique of my actions which I share with the reader now.

With me gone, and the radical curriculum gone, social work orthodoxy, obedient, sycophantic, elitist and ineffective, had, again, a clear field, which it has enjoyed to the present day. How did it come to this? To reach for this answer I need to put down a dialectical challenge to the reader. Follow me through the events that ended so badly for me and the pedagogic future of radical social work in Queensland, but don't follow me at the same time. I am only your guide. I am not the story. You must find the bigger story. I can only give you a hint. Go deep into context and locate the substratum tensions between obedience and dissent, elitism and accountability and self-interest and public interest (to name a few). Context is everything, as radical social workers used to say.

As I struggle myself to go deep into the context to find the real story for the reader, it is, beginning to end, my story. So, I hope the reader also sees my humanness, flaws and all. And you are going to see anger. While I have a lot to be resentful about, after all, my social work career was destroyed, it is up to the reader to determine whether I have gained mastery of these emotions in the story telling or my reminiscence is an attempt to get even. I hope I receive the former judgement as the chapter is a genuine effort to take a step back, now after 19 years, and examine a very momentous period in the 60-year history of the School of Social Work at the University of Queensland.

I wrote this chapter looking through my mind's eye at those young Social Work students, who each year start their courses brimming with idealism and a vague determination to do something positive in this world. The big message in this chapter for these young people is, be smarter than me in trying to change things. If you want to talk back to power don't act alone. Why? Because powerful people in powerful organisations (yes even Social Work organisations) will, if challenged, effortlessly flick the switch to meat grinder.

So, while I hope my own personal feelings about what happened to me do not highjack the narrative, it remains an account heavily tinted with a profound alienation from orthodox Social Work. Let me quickly explore this point, as many social workers would find it deeply offensive. First, my reckless use of the phrase "orthodox Social Work". It refers to the dominant, state approved style of practice that micro-manage the myriad forms of human distress that drain from broader economic and social malfunctioning. Since the end of World War II, generations of caring people the developed world over have been attracted to orthodox Social Work's laudatory intentions to bring the poor out of poverty and the oppressed out of injustice. It took the florescence of the radical social work analysis in the 1970s and beyond to expose this as a political deceit, a liberal deception; a chimera in other words. Social work is and always has been, an embedded state institution. Need I remind readers of our history here? A century before the start of social work professionalisation, our founding mothers were upper class British poor law superintendents exercising the morally bankrupt stance of *nobles oblige.*

As part of the State, orthodox Social Work answers to a higher authority then the moral imperatives of its client base. It can only help the outcast on the State's terms, which as we know, are getting harsher and more oppressive as the years pass. The winners in this captured state enterprise are first and foremost the State itself, as it gets civil serenity and obedience from the potentially disruptive disadvantaged in exchange for a few scraps of welfare. But there are other winners. Academic social workers, like I was, are also the winners. We operate the Venus Fly Traps that year after year induce the high-minded, gullible Social Work students to training. For our purposes, not our students, we determine that their boot camp will take a minimum of four years when in reality the cold charity neo-liberal "welfare" state is so lacking in generosity, change opportunities and resources that the social work that is allowed to be practiced now only needs a solid six months' training at a TAFE college. Winners too are the contented social work practice managers like those who gathered at the diamond jubilee of social work education at the University of Queensland. The idea that their practice is part of the class struggle *against* their clients remains incomprehensible within the comfort of their middle-class lifestyles. Perhaps we should have had a fringe gathering to mark 60 + years of poverty and disadvantage in Queensland in a nearby park with beer and sausages?

Bleak as it is, offensive to some, as it should be, this chapter is a piece of reminiscence, not a piece of scholarship. However, I need to refer you to my writings as I go down memory's path. I started writing published works as a social work student and only stopped at the time of my summary professional execution. Writing was an essential pathway into the oppressive character of orthodox social work. Writing took me deeper and deeper into a soft Marxist analysis. Between, generally speaking, 1970-2000, this Marxian analysis provided a rare, international-wide opportunity to critique social work practice from an external heterodox position. So effective and plausible was this critique that it was selectively absorbed into the thinking of many mainstream social work academics and practitioners. I should note here that although I grazed in many intellectual paddocks other than Marxism, to conservative social work colleagues and students I was nothing but a Stalinist apparatchik justifying the Siberian Gulags!

Knowing what could be done when people rise-up and take control of their solutions (the clenched fist) grinded against the forlorn insight that I worked in a School of Social Work which was part of the problem (the limp hand); where the dominant zeitgeist prioritised career, smart liberal talk about tolerance and freedom, Masonic-like collegial reciprocities and very definitely a fear of engaging in direct action.

The chapter first gives slight attention to my ideological formation. From there some significant moments in the years I was in practice before becoming an academic are briefly outlined. Then the chapter starts its real work of examining my life as a radical social worker in the School and the final conflict which ended my social work career forever.

The ideological formation of young Billy

Early days

If you did not live by the sea in Sydney, Saturday afternoons was the magic moment of the week as we scampered to the local pictures to see Hoppalong Cassidy, the Cisco Kid, the Lone Ranger, Kit Carson and many others. These Hollywood heroes would magically transport us out of the dreary Menzien suburban life in the 1950s. The Royal Anthem obligatorily played before each movie. It was the era. Everybody was expected to stand up. Not me! I had a simple thirteen-year old unease about automaton obedience. I don't remember the source of this opposition, but I still remember how scared I was remaining seated. I think the biggest worry was that I might be humiliated.

Don't ask where this emerging anti-authoritarian streak came from. Certainly not my parents, who got on with working hard in the post war period and paying attention to what the priest told them on Sundays, particularly about those anti-Christs in the Australian Labor Party. Certainly not my school, Marist Brothers Kogarah, where thinking for yourself was not part of God's plan for us.

As a side point, years later, in 1985, I had a *déjà vu* moment when the Vice Chancellor Brian Wilson, visited the School for talks about the headship when the renowned Edna Chamberlain retired. Everyone in the room (except me again) stood up at the same time for the Vice Chancellor. The Vice Chancellor looked uncomfortable. He glanced at me sitting and gave me a look that suggested "I get it". Am I being petty here? Was this coming to attention not just the act of normal courtesy? Maybe, but maybe I had detected something deep in the social work DNA; a mutant obedience gene?

University days

Shiftless and aimless, the wind blew me through the gates of the School of Social Work at the University of New South Wales in 1967. Given my high school results, I only got in because big changes to secondary school education meant no school kids were entering university that year. My first-year class was a wonderful eclectic mix of characters, a bit like the bar scene from *Star Wars*!

The School was probably the best in Australia at that time, and it achieved that status very rapidly. It was brand new and it felt brand new. The wonderful Norma Parker had been appointed inaugural Professor of Social Work in late 1965 and the School started in late 1967. The first chair of Social Work was taken up in mid-1968 by the brilliant John Lawrence who brought a fresh kinetic energy to the task. Lawrence mustered the tops in their fields: the incomparable Tony Vinson in social work theory and research, the kind and stolid Spencer Colliver in social administration, the brilliant and eccentric Murray Geddes in community work, Frank Pavlin and Mal McCouat, seriously mismatched, in clinical practice and Clare Bundy in group work. All these people would remain deeply influential in Social Work for many years after that.

Tony Vinson and Murray Geddes, both brilliant and charismatic, alone of all the staff assisted with my emerging radicalisation. That I would go well beyond both in my radicalism would not I think have surprised these men, such was the calibre of their characters. Murray, unintentionally, got me thinking how small minded community work can be when it moved from a similar ontological base as the other traditional methods. Years later, I would see this small-minded community work offered in the Social Work curriculum in Brisbane. This goes well into explaining why no bridges, as one would expect, were built between community work and radical social work in the School.

The Vietnam War and my involvement in the notorious Moratorium were far more significant radicalising moments for me than anything I learned in class. In fact, so profound was the Vietnam War on my young suburban consciousness that I ended up leaving the Catholic Church and forever parting from non-advocate forms of Social Work. I have a photo of a group of us in one of the Moratorium marches from UNSW to the city carrying a banner "Social Work Students against the War". It was a very small group.

Gladesville Psychiatric Hospital and other places

Fresh faced from university, in 1971 I was appointed the first community social worker in New South Wales. I operated out of Ward 18 whose catchment area was the inner western suburbs of Sydney; Ashfield, Burwood, places like that. Each day was a cognitive challenge for me. I worked in a space with a very long history of psychiatric oppression. Originally called the Gladesville Asylum, my office was just a short distance form an underground pier where patients were rowed across the river for incarceration. The metal rings used to fasten their chains on arrival were still there.

My two years at Gladesville saw me active in the contest between the dominant medical model and the minority social model, so reviled by the psychiatrists. This was the era of community psychiatry. A bogus and oppressive American import that lasted far too long in mental health policy in Australia. The wards were being forcibly emptied and hospital staff redeployed into the "community", *terra incognito,* even *terra horribilis*, to many a medical model warrior. I soon got the message that by resourcing these new community mental health centres we were just bringing psychiatric power closer to the people. In the era of second generation psychotropic drugs, pharmaceuticals took over what physical restraints had been doing for centuries. In this embroilment, I wrote two articles for the AASW Journal. The first on a social development model for Social Work[1] and the second crystallising my emerging anti-psychiatry stance.[2]

I did not hang around the hospital much. I was, after all a community social worker. With the guarded concurrence of my senior social worker, the very ethical Joy Moran, I manoeuvred myself into the position of Director of the Burwood Community Mental Health Centre. That's when the sparks started to fly. Exercising limited official power, I worked consciously on non-medical model agendas, rudimentary as they were in hindsight. Even though my style of community work at that stage was pretty safe; inter-agency committees, things like that, it still was too much for the psychiatrist in charge of the catchment, Dr Martin. I still remember the fateful meeting in the office of the Medical Superintendent, the quiet and placid David Lonie. Joy Moran was crying, I was supposed to be her *wunderkind.* Martin's voice was strong and intemperate. "It's either he or me" he bellowed. Lonie was conciliatory and asked that I return to Ward 18. I resigned and cleared out to Asia with my new girlfriend, with whom I would celebrate our ruby wedding anniversary in 2016.

My personal mode of practice was emerging from this Gladesville experience that, curiously, remained pretty much intact to the end of my career. Looking back on that now, I can see how elements in it contributed to my downfall. My emerging radicalism produced a reciprocating alienation. I found myself apart from a good deal of collegial networking, I did, however, have a natural affinity to disempowered people (including students). The pattern of my ineffectiveness was emerging; strong change advocacy, pro-

---

[1] W. De Maria, 'Social Welfare: Strategies for Social Development', *Australian Journal of Social Work*, 26(1), 1973, 11-19.

[2] W. De Maria, 'The Psychiatric Industry. A Study of Shock Absorbers, Brakes and Blunt Tools', *Australian Journal of Social Work*, 27(2), 1974, 21-3.

moted too quickly with little collegial support. The lone wolf was a pup but it was howling into the night time stillness when everyone else was asleep. Perhaps I am being too hard on myself here but this pattern followed me through my career, except in two spaces; the classroom and the manuscript. In my defence, as I have said, I found myself deeply alienated in most of my work spaces. Hospitals, universities and the like that employed me all turned against their core missions; hospitals to care, universities to offer reprisal-free spaces to think. Isn't the lone wolf just an expression of this alienation?

Returning to Australia, I was appointed the first social planner in NSW when I joined the special projects team in the Town Planning Department at Bankstown Council in 1973. After that I took on the role of Director of Social Planning for the Riverina Council for Social Developments, one of the principal funded regions under Whitlam's audacious Australian Assistance Plan. While the specific workplace imperatives of both positions took me into non-radical practice, I did somehow remain theoretically connected to the radical agenda. I conceptualised an advocacy-counselling model for social workers wanting to bridge from interpersonal work to social action. That piece went into *Australian Social Work* in 1977.[3] In the same year, and in the same area, *Australian Social Work* published my *Social Work as Social Critique*. Here I was again working the concepts between action and practice.[4]

University of Queensland School of Social Work: Summer Days 1978-1986

In 1977, after giving a lecture at Brandeis University (where I was travelling on a Churchill Scholarship), I threw caution to the wind

[3] W. De Maria, 'Advocacy-Counselling: A Double Entry System of Social Welfare', *Australian Journal of Social Work*, 30(1), 1977, 5-8.
[4] W. De Maria, 'Social Work as Social Critique', *Australian Journal of Social Work*, 32A, 1979, 9-13.

and wrote to Edna Chamberlain, the Head of School at the University of Queensland. I told her I was returning to Australia and was there any chance of a job. I had known Edna since my days as Secretary of the NSW Branch of the Australian Association of Social Workers. Can I pause briefly to say that my alienation from orthodox social work was a progressive thing. In the beginning, I made an effort to reform within the orthodoxy, hence my AAASW position.

Edna wrote back the most encouraging letter. I applied and got a job as a Tutor Grade IV. The unanimous conclusion of my selection panel is instructive:

> The committee discussed the application of Mr. W.A. De Maria ... It was agreed that he is a challenging person who, while occasionally "rocking the boat" would be of great value in the department.

As events will show, my "great value in the department" would not last.

Edna's illustrious and compassionate career is on the public record. Unlike me, she embraced the wholeness of social work and championed equally all its practice modalities. She was, in this respect, a true post-enlightenment liberal. But this is not what I remember most about Edna. It was her solid moral leadership that I recall the most. Under her leadership, the School was a vibrant, ethical space. There were no visible factions, no bullying, no posturing for power and certainly no nepotism. All this came later. There was a high level of collegial respect and morale was high. It was a good place to go to work. Putting the School in such a moral place was Edna's great, untold contribution.

The reader is at liberty to dispense with my aims for this chapter and to see it instead as a tale of the absolute indispensability of moral leadership to an organisation's wellbeing. When Edna retired, she left a moral vacuum that has never been filled. Over the years, up to the present, into this vacuum, so regrettably, has poured vindictiveness, nepotism, dishonesty, confusion and above all fear.

Although I know I strained our friendship at times, I always knew Edna had my back. She wouldn't use these words but she clearly mentored me and gave me protected space to think outside the orthodoxy. I remember she handed over to me her own flagship undergraduate course, *SW250: Philosophy and Social Work.* It was like receiving a bequest from a favourite aunt. Even though I changed the course considerably, I like to think I never disappointed her with my custodianship of it. I co-ordinated this course for 16 years until it was taken away from me as part of the School's reprisal package.

Edna and I collaborated on some trailblazing research on the legal needs of social security clients. We then developed a course for lay advocates to assist social security appellants with their reviews and appeals on social security matters. We also co-jointly founded the Brisbane Welfare Rights Centre in 1985 which still exists today by another name. I feel privileged to know that these projects were amongst the last that Edna worked on before her portentous retirement.

My Masters of Social Work degree was another strongly conceptualised, if not over-elaborated account of the relationship between ideology and social work. Edna was my very enthusiastic and supportive thesis supervisor. It was marked by two eminent British social workers in the radical field, Vic George and Paul Wilding.

From that thesis flowed three articles in 1982. The first one "Fumbling with the kaleidoscope: Worldview Clashes in Social Work" for the *Canadian Journal of Social Work Education,*[5] established, at least for myself, that Social Work is a marketplace of contend-

---

[5] W. De Maria, 'Fumbling with the Kaleidoscope: Worldview Clashes in Social Work', *Canadian Journal of Social Work Education*, 8(1-2), 1982, 31-43.

ing values and aspirations. This paper marked an early assault on hegemony and obedience. In the same year, *Australian Social Work* published my "Empiricism: An Impoverished Philosophy for Social Work Research".[6] This came about in two ways. First, my feelings of suffocation as researchers in the School were pushed into the quantitative model which had absolutely no bridges into action. I was also moved to write the piece from something a caseworker colleague said one day in a staff meeting in 1981. "Social work is a science" she confidently proclaimed. The follow up "just joking" never came; my colleague was deadly serious. How, I thought can an academic social worker proclaim this antediluvian nonsense in the 1980s. The third piece, for the American *Journal of Sociology and Social Welfare* was titled "The Dreaming and the Doing: Utopian Foundations of Social Action".[7] Then a year later, in 1983, "Dialectics and Dominations: Reflections on Social Action" for the *Australian & New Zealand Journal of Sociology.*[8] More attempts to build a conceptual exoskeleton for social action in social work.

I did not publish in this genre again until 1991. The period in-between was used to publish works from my 1988 welfare history PhD (supervised outside the School) and for my work as a member of the Commonwealth Administrative Appeals Tribunal that I was appointed to in 1983. Those AAT articles got me into enormous trouble, but that's another story.

Between 1991-93 six articles by me on the teaching of radical social work were published in various journals such as *British Journal of Social Work, Journal of Sociology and Social Welfare,* and of course *Australian Social Work* which developed a surpris-

[6] W. De Maria, 'Empiricism: An Impoverished Philosophy for Social Work Research', *Australian Journal* of *Social Work*, 34(4), 1982, 3-8.
[7] W. De Maria, 'The Dreaming and the Doing: Utopian Foundations of Social Action', *Journal of Sociology and Social Welfare*, 9(2), 1982, 186-202.
[8] W. De Maria, 'Dialectics and Domination: Reflections on Social Action', *Australia & New Zealand Journal of Sociology*, 19(1), 1983, 50-78.

ing support for my work over the years.[9] This batch of papers cross-fertilised with the radical social work course I was teaching to fourth year students.

The teaching pattern stabilised for a few years. In first semester, my main intervention was *Philosophy and Social Work* where my first lecture, "Social Work as Social Control" set the theme. In second semester, my main teaching was in *Social work and Social change*. Here, with Mal McCouat and Yaro Starak, I would introduce students to conflict theory with the subversive twist that change waits on conflict.

School of Social Work: Winter Days 1986-1998

1985 is a critical watershed year in this account. That was when Edna Chamberlain retired. The University advertised Edna's position internationally. My heart soared when it attracted the attention of Professor Peter Leonard, the world leading exponent of radical social work. He had been, among many other things, the youngest member of the influential *Seebohm Committee* whose report in 1968 led to unified social work practice in the UK. Ten years later, with co-author Paul Corrigan, he published one of the definitive books on radical social work, *Social Work Practice under Capitalism: A Marxist Approach*.[10] This book was published in the same

---

[9] W. De Maria, 'Re-possessing the Neo-Conservative Classroom: Social Work Strategies for a Radical Pedagogy', *Advances in Social Welfare Education*, 1991. W. De Maria, 'Social Work and Mediation: Hemlock in the Flavour of the Month', *Australian Social Work*, 45(1), March 1992, 17-28. W. De Maria, 'On the trail of a Radical Pedagogy for Social Work', *British Journal of Social Work*, 22(3), June 1992, 231-252. W. De Maria, 'Alive on the Streets, Dead in the Classroom: The Return of Radical Social Work and the Manufacture of Radicalism', *Journal of Sociology and Social Welfare*. IX: 3, September 1992, 137-158. W. De Maria, 'Critical Pedagogy and the Forgotten Social Work Student: The Return of Radical Practice', *Australian Social Work*, March 1993. W. De Maria, 'Exploring radical Social Work Teaching in Australia', *Journal of Progressive Human Services*, 4(2), 1993, 45-63.

[10] P. Corrigan & P. Leonard, *Social Work Practice under Capitalism: A Marxist Approach* (Palgrave Macmillan, 1978).

year I started in the School. From the beginning, I had an authoritative radical social work text to work with.

Peter and I had a friendship going back to the days when I was the Director of Social Planning for the Riverina Council for Social Development based in Wagga Wagga. Peter was on sabbatical from the University of Warwick and the Department of Foreign Affairs encouraged him to come and see the new community engagement programs I was establishing in the Riverina under the Australian Assistance Plan.

Staff in the School of Social Work took a unanimous vote to endorse Peter Leonard in February 1986, one month *before* he came out to Brisbane for the selection process. That was the last time staff showed common cause to fashioning a School on social justice lines. A virus was entering the social work school's body politic, which was just starting to show symptoms.

Leonard met staff and gave a lecture on radical social work. There were two others on the short list, including Jan Carter, one of the great social work practitioners in Australia who had achieved much at the Brotherhood of St. Laurence in Melbourne. For reasons I am not aware of, Jan Carter pulled out. So too did Peter Leonard. He astutely picked up a worrying vibe in the School. He turned down the job offer, going to McGill University instead where he felt he was more able to develop his vision of social work and social justice. That missed opportunity to have Leonard as Head of School in Brisbane was nothing short of a tragedy.

With Carter and Leonard out of contention, the offer was made and accepted by the third person on the list. I was not the only one who opposed this appointment. I was, however, the only one who made my views public. I would like to pause momentarily and reconnoitre this issue of going public. It was clearly my undoing, as it is for the majority of dissenters and whistle blowers. Going public will always be lethal for the discloser because it alone, of all the strategies in the activist's arsenal, is the one that exposes the *reputation* of the organisation. This *reputation* is the core of an organisation's survival. We know from a mountain of research evidence (most recently from the Royal Commission into Institutional Responses to Child Sexual Abuse) that so exposed, organisations will fight back with a lethal vengeance.

So I argued for re-advertisement of the position, claiming that such a central position should not go to someone who was only able to achieve the confidence of the selection committee once two other candidates were out of contention. Torvil and Dean, the British master skaters were in town that week. Little did I know that it was I who had just slipped onto the thin ice. I did not find out until many years later that the third placed candidate was only in the position of Head of School for about eighteen months when that person wrote a secret memo to the Vice-Chancellor, Brian Wilson, in October 1990:

> [There is] a fairly consistent pattern of harassment of students and staff both within the Social Work Department and in other departments by Dr. De Maria. This has continued over several years, and has been the cause of numerous complaints...to the Department, appeals to the Student Union and appeals to the [University] Senate.

The third placed candidate, as Head of School, and apparently on "behalf of the Department" asked the Vice-Chancellor to have me investigated. This vexatious and libellous complaint went the same way as all the other behind my back accusations – nowhere. As for my reputation outside the radical social work class; it was goodbye to that.

The third placed candidate took over a year to take up the appointment because the University was put into a position of trying to find employment for the candidate's spouse. Despite the best intentions of the interim Head during this interregnum, the very spiritual Alan Halliday, the School went into a deep policy ennui. All major policy initiatives were met with the same riposte, "We will have to wait until the head gets here". School morale was slipping. Staff retreated into their offices. But in that year, something remarkable happened.

SW402 Stream D: D for Danger?

When I look back at my rocky time in the School, my most surprising teaching achievement was that I was able to offer a radical social work course continuously for 11 years, from 1987 to 1997. How this happened is a story ready for retelling.

In 1982 I was prominent in driving a curriculum reform into offerings in the final academic semester in the degree program. The changes went through, allowing students to spend double the normal time in their chosen practice option before their last practicum. Five years later this was to be the logical nest in which to lay the radical social work egg.

On 14 November 1986, a meeting was convened to discuss my proposal for a new course with the deliberately innocuous title "Social Work in Bureaucracies", to go onto the coveted option list for first semester fourth year. The meeting, ignored by some staff, boycotted by others, recommended the go ahead and this was accepted by the interim Head.

The success of the proposal was largely accounted for by the support of students. The proposal listed 22 students who were interested in doing the first course in 1987. Of this total 13, students pulled out and picked up other options. Some of these students had listened very carefully to reports of a staff member at a meeting saying that the "field" would be displeased if the stream went ahead. One student was told by her student unit supervisor that if she did my stream, she would not expect a reference from that supervisor. To her credit the student overrode this blackmail (how valuable can a supervisor's reference be anyhow?).

After she did the course, this student, who went on to an impressive leadership role in the Brisbane welfare scene said:

> Upon entering Stream D, I had many pre-conceived ideas about not only the content but the personal repercussions that would result from partaking in such a subject. Instilled by fear, these repercussions included: diminished job prospects, severed field and social contact, and what I felt was the most threatening, the loss of respect and credibility from people whose judgments and friendships I felt were very precious to me.
>
> I now believe that I have gained a far deeper and more personal learning from "Social Work in Bureaucracies" than I had anticipated.... I do feel I have come a long way since the beginning of the semester. The forms of collective action and indeed the forms of social work which we as a group are endeavouring to practice involves incredible risk taking and I have to state that I have amazed myself with how much I am willing to risk in comparison to three months ago. Coming into the group as a non-assertive personality, I have been placed in role plays that have attempted to draw out of me the very confidence that I have been lacking. But more importantly, I have learned and experienced how being part of a collective minimises the personal and social risks involved in social action, that otherwise serve to steal your confidence.

Re-reading this statement, all these years later, I realised how un-switched on I was to the risks students took in signing up for my course. That now counts as a big failing on my part.

Over my 11-year run with the course, it changed shape a few

times in response to student feedback and my own growing experience in offering a fringe program. One constant was that course design offered working practice and working perspectives. It was never my intention to produce unemployable misfits. The students who crossed the Rubicon to do my course did so with the expectation that they would have a remunerated career and that I would assist with this aspiration.

One important innovation in this regard was a design component called *Fieldlink*. At the start of each course, students were asked to make contact with a social worker, spend half a day with this person to obtain agency case material in four areas: a recent first client contact, a recent groupwork or family intervention matter, a recent piece of social action (rarely found) and a recent issue over staff or resources. Students brought these anonymised real time matters into class. This was our solid case bank that we drew on for the entirety of the semester. There were no more practice ready students graduating from UQ Social Work in that time then Stream D students. For every week of semester, the class became both a laboratory and an architectural workshop. In "laboratory" mode we dissected and critiqued the orthodox, State permitted practice as reported by the social workers who had been interviewed at the start of semester. I insisted students always maintained respect for these social workers' confidantes. In "architect" mode, we designed new ways of intervening on the same case facts in ways consistent with radical social work principles. Students then went back to their social work sources to engage them with these new ideas. Sometimes these engagements worked; other times they didn't.

Running the course was a bit like walking in front of a tiger's cage. Menace was in the air. It came in many forms from the pettiness of other students (replacing my nameplate with "Dr. De Marxia) to the secretive belligerence of staff, who amongst other things were displeased that Stream D students were coming into their classes with lots of new questions. There was, however, an unwritten rule. If I got too popular, if Stream D enrolments exceeded more than 20% of the total class enrolments then the School leadership would have moved against the course. I was never able to get more than 10% of the year. Small and safe.

Reflections

The engagement between the powerful social work orthodoxy and radical social work could not be anything other than deeply conflictual, for radical social work (at least my version) questioned the very legitimacy of all forms of social work practice (including its own). The smoke of this ideological battle wafted over many schools of social work in the developed world during the eighties and nineties. Looking back on that period now, it is clear that radical social work never had a chance. When the battle smoke cleared by the late nineteen nineties, orthodox social work stood shaken but triumphant, ready, once again to do the State's bidding.

There were no ideological battles in my School in the sense of open engagements about different outlooks. I recall May 1996. By now times were really tough for me in the School. I was visited by Professor Bob Mullaly, a Canadian academic who had published valuable works in the radical social work field. He was on a national tour and had been well received in other Schools of Social Work throughout Australia. I organised a seminar for him for the 31 May. There was an enormous turnout of Brisbane social workers and students. In fact, it was one of the best attended seminars in the School for a long time. Other than me, not one member of the academic staff bothered to attend.

The post-Chamberlain School of Social Work was a place of factions, fear and nepotism. There was nothing conducive here for free and frank discussion about radical social work. It seems that this culture went dark very quickly. The victory of an 11-year run of Stream D was not achieved by force of argument, for that would never work. It was attained by stealth and persistence: the *modus operandi* of the guerrilla. It was also achieved by my loyal compatriots in arms; students whose real hunger for social justice was not satisfied in any other parts of the curriculum.

The post-Chamberlain School, being what it was, meant that the ideological tension over radical social work was never exercised openly. There were many reasons for this. I think I understand a few of them. The power group in the School had built, or were building, their careers on solid, non-reflective conservative ground. They were not about to allow the radical challenge to their practice go unimpeded. Secondly the radical spirit in the School had evaporated by the mid-1970s. I could not access a likeminded community of scholars.

Little wonder that failed open engagement soon found proxy equivalents in clandestine personal attacks. The post-Chamberlain School became a gossip culture. The most outrageous things were said about colleagues. Gossip was not discouraged because it had utility with the power elite and the upwardly aspiring camp followers because it was a way of keeping tabs on *everyone*.

I was the target of a lot of this gossip. As whistle blowers well know, take out the messenger and you take down the message. I remember the ostracism. Such a psychologically powerful weapon; the organisational equivalent of death. I remember the loneliness. I remember snippets of conversation showing that School social events had come and gone without my knowledge or involvement. I remember my self-imposed exile from staff meetings. By now, I was only coming to work for my students. I did my research at home. The atmosphere went on for 11 years; sustained, secret, and completely off the ethical Richter Scale. I hung in there because I totally believed in what I was doing, and the world was not exactly beating a path to my door with new job offers. Time, I knew, was running out for me.

In the end, mimicking an embattled Prime Minister of Australia, I had to crash or crash through. Well I did both! I crashed through and then I crashed. A report detailing 19 allegations of organisational wrongdoing against me was tabled in the Commonwealth Senate on 27 May 1997 by Senator John Woodley. In his tabling speech Woodley referred to one of my allegations, the failure of the School and the University to protect me from political attack.

> I want to make mention tonight of Dr. William De Maria...[He] has done some pioneering work in researching...whistle blowers. It is important to highlight the value of the work done by Dr. De Maria and his researchers... Certainly Dr. De Maria's work should be seen as bringing credit to the University of Queensland's social work department.
>
> However, there was one disturbing aspect of Dr. De Maria's study into whistle blowing which comes not from his report but from the reaction which he received as a consequence of it.
>
> When the details from the study were released, the credibility of the research and the researcher was attacked by the then Premier, Mr. Goss. Mr. Goss was reported in the *Australian* newspaper alleging that Dr. De Maria had made up details in at least one of the cases contained in his research-a serious allegation. In the State Parliament on 12 April 1994, Mr. Goss again attacked Dr. De Maria.

As mentioned, Senator Woodley's statement was made in the Senate on 29 May 1997. Then something happened that was pernicious but not unexpected. With my main enemies working the phones over the following weekend, it took only one working day for the *entire* Social Work School to issue a three-page refutation of all my allegations and a unanimous support for the Head of School. This refutation, with defamatory material lurking in every sentence, was then sent to the Australian Senate in an unsuccessful bid to derail my complaints.

The document deserves our attention. In all the years of examining workplace violence and ostracism, I have never heard of a case where an *entire* work unit attacked with a single voice a fellow worker. Yet here it was happening to me! This is a document that could only come out of a workplace riven by fear and nepotism. The document, which is on the public record, is clearly the product of a master's class in sycophantic writing. The School, the document asserts, is managed "exceptionally well", the Head of School is "outstanding", no staff "engage in self-censorship", there is "no ruling orthodoxy" and imputations of nepotism are "a slur on us all and are completely without foundation".

Inscrutable as this aspect of the School's reprisal culture was, I owe it to the reader to make some sense of it all. We can toss many elements into the explanatory mix. I will focus on one; the power of the Head of School. This power, bloated during this period as a consequence of decentralising models of decision making that were all the rage back then, took on a venal sharpness when that power was exercised over a cowered and compliant collegial community. Heads of School hold in their hand the careers of all academics under their authority. They can open their hands and let these careers fly like birds, or they can close their hand and crunch the life out of them. Heads of School use this power to recommend, *inter alia*, promotions, endorse research applications, support tenure, appoint subject coordinators, write references and approve the allocation of resources. All these are the life sources of careers. All of my former colleagues who signed the three- page refutation needed one or more of these "gifts" at the time of signing. This explanation does not need a malevolent force sitting in the Head of School's office.

It just needs an exercise of enlightened self-interest by staff. Ninety two percent of the staff who signed were at the level lecturer and below of which 41% were very junior members in the School who could not possibly form a considered view of the background to the Senate submission. Decent individuals all of them. However, when they signed they joined the mob, they lost their individuality and they turned their backs on their own ethical identification. They became accomplices.

In conclusion, around 1000 students have now passed through the School since my failed insurrection. They have graduated into resource-starved, stressed, unsupportive work environments, so well described in Ken Loach's heart-breaking account of the bleak and punitive social security system in *I, Daniel Blake*. They will toil in this bleak, unrewarded welfare factory without the support of the School or the AAASW, who steadfastly refuse to speak out against the amputation of welfare services and the constant denigration of the poor and disadvantaged. How long will this indifference be tolerated?

In 2015 the School was translocated into the School of Nursing, Midwifery and Social Work. Back home to its medical model roots? Maybe. Or is this the start of a process of death by amalgamation? After 60 years of faithful service to the State in holding the limp hand of the oppressed, there are early signs that the School is being shown the door. The State has learnt much during its neo-liberal ascendency. It has found quicker, cheaper and more efficient ways to control the poor and disadvantaged. Maybe it no longer needs to use the services of Social Work to achieve its control agenda.

I hope those at the 60th anniversary dinner enjoyed the expensive wine because it could be last drinks!

7

SOCIAL WORK, SCIENCE AND GREEN POLITICS

Jim Ife

This chapter recounts my engagement with green politics, and my interest in linking this radical world view to social work and social policy. It describes events in Perth in the late 1980s and early 1990s, but like all intellectual and practice journeys it had earlier origins, and later consequences, which need to be briefly recounted in order to place the chapter in its historical context, and within my own biographical experience.

I had started my university studies, at Sydney University in 1963, enrolled in a science degree; my high school years had emphasised science, and science had excited me as a way of learning about, and wondering at, the natural world. One year of university science study was enough, however, to convince me that I should change course, and, young and idealistic, I chose social work. It seemed like a good way to change the world, and that fitted in with the general mood at Sydney University in the 1960s. I have, however, always retained a fascination with science and a degree of comfort with scientific ways of thinking, which was subsequently to serve me well (I still devour popular science books, especially about the ecological crisis in its various manifestations). At that time, social work study was a two-year program, following all or part of an Arts degree. I enjoyed the Arts subjects – Philosophy, Anthropology, Politics and Psychology – and also gained a great deal from the general intellectual and political climate at the university at that time, which introduced me to earnest discussions about the meaning of life, and radical political ideas and activism, with heavy doses of Bob Dylan, Joan Baez and Pete Seeger. It was the time of the Freedom Ride, Vietnam demonstrations, Civil Rights in the USA, anti-Apartheid, and so on; heady days indeed. Following this, social work study was a disappointment; a very conservative and therapeutically-oriented social work course, including lots of psychoanalytic theory, Rogerian counselling, conservative sociology, Political and Moral Philosophy, and two full years of 'Physical and Mental Health'. There was no community work at all, very little social policy, and nothing about activism. In retrospect, the Political and Moral Philosophy, taught by John Lawrence, was for me the most valuable part of the course.

My social work career has been characterised by developing interests outside social work, and then finding ways for these interests to integrate with, and inform, social work theory and practice. This happened first with my interest in politics. Social work at Sydney University at the time was apolitical, but the story was very different when, in the early 1970s, I undertook further study at McGill University, Montreal. There I was strongly influenced by the Head of the Social Work School, Professor David Woodsworth, a powerful intellectual and a generous human being, who came from one of Canada's best known socialist political families, and for whom social work was strongly linked to political theory and political practice. David was a key mentor, who helped me to define social work as political, and from that point on I had no difficulty in reconciling my interest in radical politics with my practice as a social worker, though of course in the world of practice this is never easy. This was further reinforced in my first academic job, in Hobart at the Tasmanian College of Advanced Education, from 1974 to 1980, working with another important mentor, Adam Jamrozik.

120

Another life-changing event in the early 1970s was reading *The Limits to Growth*,[1] the well-known publication by Meadows et al. from the Club of Rome published in 1972. At McGill I had read some of the work of Jay Forrester at MIT, which laid the foundations for *The Limits to Growth*, and I had been fascinated by it. My interest in science meant that I had no difficulty understanding the early projections involved in this work, and in recognising their stark implications. The argument is both simple and logical: even though we have accepted 'growth' (economic, population, resource use, pollution, etc.) as both normal and beneficial, the simple fact is that you cannot have continuing growth in a finite world – something has to give. The projections of the study showed that with continuing growth the earth was going to reach crisis point around the year 2030, at which point the graphs just fell off the page. The study was strongly criticised at the time, mostly by those with the most invested in the economy of continuous growth, but over the years the projections have proved remarkably accurate, and global crisis by 2030 no longer seems such an unthinkable idea. Indeed, Dennis Meadows, the lead author of *The Limits to Growth*, has recently suggested that 2020 may be a more likely estimate.[2]

More than any other influence, it was *The Limits to Growth* that awakened my interest not only in environmental issues, but in Green political theory more generally, as it was obvious to me that incremental environmentalism was not enough to avert the major crisis which was inevitable if the social, economic and political order remained unchanged. Radical, fundamental change was needed. This, of course, has been reiterated since by many other writers, most notably in recent years by Naomi Klein in relation specifically

---

[1] D. H. Meadows, D. L. Meadows, J. Randers and W. Behrens III, *The Limits to Growth: A Report for the Club of Rome's Project on the Predicament of Mankind* (Signet, 1972).

[2] D. Meadows, *http://www.resilience.org/stories/2014-06-03/a-gathering-of-silverbacks-age-of-limits-2014*

to climate change[3] (of which we were ignorant in the early 1970s, but which makes the need for radical change all the more urgent). I would now class *The Limits to Growth* as one of the three books, all published in the 1970s, that have most influenced my career (the other two being Brian Fay's *Social Theory and Political Practice*[4] and Paolo Freire's *Pedagogy of the Oppressed*[5]).

So much for the background. During the later 1970s and early 1980s, parenting, heavy workloads and PhD research necessitated a lessening of engagement and activism, but then in the late 1980s, working in a university with less demanding workloads, and urged on by two idealistic daughters, I began to engage with various environmental and political groups in Perth, where I then lived. It is that experience, and its implications for social work, that I explore in the remainder of the chapter.

The Greens (WA)

The Greens (WA) initially began as a separate party, not formally affiliated with the Greens in the Eastern States, led by Bob Brown and others. They subsequently became part of the national Greens Party, but in the period I am discussing, roughly 1988 to 1993, the WA version of 'The Greens' was independent. From its inception, the Greens (WA) was not 'just an environmental party'. Indeed, it was formed from a merging of three different groups: The Nuclear Disarmament Party, with its affiliation to the peace movement, a small Green Party concerned with environmental issues, and a Social Justice Coalition involving various psychologists, social workers and others who were pursuing more progressive social policies. Jo Vallentine was already an elected Senator for the Nuclear Dis-

---

[3] N. Klein, *This Changes Everything: Capitalism versus the Climate* (Allen Lane, 2014).

[4] B. Fay, *Social Theory and Political Practice*, (Allen & Unwin, 1975).

[5] P. Freire, *Pedagogy of the Oppressed*, (Penguin, 1972).

armament Party, but she switched her allegiance to the The Greens several months prior to the March 1990 election, when she was re-elected, this time as a Greens Senator. Following her resignation from the Senate in 1992, she was replaced by Christabel Chamarette, a psychologist who had been prominent in the Social Justice Coalition. Christabel was subsequently joined in the Senate by Dee Margetts who was elected in 1993, and whose origin was in the Nuclear Disarmament Party. Thus of the first three Greens (WA) Senators, none had their activist origins in environmentalism; their primary orientations were peace and social justice, though of course all three were strongly committed to environmental sustainability as well. It was only with the election of Rachel Siewert in 2004 that the Greens (WA) finally had a Senator whose activist origins were in the environmental movement.

This background is important, because it shows how The Greens (WA) was, from its inception, more than an environmental party. It adopted the 'four pillars', common to a number of Green parties: environmental sustainability, peace and disarmament, social and economic justice, and participatory democracy. This articulation of a holistic political platform meant many interesting discussions about how the four pillars related to and supported each other, and how policies needed always to address all four. Each of us came with different background and expertise across the four 'pillars'; in my case it was a strong background in social justice, with a long-term interest in environmentalism, a commitment (through community development) to participatory democracy, and less expertise in (though a strong commitment to) peace and disarmament. It soon became clear that I had a stronger background in social policy than anyone else in The Greens (WA) at the time, and this was readily acknowledged by others.

We had an urgent job on our hands. The Greens (WA) was formed in late 1989, and there was a Federal Election coming in

March 1990. Jo Vallentine was our Number 1 Senate candidate, and because of her high profile as a peace campaigner and an outspoken Senator she had a strong chance of re-election. But what policies would she bring to the campaign? Just what did this new party stand for across a whole range of policy areas? Many Greens members had very strong views on particular issues – after all we were a group of optimistic and committed activists, and we were wrestling with the tension between idealism of a social movement and the pragmatic realities of electoral politics. Because of our commitment to participatory democracy, it would have been ideal to have a longer deliberative process involving all the Greens membership, but there were only a few weeks available to us, including the summer holiday period. We devised a 'fast track' participatory process which proved to be remarkably effective. A small group of us – perhaps four or five from memory – wrote draft summary policies (about two pages per policy) in our areas of expertise. I found myself writing draft policies across the whole social policy range: health, education, housing, poverty, multiculturalism, Indigenous issues, and so on. We then hired a church hall for an entire Saturday, and invited all Greens (WA) members to participate in our policy exercise. We displayed our draft policies around the walls, surrounded by lots of butchers' paper on which people were asked to write their comments, suggestions, disagreements, additions, and so on. The members of the policy group stayed for most of the day, happy to discuss the issues with Greens members. The day was well-attended, and there was a lot of energy in the hall, as we talked about the various issues people raised. At the end of the day the policy group collected up the butcher's paper and we sat around on the floor of Jo Vallentine's electoral office, sorting through people's suggestions, discussing and incorporating their ideas where we could (inevitably some suggestions contradicted others). In the end, we came up with a reasonably coherent set of policies, covering all aspects of government activity, informed by the principles of the 'four pillars'. It turned out to be a fairly robust document that was used, with amendments, for some years afterwards. And Jo Vallentine was easily re-elected to the Senate.

These were heady times. It was a time when there had been a strong awakening of environmental issues, and the dangers of global warming, over-fishing, top-soil erosion, wilderness destruction, species extinction, and so on were receiving significant coverage in mainstream media. Environmental activist groups were strong, and there were plenty of idealistic activists wanting to be involved with the Greens, who were becoming a political force on the national scene for the first time. In such an environment it was not surprising that there were some people with strong, and extreme, views on particular issues, which often would not be supported by many of the Greens membership. I recall, for example, heated discussions about vaccinations, and a meeting with some Greens members who fervently believed in the influence of 'The Illuminati'. While recognising that such views were sincerely held, wishing to respect the differing views of others, and being open to dialogue, there was no way that such views, in opposition to those of most Greens members, could determine official Greens policy. This will always be a point of tension in parties that seek to be inclusive and participatory. In retrospect, I think we handled these differences reasonably well, though inevitably some people left the party when they felt their views were not included.

The Greens had a strong commitment to consensus decision-making, but it was not always easy to achieve when people held strong opinions. Some Greens members had joined because of their disillusion with other political parties (usually the ALP), but brought with them their socialisation into less consensual ways of working. Coming from a background of 'getting the numbers', pushing through a position in spite of objections; such people (usually men) did not fit easily into the consensus style adopted by The Greens as a whole; it was a learning process for all of us. These political veterans were, however, very useful when it came to such things as doing preference deals with other parties, which were crucial in enabling Jo Vallentine to be re-elected. Hard-nosed pragmatic political operators have important contributions to make, when consensus-based groups have to operate in the world of *realpolitik*. The compromise between the ideal and the pragmatic is always present, and cannot be avoided even by the most idealistic of holistic change activists. This tension also raises the question for activists as to whether electoral politics is the best way to channel their commitments. Inevitably, those commitments will be compromised, and so electoral politics can never be the only vehicle for a social movement. Electoral politics can be important, indeed essential, if results are to be achieved within a framework of liberal democracy, but other forms of activism are also necessary if passion and commitment are to be maintained, and if a social movement is to retain its integrity.

Coming from a social work background, and with the critical orientation I had developed from my earlier experiences, two things particularly struck me about my colleagues within Green politics, and emphasised the important contributions that social workers had to make. One concerned the social justice orientation that Greens professed, but often did not fully understand. For example, the idea of a carbon tax was widely discussed and advocated, but with very little consideration of what this might mean for low-income families, living away from public transport, and dependent on cheap old-model petrol-guzzling cars. Clearly a more integrated and holistic policy perspective was required, consistent with Green holistic ideals. When I raised these issues, people in The Greens were quick to acknowledge their importance and to seek more appropriate policy solutions. There was no resistance to my arguments, but rather it was a case of people with a strong environmental aware-ness who had not thought through the social justice implications of particular policies. A social justice perspective, inherent in but not limited to social work, was sometimes missing, and this was a very significant contribution that critical social workers could make to the Green movement.

The other area where I could see potential contributions from social work was more process-oriented. Given their interest in con-sensus decision-making and democracy in small groups, it was in-teresting to see that The Greens were running workshops in these areas, using the same books we were using in social work educa-tion at the university, in group and community work. This led me to think about the commonalities between what The Greens and social workers were trying to achieve; motivated by the same commit-ments to social justice and to the importance of inclusive process, it was hardly surprising that they were using the same books. I realised that there was a strong commonality, and as social work-ers had been doing it for years, while many Greens were relative newcomers to all this, it seemed to me that social work had some important contributions to make to the Green movement. Later in my career I drew the same conclusion about the human rights movement;[6] while that is outside the scope of this chapter, the important point to note is that social workers have real expertise in areas that social movements are often lacking.

Working with scientists

At the same time as my engagement with the Greens (WA), I also became involved with a group largely composed of Physical Scien-tists – physicists, biologists, and so on – who were particularly con-cerned with peace and social justice; they were members of groups

---

[6] J. Ife, *Human Rights and Social Work: Towards Rights-Based Practice*, (Cam-bridge University Press, 2012).

such as SANA (Scientists Against Nuclear Arms) and some were from Quaker backgrounds. Through an organisation named Peace Education Foundation, they ran workshops for senior high school students around issues such as peace and environmental sustainability, aiming to encourage social and environmental awareness. They welcomed me into their group, even though I was something of an outsider. There was one other person with a social science background, the remarkable John Croft whose wide-ranging intellect, total commitment and infectious enthusiasm has led him to undertake amazing work raising awareness of holistic understandings of human and non-human interdependence and Gaia awareness, which has had great impact on activists in many countries. John was also involved in The Greens at the same time.

In this group of physical scientists, we had some very interesting dialogues. Here I valued my much earlier science study and my interest in science at school and first year university. Although my scientific knowledge was nowhere near that of the other members of the group, I could at least understand their world view, and had enough basic knowledge to engage in some useful discussion about the intersection of the social and the scientific. Again, as with The Greens, there was a genuine willingness by the scientists to engage with the social, in a spirit of dialogue. Like the Greens members, they were committed to ideas of social justice, but without the background to understand their complexity. They were prepared to question the traditional role of scientists as simply the messengers, coming up with the data and trusting others to make the important policy decisions. These were scientists who took their responsibilities as concerned citizens seriously, who wanted not only to make a difference but to encourage young people to do so as well. There was a strong commitment to dialogue, and to learning from each other. I even managed to organise a session at the state conference of AASW where one of these scientists and I tried to hold a dialogical discussion about our different world views for a social work audience. It was not particularly successful, and in retrospect I think we should have done more background presentation as to why such dialogue is significant. But at least we tried.

And so to the present

We now live at a time when the value of expertise is being attacked. There is wide mistrust of experts as belonging to the 'elites', and expertise is confused with opinion, in the name of a perverted understanding of democracy. Even the expertise of scientists is constantly questioned, by the ideologically-driven opponents of climate change. Media outlets assume that there are two valid sides to a debate about climate change, and set up debates where a climate scientist debates a climate sceptic with little or no scientific background, as if the views of the two are equally valid. In such debates, the scientists are often at a disadvantage, as they have little experience of political rhetoric and their dry rational arguments are readily trumped (now in more than one sense!) by emotive rhetoric. Anti-intellectualism seems to be on the rise, with the idea that everyone's opinion counts the same, however well-informed or otherwise. Some people take a perverse pride in ignorance, never reading a book, and so on, as if this somehow makes their views more 'authentic' and 'real world'. And the ultimate test of any policy is whether it can 'pass the pub test'.

Social workers have often not been very good at recognising the value of their own expertise, in understanding the complexities of 'social justice', in understanding 'social problems', in connecting private troubles to public issues, in linking values with action, and in taking a holistic perspective in understanding the connections between apparently unrelated phenomena. This was an important lesson I learned in my encounters with The Greens and the concerned scientists. I realised that I did have important expertise to

129

contribute, and that others could learn from me, just as I could learn from them. Fortunately, my expertise was readily acknowledged by those I was working with; it is much harder when more powerful professional knowledges (such as medicine, law and economics) assert their primary authority and fail to validate the expertise that social workers have. But it is very important to remember that we do have important things to say, and that we can contribute significantly to social movements committed to change (I have elsewhere made the same argument in relation to social workers and the human rights movement[7]).

As many writers and commentators now remind us, we are living in the Anthropocene. Human activity has significantly and permanently altered the earth, in such a way that humans have ushered in a new geological epoch. In such a context, it is imperative that we re-evaluate our position in the natural world, understanding that we are interdependent with other species and the inanimate world.[8] We are confronted by the need do redefine the 'social' and 'community' – with which social workers work – in less anthropocentric terms, and in this context our capacity to work in dialogue with physical scientists is more important than ever. Social workers need a scientific literacy, and to develop their already-existing ecological literacy, if they are to remain relevant, and to influence policy and social movements.

A simple example: in the above paragraph I deliberately used the language adopted by many scientists – 'human activity' as hav-

---

[7] Ibid.

[8] For more detailed discussion of the reality, extent and implications Anthropocene, see I. Angus, 2016, *Facing the Anthropocene: Fossil Capitalism and the Crisis of the Earth System* (Monthly Review Press, 2016). For a consideration of the Anthropocene from a more social science/humanities perspective, see C. Bonneuil & J-B Fressoz, 2016, *The Shock of the Anthropocene* (Verso, 2016) and A. Ghosh, *The Great Derangement: Climate Change and the Unthinkable* (University of Chicago Press, 2016).

ing 'altered the earth', and so on. Yet to a social worker such language is troubling. We know that 'humanity' is not all the same, and that the environmental disasters we now face are the result overwhelmingly of the actions of the global north, and of global elites, who have benefited most from environmental destruction. We also know that environmental and ecological disasters tend to affect most heavily the most disadvantaged, who are the least responsible for the causes of the disaster, and who have the fewest resources to cope with it. To understand this we need to understand phenomena such as industrialisation, colonisation, globalisation, power, patriarchy, white privilege, capitalism, social class, and so on. To simply blame 'humanity' and to say that 'humanity' must change its ways is far too simplistic and denies many of the important exploitative relationships at the heart of the ecological crisis. There is surely no chance of adequately addressing the ecological crisis unless the ways forward also take account of these classical issues of social justice, so familiar to social workers, but usually ignored by the scientists who write about climate change. Social workers are also likely to point out the importance of Indigenous knowledge and world views in contributing to alternative ways of living in the world; again this is overlooked by a narrative that talks about an undifferentiated 'humanity' as both the cause of the ecological crisis, and as the solution to it.

The relationship between the sciences and the humanities/'social sciences' has changed over the years. In the early 19th century, scientists and poets/philosophers had a lot to do with each other, and used to dialogue about how their different work supported and enriched each other in their attempts to understand the world.[9] But as industrialisation and modernity really took hold, this collaboration weakened, and by the mid 20th century, C.P. Snow, in

---

[9] R. Holmes, *The Age of Wonder: How the Romantic Generation Discovered the Beauty and Terror of Science* (Harper, 2008).

a widely-read essay and book,[10] was criticising the 'two cultures', where each group really had nothing to say to the other and did not understand the other's world, or even vocabulary. It was as if scientists and humanities scholars lived in different worlds, seeing the other as largely irrelevant to what was important, and their graduates followed suit, with one group knowing little of the works of Shakespeare, while the other was ignorant of the Second Law of Thermodynamics. The sharp divide between science and humanities (with 'social sciences' trying to straddle the divide but usually finding themselves in the humanities camp) remains in universities to this day, and this has been to the detriment of professions such as social work, who have felt forced either to adopt a 'scientific' world view uncritically, or to totally reject it.

This is now changing. With the looming environmental crisis, scientists are finding that simply doing and publishing the research, in the expectation that policy-makers will act accordingly, is not enough. They also have to understand how society works, how politics work, how 'the market' works, how attitudes do or do not change, and 'human nature', if their research and their dire warnings of catastrophe are to have any impact. Scientists are thus becoming aware of how they need the humanities and the social sciences. At the same time, those of us concerned for social justice, human rights and democratic participation have come to realise that these things can only be achieved in an ecologically sustainable world. We need to pay attention to ideas of sustainability, energy and entropy, and we need to understand the primary importance of the physical world (place, environment, land, biology, energy sources, water, food security, etc) for humanity. It is as if C.P. Snow's two cultures are each starting to realise that ignoring the other is a recipe for irrelevance, and are starting to come together again.

---

[10] C.P. Snow, 2001 (1959), *The Two Cultures* (Cambridge University Press, 2001 (1959) also C.P Snow, 'The Two Cultures', *The New Statesman*, 6 October 1956.

Social workers will only be able to participate in such discussions if we have a level of scientific literacy: we need to understand how scientists think, how science 'works', and how to talk meaningfully with scientists about their work and its social impacts. This does not mean, however, that we have to accept uncritically a positivist and empiricist world view, as this is a misinterpretation of the nature of contemporary science (and especially ecological science) which has moved well beyond crass empiricism. Rather, we need to break down the false binaries of science/humanities, positivist/ interpretive, empirical/phenomenological, and so on, in creating a broader discursive space for the exploration of humanity, and the achievement of social justice. This, for me, was the important lesson from my engagement with The Greens and with the concerned scientists. Social work has a lot to contribute – not just by itself, but also in partnership with other disciplines, occupational groups and social movements. And at the present time, with the threat of ecological catastrophe looming stronger ever year, this means that critical social workers can play an important role in addressing perhaps the most pressing issue of our time. It is essential that social justice values be strongly represented, and yet social justice values are under threat in ways we would not have imagined possible ten years ago. If there was ever a time for strong, radical, social-justice-oriented social work advocacy and activism, it is surely now.

My interest in environmentalism and Green politics, followed by the encounters with The Greens and with concerned scientists, had a profound effect on my social work career. The realisation that social workers had much to contribute to the Green movement was matched by the reverse realisation, that social workers needed to learn from the Green movement, as ideas of sustainability and the finite nature of resources were essential in understanding the context for a future social work. In 1989 I first started to articulate a social work beyond the decline of the welfare state, based more on Green principles, at an AASW conference (where I first met the wonderful Mary Lane, a marvellous community worker and academic who had herself been exploring similar ideas). In 1991 I presented papers at both social work and social policy conferences, exploring the implications of Green political theory. This was radical indeed for the time: the organisers of the National Social Policy Conference did not know which session to put me in, as my topic was so left-field compared with all other papers at the conference. Of course, it would not be so today; Green ideas that seemed radical then are at least given a legitimacy today, even though they are still seen as 'fringe' by mainstream political parties and the Murdoch Press.

After this, I was able to develop Green political theory into an approach to community development, published in the first edition of the book *Community Development* in 1995[11], and it has since become well and truly incorporated into mainstream social work, though it might be argued that in doing so it has lost some of its radical analysis. But it was a long process. My integration of the Green analysis into social work took much longer than my integration of a political analysis, as described above. But I think this illustrates an important point about social work knowledge and practice. I managed to take interests that I had originally developed right outside social work, and later understand their relevance for social work, and try to bring them in to the way I understood social work theory, ideology and practice. I know this process has also been followed by other social workers in different fields, and it is the way that we can keep social work stimulating, exciting, and relevant to the changing context in which we find ourselves.

---

[11] J. Ife, *Community Development: Creating Community Alternatives – Vision, Analysis and Practice* (Longman, 1995) (subsequent editions up to 2016 published by Pearson and by Cambridge University Press.

8

MEDICARE AND SOCIAL WORK ACTIVISM

Stuart Rees

Universal health insurance is a vital feature of Australian citizens' rights and entitlements. In 1974, legislation to ensure such rights required a double dissolution of the Federal parliament, a Labor Government's success in the election of May 18th of that year, and a subsequent joint sitting of both houses.

That controversial process had been preceded by decades of disputes concerning the medical profession's claims that they should be free to choose how to practice and to decide the fee arrangements to pay for their services. In political and policy circles, the elephant in the room remained, whose freedom should be protected and promoted?

Successive Labor governments insisted that medical services from doctors and in hospitals should depend on assessments of need and not on a patient's ability to pay. This interpretation of freedom envisaged intervention by governments in order to bolster citizens' chances of obtaining treatment in public hospitals irrespective of their – the citizen's – financial resources.

Conflict over the freedom to choose came to a head in 1984 when orthopaedic and general surgeons resigned from New South Wales public hospitals. They opposed what they called government interference, in particular regarding the Minister of Health's power to control the conditions of employment of visiting medical officers in public hospitals. These specialists believed that patients with private health insurance should always be given priority over those who were only covered by universal health insurance – Medicare.

Values underpinning private or public health care policy became the inflammable centre of the dispute. Battle lines were drawn. Influential specialists supported private patients. A Labor government insisted that treatment should not depend on an ability to pay.

Government versus medical specialists

During several months in 1984, it looked as though there were only two parties to the dispute: the procedural specialists on the one hand and the Federal government on the other. I watched the ping pong arguments between the government and the doctors' representatives. Patients and prospective patients stayed invisible and powerless. The dispute continued as though they did not exist.

At that time, health care policy was not my responsibility. I was a Professor of Social Work, and I assumed that health policy academics and analysts would speak out against this attempt to bring down universal health insurance. Nothing happened. Noone spoke.

On January 24th 1985, an orthopaedic surgeon and leader of the NSW procedural specialists, commented on why an injured miner from Wollongong had been moved from hospital to hospital. Surgeons had refused to operate on the man's crushed fingers, apparently because he did not have private health insurance. Asked by a Sydney Channel 10 reporter to explain why this had happened, the surgeons' leader justified the action by attacking another universal health care system, the British NHS. 'In England I can tell you, it would take even longer to treat this man.'[1]

Outraged by the procedural specialists' behaviour and disappointed by the silence of colleagues who were supposed to be conversant with health care policy I contacted trade union leaders, the

---

[1] S. Rees, 'Medical Malpractice', *Australian Society*, March, 1985, 27.

following day whose members benefitted from universal health insurance and would suffer from any revival of only a fee pay system.

Social work as justice

I assumed that if social work practice was not concerned with justice, it should not be called social work. I also believed that the availability of universal health insurance provided the foundations of a civil society, that it was and is uncivil to financially penalise people for being sick. Long held convictions prompted my intervention.

Consistent with that last assumption, I believed that a purpose of social policies should be concerned with altruism not egoism. In his study of the international blood donor system, Professor Richard Titmuss had elaborated such values. He referred to 'the gift relationship', a service given to help a stranger without any expectation of reward.[2] Universal health insurance is based on the same principle.

I regarded cruelty as always abhorrent, especially when it is practiced by privileged professionals. The indifference to the Wollongong miner's condition looked like cruelty. In response to such behaviour, one could hardly sit still and stay silent. What to do became the next question. Write a letter. Ring a friend. Phone a politician. Perhaps write an opinion piece for a newspaper or craft a poem. These appear to be worthy reactions but they represent individual initiatives, unlikely to cause ripple effects beyond one's conscience.

At that point, my assumptions about radical social work and community activism took over. In response to injustice, concerned individuals needed to be in conversation with people of like mind,

---

[2] R. Titmuss, *The Gift Relationship: From Human Blood to Social Policy* (George Allen & Unwin, 1970).

alliances needed to be formed, the opportunity for problem solving enhanced.

Pursuing radical social work

Radical social work assumes that conflict is inevitable and desirable. The alternative is to stick with an easy consensus, which in this case might have allowed the procedural specialists to achieve some of their objectives and the government to claim that it had not really given way. The Murdoch dominated media which supported the doctors could have argued that unnecessary conflict had been avoided.

The value of conflict theory should be made explicit. When conflict occurs, realities are revealed and the usually voiceless stand a chance of being heard. Once you engage in a campaign which challenges powerful interests, you should prepare yourself for conflict and be sure you have the physical and mental stamina to resist.

Within a week of viewing the television report on the fate of the Wollongong miner, I had made contact with representatives from the Doctors Reform Society (DRS), with members of the nurses' union and with office holders in the Waterside Workers Federation, a forerunner of the Maritime Union of Australia (the MUA). A couple of meetings later, this alliance of unionists, doctors and myself as an academic, had created the Defend and Extend Medicare campaign.

Reasons for the campaign were announced in an overflow public meeting in Sydney. We argued that the procedural specialists' desire to control health care policy ran counter to the Hippocratic Oath which said that a doctor promises 'to follow that method of treatment which according to my ability and judgement I consider for the benefit of my patients and abstain from whatever is deleterious and mischievous … with purity and holiness I will, pass my life and practice my art.'[3]

At that initial public meeting, we explained our intention to defend the principles of Medicare, as issued in December 1983 by the NSW Department of Health. That Department's statement read, '… it is government policy that there shall be no discrimination against persons seeking inpatient treatment in public hospitals as non-chargeable patients.'[4] We also wanted the dispute to be judged in terms of accountability to patients and not seen merely as a conflict between government and members of the medical profession.

Members of the campaign met two to three times a week in the offices of the MUA on the Sydney dockside. At such meetings, we shared food and drink, discussed the rules governing the operation of Medicare, considered the political significance of the Hippocratic Oath and the goal of holding politicians and doctors accountable to patients.

Representing patients' interests

After several meetings, we acknowledged that we could not claim to represent patients' interests if we had not directly heard their stories. We also realised, and this should be apparent in any social work activism, that information is power. We needed information about patients which the government and the doctors did not have. Only if we had details of patients' experiences would the media take an interest and begin to report the dispute as having at least three sides not two.

Together with social work and sociology colleagues, we wrote a research proposal with the objective of documenting the views

---

[3] British Medical Association, *The Handbook of Medical Ethics* (BMA House, 1981, 5).

[4] Department of Health, NSW. NSW Information Manual (State Health Publications, 1983).

of people who were experiencing difficulties in seeking medical treatment in public hospitals. We aimed to record the experiences of people who, despite their illness or injury, were having difficulty in even becoming patients. To overcome this problem of access to patients, we needed to publicise the proposed research, interview patients and gain the co-operation of medical experts who would assess the seriousness of each patient's condition.

We then trained six interviewers who would obtain details of patients' age, ethnic backgrounds, income, employment status, their patterns of referral to specialists and their experience on try-ing to obtain treatment. I used my position as Professor of Social Work to not only train students as interviewers but to also gain the cooperation of medical colleagues who could assess each patient's condition.

With the financial support of the Australian Consumers' Asso-ciation, we publicised our request to hear from individuals who claimed to have been disqualified from receiving treatment because they did not possess private health insurance. The purpose of the research was explained on radio programmes, in newspaper articles and in advertisements. Within four months our interviewers had obtained the names, income, ethnic background and employment status of 128 patients.

The patients described the conditions for which they sought help. These descriptions were given to a panel of doctors who classified the conditions into ten categories based on international classifica-tion of diseases.As patients contacted my office and as the number of interviewees increased, we confronted the criticism – from psy-chologists – that the patients did not represent a random sample and the research would therefore be regarded as academically unwor-thy. To me that that sounded like privileged and predictable ivory tower commentary. If we had changed the research to comply with such criticism, the project would hardly have begun, let alone been completed. We needed to conduct the interviews simultaneous with patients' difficulties in obtaining treatment. The research had something in common with participant observation, an appraisal of ongoing events in which interviewers' observations become part of the story. It could not be an evaluation after the events, almost certainly after some patients had died.

Gaining access

Even if procedural specialists had not withdrawn their services from public hospitals, patients would have experienced delay in obtaining treatment. Waiting lists for operations regarded as non-urgent existed before the dispute began. It should also be acknowledged that medical diagnosis takes time and may involve several kinds of carefully conducted tests before decisions can be made about treatment.

Nevertheless, patients' account of their experiences provided insight into whether treatment was obtained or denied. Given that Medicare was intended to facilitate access through universal health insurance, the patients' experiences were also an important test of policy and of the attitudes of professionals who were in a position to make the policy work.

As a key feature of the Defend and Extend Medicare campaign, this research into patients' experiences had to be credible. We had to defend the findings in several forums – with our peers, in the media and in meetings with doctors. In the campaign alliance, roles and responsibilities for organising public meetings, for printing and distributing campaign material, for writing press releases and for conducting the research were regularly assessed, defined and re-defined.

Friendships in a year-long campaign affected motivation, stamina and the sense of achievement. Within friendship came humour and insight, the latter often derived from patients. We learned from them. A middle-aged man explained why he did not complain, 'I didn't know who there'd be to complain to. And, after all, Jesus gave a sermon on the mount and no-one listened.'

A son who was trying to get his elderly father into a hospital for urological surgery explained, 'I kept being confronted with the merits of private hospitals. The surgeon's secretary rang and offered the private hospital at a discount price of $50.00 per day. They'll do everything to get you into a private hospital, even if you complain. The newspapers say there are empty beds (in public hospitals). The specialists' secretary says there are no beds.'

A significant outcome

With the wisdom of hindsight, it is worth commenting that activists in social work seldom need to be always on the barricades, always on the crest of a wave ready to confront opponents. There are troughs to waves before they begin to build. During such calmer periods, while momentum gathers, important preparation occurs ready for a wave to break, ready for the days of protest.

The key ongoing preparation in the Defend and Extend Medicare campaign concerned the building and sustaining of crucial alliances, with immediate colleagues, with cooperating doctors, with representatives of the media, with patients and their families. Without such friendships, networks and highly professional, effective cooperation, the campaign would not have developed and would not have resulted in successful outcomes.

At regular intervals, case studies of particular patients were published in mainstream press and aired on radio and television. At the beginning of 1986 the book *A Brutal Game: Patients and the Doctors' Dispute* was published.[5] In response to that book, an expe-

---

[5] S. Rees, S. and L. Gibbons, *A Brutal Game: Patients and the Doctors' Dispute* (Angus & Robertson, 1986).

rienced historian said, 'Given the decades of conflicts over efforts to introduce universal health insurance, at least we now have a detailed record of what happened to patients, why and how universal health insurance survived to have a crucial effect on people's lives.'

Ultimately, Medicare was defended and remains a foundation of health care policy, and a crucial cement in sustaining a civil society.

9

WHITHER FEMINISM IN SOCIAL WORK:

What is the Outcome of Four Decades of a Feminist Agenda in Social Work in Australia?

Carolyn Noble

Introduction

Using a feminist lens, this chapter takes a retrospective and reflective view of the author's 'discovery' of feminism in the late 1960s and how this provides a useful lens to review the issue of women and social work, especially women's leadership roles over the last 40 years. From the early 1970s, when scarcely a woman's voice was visible in societal politics, the feminist voice emerged- full throttled and loud and clear. Its voice was directed towards empowering women's development and providing challenges to the power dynamics and unequal hierarchical relationships between men and women, and consequentially some gender re-balancing occurred. Even though social work is still predominately a female majority profession and where men hold positions of leadership, there was a time in social work history when the influence of feminist practice and values did challenge male privilege quite significantly. The fact that this repositioning of gender politics has been undercut by the pervasive influence of the new liberalism and a steady return to masculinist politics from the noughties onwards does not mean that lessons learnt and successes achieved can't be revisited today in social work particularly, and new challenges mounted as yet another wave of feminism emerges across the world.

Back at the beginning

It is oddly poignant as I sit down today to write this chapter that it is also International Women's Day (2017) and I see from the internet the same fury and backlash towards women having a day for themselves and taking up front page space in the media and workplace (for example, Radio National had all women presenters for the day) that the early days of the women's movement engendered. It is more disheartening to see after four decades of feminist critique prominent and successful women in the media still see their role as supporting their male colleagues by joining them in the predictable male pushback. This pushback is disingenuous, as men still dominate the public space and women are still subjected to all forms of violence, and lack political and cultural representation and equal access to childcare, equal wages and secure jobs. For example, in 2013 the Abbott (Liberal National Party) Commonwealth Government's senior ministry had only one woman! The same slogans appearing at the 2017 International Women's Day march, such as equal pay, stop sexual assault and protection of women from domestic violence, are the same urgent pleas from new generations of women as they were for me as a fledging second-wave feminist in the late 1960s as I was just entering adulthood. As a lifelong feminist charged with making women's lives more equal, I am as dismayed now, as I was then, at the position of women vis a vis men. While I have been relatively successful as a senior academic, it is still not a path well-travelled by many women. Why has change been erratic and what sense can I make of this for myself and my women colleagues who travelled the same path as me and for those yet to embark on that journey?

Where to start?

It is a matter of luck, I guess, where one is born and the circumstances in which one lives, and the early environmental, parental and cultural influences, the relationships encountered and then fostered, and of course happenstance that comes our way. I was already privileged with my middle-class background and Catholic educational opportunities when I met my first happenstance. I began my undergraduate social work degree at the University of New South Wales in 1968. What a time to enter the gates of higher education as the rumblings of the European and the USA students' revolt was gathering forces. The discontent about capitalism, the conservative status quo of family and gender stereotypes, the challenge to the restrictive roles for women as primarily mothers and wives and their deliberate exclusion from public life, leadership and decision-making roles seemed obvious to me the moment it was named, despite my rather privileged and middle-class background.

While encountering the student protests was happenstance for me, it was much more significant for my generation. The period from 1968 has been attributed to fostering new social movements, such as the civil rights and women's movements and all the other mass movement protests that followed. With regard to women, traditional institutions, values and morals were deemed oppressive and discriminatory and thus were unhealthy for women but offered many advantages for men who benefited from these social arrangements. This led to the emergence of many women forming spontaneous group huddles seeking new empowering experiences through group consciousness raising and sharing personal stories. These group experiences were surprisingly empowering, especially because of the critique of men and their power and privilege. A cultural taboo was broken. I can still feel the power of naming patriarchy as the problem and its elimination as the solution. Male

dominance in all institutions that govern social, economic and political discourse needed to be challenged and critiqued and alternatives found. It was not women's fault that they found themselves
in this situation.

These early consciousness raining groups expressed an urgency
for a different world where women and men were equal, or early on
when the most obvious and easiest solution, it seemed then, was to
push men aside to make space for all the disposed and marginalised
women. This critique had resonance for me and many other young
women who were already sceptical about marriage and the limited
public roles available for them. Without knowing it, I was already
seeking paths to a more autonomous, independent life when I went
to university, instead of choosing early engagement and marriage.
Happening upon this discontent was life changing – how it would
manifest itself was still unknown, but the seeds were now firmly
planted.

Early career: Feminist practitioner

In 1973 after 18 months as a psychiatric social worker in Sydney
Hospital I went overseas to the United Kingdom to seek a bigger
life and got a position in my local government/council as a mental
health social worker. Almost immediately, I was confronted with
the unrest that was brewing from social workers as government
funding restrictions (beginning of what we now know as New Public Management or NPM) began to take hold. Social workers concerned with the growing influence of the new right and changing
work conditions began to get organised. This growing militancy
aimed its critique towards the public policy discourse that clients
are responsible for their own welfare and social problems are the
result of individual failures rather than the growing inequality and
structural readjustment occurring at the time. Many local govern-

ment/council social workers went on strike over changing work conditions and reduced wages, the move towards the corporation of welfare and significantly the ideological challenges to their professionalism.

Case Con, a revolutionary magazine aimed directly to those social workers who wanted to have a platform to critique the rise of managerialism in their workplace and neoliberalism increasingly dominating the social, political and cultural landscape, had been launched a couple of years earlier and Bailey and Brake's *Radical Social Work* published in 1975 and Corrigan and Leonard's critical text titled *Social Work Practice under Capitalism* which followed in 1977 gave the emerging radial critique academic status and a forum for dissemination.[1] Social work had become complicit, the radical voice contended, in a culture of silence around social justice and their unconscious bias towards bourgeois values and capitalist models of welfare. What was needed was a revolutionary theory and a revolutionary practice and a critical consciousness of power relations and their economic, social and cultural impact. This was an exhilarating time and certainly disruptive to the establishment and the conservative social work practice of the day!

In the mid 1970s I moved into acute mental health hospital work and was for a few years caught up in the new anti- psychiatric and consumer mental health movement that attached itself at last initially with leftist social movements and radical critique of the time because of its overlapping membership and its anti-establishment critique. The anti-psychiatric critique of the hegemonic definition of normalcy imposed by organised (scientifically and pharmaceutically dominated) psychiatry had hit a nerve with radical mental health workers who saw this as an opportunity to argue that the so-

---

[1] R. Bailey and M. Brake, *Radical Social Work* (Edward Arnold, 1975); P. Corrigan & P. Leonard, *Social Work Practice under Capitalism: A Marxist Approach* (Macmillan, 1977).

cial, political, cultural and economic context of health needed to be considered in assessing mental ill health rather than purely relying on biological aetiology. As resistances have their ebb and flow, this movement gradually lost its relevance in the late 80s for being too academic and too intellectual, and as many of their demands were adopted into mainstream, its professional influence faded. However, consumers empowered by this critique continued to keep the movement alive. Now in the hands of 'prior' patients, this movement survived as a consumer/survivor-based action group and continues to exercise its socio-political influence on mental health policy and practice. An important determinant that I never lost sight of though, and which has left an inedible mark on my professional thinking, was the number of women who were in psychiatric hospitals who were there because of early childhood sexual abuse and the yet unexplored and unrecognised impact of domestic and social violence. My head was spinning from all these ideas; my emotions were renewed with hope for a more humane and socially just social work practice if the profession became more readily informed by feminist and other structuralist analyses. I returned home from the UK ready for a new future.

Academic career: Feminist scholarship

My career in academe mirrors other feminist colleagues writing in this book; so there are some common experiences. I was interested in teaching, as a young mother, full-time mental health work seemed too daunting and so with a friend in a similar position we applied for a position at MacArthur Institute of Higher Education (MIHE) – now Western Sydney University (WSU) as a job-share lecturer. Between us, we had five children and could realistically only work part-time. As I was doing my Masters of Social Work, and as she was already a casual teacher in this institution, we presented ourselves as a ready and willing partnership for the new welfare program being delivered. This was in 1984 and our appointment was the first such position in an academic institution in Australia. In 1986, in my final year of study, I published a chapter with Brenda Smith in the landmark social work book edited by Betsy Wearing and Helen Marchant called *Gender Reclaimed*[2]. This book was a result of the research being done by MSW students and academics in a cross-institutional women's studies subject at the University of New South Wales and the University of Sydney. It was the first feminist analysis of social policy, practice and scholarship in social work in Australia. This chapter was my first serious scholarly effort and, as a result my career as an academic began to take hold.

Two years later, when I was promoted to a full-time position, women's studies programs burst onto the academic landscape heralding a critique of current social policies and brought the feminist voice onto the campus. Specific women studies units were introduced in the sociology curricula and they shook up the patriarchal academy. The advances made by women in the Whitlam era such as supporting family benefits, childcare and safe houses for women running from abusive men, women's pensions, equal pay legislation, land rights for Australian and Torres Strait Islander peoples and for a time free university education for all, always felt transient, needing constant vigilance to keep them on the social policy agenda. Women's studies programs were in part an attempt to keep these priorities and successes in the forefront.

Inspired by this feminist activism and scholarship, and taking lead from the success of women's studies programs in sociology departments I wrote the first women's studies unit for the welfare program at (now) Western Sydney University (WSU) in late 1980s. This unit addressed women's structural disadvantage, highlighting

---

[2] H. Marchant and B. Wearing, (eds), *Gender Reclaimed: Women in Social Work* (Hale and Ironmonger, 1986).

how current social policies inevitably disadvantaged women, as the needs of the male bread winners and their salary were the yardstick of the family wage. Using a feminist lens and feminist social policy analysis demonstrated that the impact of informal care, family responsibilities and employment affected disproportionately on women and children and needed addressing both in social work scholarship and practice. Despite this, I had to argue in a full staff meeting for its inclusion and counteract the patriarchal resistance from my male colleagues. I then taught a feminist social work theory and practice subject in the new social work program and experimented with feminist pedagogy in its delivery. Fostering women only learning spaces, these classes were held over weekends and off campus. In a supportive setting, such as this, students could deconstruct social conditioning and reflect on their lives. This was my first exposure to what is now known as critical reflection informed by critical thinking and the educative and transformative potential of these personal stories framed by feminist analysis. These powerful personal stories were used as basis for new ways of experiencing agency and for a time in the social work program the demarcation between the teacher and the student was blurred. We learnt from each other and it was in these inspiring situations that my firm commitment to feminism, feminist pedagogy and addressing women's disadvantage was reinforced as crucial to my life and well-being, as well as to my teaching. This subject was an attempt to make sure beginning students and future practitioners were cognisant of women's issues and that women centred social policy initiatives were seen as relevant to social work practice and their lives as well.

In 1988 I attended my first international social work conference in Vienna which was organised by the International Association of Schools of Social Work (IASSW) and inspired by my early success in my academic career, I worked with Lena Dominelli to establish the first woman's caucus Chair (with its own vote) in the male-dominated IASSW board. I can still remember the surprise that the current composition of mainly men expressed when the argument was present to them that the male dominance on the Board was a problem for women and their response was: "What could a woman's Chair add to the conversation and activities of the organisation that the current board could not"? However, the need to focus on gender representation was met with begrudging acceptance in the General Council when it was put up for voting at the next bi-annual conference in Amsterdam. This role was to work with the local organising committee of each international conference to have a women's stream in the program and women events if possible or at least a lunchtime workshop to discuss issues facing women in their country and academic community. I held this position for several years and gradually saw the gender balance on the IASSW Board change after Lena was elected international president, which she served for eight years from 1996 -2004.

This period from the mid-1980s to the end of the 1990s was a flourishing time for feminism and social work. From as early as 1983, I was a part of a small group of welfare/social work women who spontaneously met at Australian Association of Social Work and Welfare Education (AASWWE) conference held at Sydney University to discuss (and complain about) the lack of gender analysis in both the social work and social welfare programs we were all involved in. The late and much-missed Wendy Weeks was a powerful influential feminist at the time, leading many of the group meetings and agenda setting. Women in Welfare Education (WIWE) was formally launched at this conference and we met as a 'women only group' annually at the AASWWE and Australian Association of Social Workers (AASW) conferences until a few years ago. The group bubbled along, while we established our academic careers and raised our families and when space emerged, the group became more public and we began to develop a national profile. WIWE's first national conference was held at WSU in 1992 where I was a lecturer in the welfare program. It was here that a Sydney-based writing group was formed, based on the RMIT women's writing group. Women students and lecturers from across the post-secondary education sector wanted to discuss and mentor their 'work in progress', support and consolidate a feminist voice in welfare and social work education and promote women's scholarship more generally. Several of us decided then that we would study for a PhD no matter what obstacles might lie ahead. As a founding member of WIWE, along with Karen Heycox, Lesley Hughes and Jude Irwin, we established a journal exclusively for welfare women's scholarship. The first edition of the journal *Women in Welfare Education* was published in 1994 and this ground-breaking venture stopped production with volume 10 in 2011. I guess we assumed that women's publishing option were less restrictive. Here's an edited snippet from this first edition:

> As women educators, we know that we ourselves are educated in and surrounded by phallocentric knowledge; we occupy institutional structures dominated by male epistemology and we work in a feminised and caring discipline which remains the theoretical and administrative custody of men…It is within this context that we attempt to arm (sic) our students with intellectual tools of critical thinking, a language of critique and possibility, and a recognition of historical structures of domination and exploitation.[3]

While these critiques had hit a nerve and we had some success with women's programs, feminist collectives and women's studies courses, these accomplishments were, like the Whitlam

---

[3] T. Stephens, 'Feminist Backlash: New Enemy of Women in the 90s' (1994), *Women and Welfare Education*, 1, 17.

changes, always under threat and constant vigilance was needed to keep these achievements in practice and in the curriculum. In late 1990s, neoliberalism was taking hold and gender analysis was mainstreamed into the core curricula and these empowering workshops and stand-alone units were stopped. The backlash against feminism had begun along with an era of austerity and with the consolidation of neoliberalism, it meant that the very identity politics that supported women's visibility and issues and importantly their demands to be included in academe specifically and the public space more generally became under attack and gradually the feminist voice was silenced.

The question of feminist leadership

When I think back to the early days as a lecturer at WSU there were between 30- 40% male lecturing staff in the welfare and soon to become social work discipline. Here a new challenge presented itself. The men were applying and getting promoted and the women were doing most of the administration (for example, chairing and serving on committees, community networking and working in the field education component of the degrees) and doing most of the practice teaching required for a successful program. As staff representative and the mandatory woman member, I sat on my first promotions committee. To my utter surprise, I saw that male applicants were applying for promotion with significant success and with less experience and academic profile than myself. It then occurred to me that not only was a gender analysis needed in the curricula but institutional sexism was the next battle.

In 1987 the Commonwealth introduced the Equal Employment Opportunity (Commonwealth Authorities) Legislation and all States followed over the next five years to introduced Anti-Discrimination legislation and Affirmative Action strategies. Women were to be treated equally in the workplace and unconscious male privilege was too be named and challenged. EEO/AA policies and strategies, maternity and family leave, childcare (many in the workplace), grievance procedures, leadership and mentoring programs were introduced across both the public and private sector to support women's advancement and help workers stuck at 'junior' levels. These policies gave some women hope for a changed future and that leadership roles were a possibility.

This was another light bulb moment for me. Many of my male contemporaries had already passed me on the way and had secured senior academic positions in greater proportion than their numbers in the discipline (a phenomenon now called the 'glass escalator'). This was true for the professional associations such as AASW, AASWWE, IFSW, IASSW and the social work professoriate. Still convinced that feminist politics was the answer, when my institution set up their Equal Employment Opportunity (EEO) committee, I put up my hand and was elected as inaugural member and was soon elected chair. This committee was responsible to work with the EEO Coordinator (EEOC) to develop and implement EEO/AA polices and strategies that would enhance women's advancement and make sure women were equally represented in committees and leadership positions and to run programs to help them along the way. I held this position for a few years but while the policies were developed, little change occurred in general as gender balance above senior lecturer position remained largely unchanged. The way women and men prioritised academic work was a factor in the selection criteria favouring publication and research over teaching, administration and community engagement. However, that was not the only factor. Several of my women colleagues who failed to get promoted opted out of the dominant masculine culture and settled early on for work/life balance and expressed little interest in continuing to apply for promotion. Other women explicitly refused to seek promotion, seeing the game as rigged. According to them, there was no way the 'thick' male culture was to be diluted! A few women tried to work within the system and carve out an academic career for themselves. What was going on? And what was the reason little improvement occurred?

Between 1992 and 2000 Jane Mears and I conduced a longitudinal study to explore the effects of EEO/AA legislation and programs in Australian Universities. After interviewing VCs and PVCs charged with implementing EEO/AA in their universities, it will come as no surprise to know that empirical evidence supported the 'on the ground' experience that these initiatives had little impact on creating a more equal playing field for women to access promotion and secure leadership roles. Bullying, intimation, harassment, men's fear of being taken over and losing their jobs and being answerable to women meant there was conscious and unconscious resistance from the top down which resulted in delays and EEO/AA strategies and resources being placed low on the list of the university's priorities. This meant that structural and cultural change was not addressed by these initiatives, suggesting that these attempts at policy change to lead to behaviour change were doomed from the start. [4]Indeed the 'thick' male culture was impenetrable. Women alone could not shift the organisational culture which supported male privilege, entitlement and male behavioural norms. In fact, the organisation of knowledge was underpinned with masculinist imaginary and the doing of gender scripts where men and women act out (unconsciously in many cases) the gender stereotyping as socially constructed behaviour was alive and functioning

---

[4] C. Noble, 'The Paradox for Advancing Women in Paid Work and Public Life in Post-EEO Era'. In M. Paludi (ed), *Women, Work and Family: How Companies Thrive with a 21st Century Multi-cultural Workforce* (Praeger, CA 2014). C. Noble and J. Mears, 'The Impact of Affirmation Action Legislation on Women Working in Higher Education in Australia: Progress or Procrastination? Women in Management Review', 19(8), 404-11 (Manchester, 2000).

well. This is the key issue which needed addressing if women were to break through the glass ceiling or maternal wall. The undoing of male privilege and the promotion of profeminist response from men meant that for now men need to deconstruct their unearned advantage and undo the economic and political and organisational power attached to this privilege. [5] This challenge remains, as in 2016, the gender pay gap for women academics is 19%, 10 out of 31 VCs are women, 43% of women have research only positions and 57% are teaching only. Currently 29% of all parliamentarians are women and 7% hold ministerial posts. Interestingly, there are fewer women CEOs and chairs of the top 200 ASX companies than men named Peter, David or John! According to National Tertiary Education Union (NTEU) National President, it will be over a century before Australian boards even get towards a gender balance. [6] That is, if EEO/AA policies aren't demolished altogether!

Feminist social work leadership: Are we there yet?

In 2001 I was successful in my promotion application to Associate Professor and in 2005 I accepted the position of Professor of Social Work at Victoria University, Melbourne. I was one of the 29% of women in the professoriate across Australia. I had broken through the glass ceiling and many of my women colleagues in social work (not so in the STEM faculties) were doing the same. What had changed over the last decade? Certainly, the numerical dominance of women in the profession and the proliferation of programs across the country meant there were more opportunities for promotion and leadership roles for women. Children had grown up and women were more mobile. And certainly, the remnants of

---

[5] C. Noble and B. Pease, 'Interrogating Male Privilege in the Human Services and Social Work Education' *Women and Welfare Education*, (2011), 10: 29-38.

[6] J. Rea, 'More Qualified Women But Jobs and Prospects Still More Precarious', *Agenda* 24, Sept (NTEU 2016, 18-9).

EEO/AA strategies influenced the broadening of the promotion criteria to include teaching, community engagement and university service as having significant value to the workplace. As I balanced my career with research, scholarship, administration, service and teaching and like many of my colleagues chose to work long hours to manage the workload, I eventually had a profile acceptable for promotion. My international work and overseas secondment to a University in Canada also helped but I think another happenstance was also influential for me once again. The rise in women in middle management and the changing nature of work demanded a rethinking of work and the type of leaders needed to respond to these changes. [7]Innovation, flexibility, multi-skilling, team work, response to client needs, workplace complexity and increasing diversity, resulted in women's skills being valued, as it was argued that women could deal with internal contradictions, ambiguity and complexity and are more 'naturally' adaptable to responding to the demands of rapidly changing workforce. [8] Feminist theory began to influence leadership theory as women as leaders was now a topic of research and scholarship.

The interlinking of feminist theory and leadership theory began to influence the emergence of a new type of leadership trait. Transformational leadership was regarded as a more successful and a more potent style of leadership and, consequentially was becoming persuasive in leading the move away from the leader-dominated view to a broader follower-involvement where shared leadership, participatory decision-making, power sharing through team building, forming coalitions, networking and supportive and collaborative decision-making was seen as fostering a positive

---

[7] M. Paludi (ed), *Women, Work and Family: How Companies Thrive with a 21st Century Multicultural Workforce* (Praeder, CA 2014).

[8] M. Gray and L. Schubert, 'Do Something, Change Something: Feminist Leadership in Social Work' In S. Wendt and N. Moulding (eds) *Contemporary Feminisms in Social Work*, (Routledge, 2016), 133-131.

work environment. Emotion work and relationship work was also seen as successful to achieving employee and client satisfaction. The noughties and early millennia did see an increase in women's leadership roles and again for a time the future for women in the workplace looked positive. On leaving Victoria University in 2005, I was appointed Professor Emerita and not long afterwards was appointed Foundation Professor of Social Work at the Australian College of Applied Psychology (ACAP) in Sydney. In this role, I was able to write and establish a stand-alone social work program in a reputable private Higher Education Provider. Having a free hand, I could get TESQA and AASW accreditation for an anti-oppressive program where leadership and international social work are also core curricula. Critical reflection underpins the practice strand and community partnerships in undertaking research is also a feature. Placing social work in a globalised arena and making links with social action and social movements means these students are well placed for the challenges ahead for the profession.

While women are in the majority of social work leadership now; for example, at the 2017 Australian Council of Heads of Schools of Social Work meeting, from the 20 plus attendees, there were three men leaders, it does not mean that the male patriarchal power is content with these changes and impediments are still evident. For aspiring future social work academic leaders, obstacles like lack of family-friendly work polices, affordable childcare and the strong boy's network and excessive work hours remain barriers. Women still have to work harder and longer than men to get the same take-home pay. Promotions criteria still favour a traditional research profile and it remains a constant challenge to achieve publications. These impediments continue to make it difficult for women seeking to make a valuable contribution to academic leadership. However, almost as expected, more sinister backlashes are afoot.

And now? Where is feminism and social work?

As women begin to fill the ranks of the social work professoriate, another wave of anti-feminist backlash began in earnest and with the recent election of a misogynist world leader in the United States, all indications are that the backlash is global. The resentment of women's authority in general and woman holding power over men specifically was always been a bitter struggle and still results in questioning, debating and in some cases exposing women leaders to debasement (cf PM Julia Guliard's "ditch the witch").[9]

The stranglehold of neoliberalism and New Public Management (NPM) in all spheres of work, both public and private, is another factor that undermined feminist contributions to empowering workplaces for women. During the last 25 years of my academic career, I can count at least eight restructures (across three institutions) that immediately come to mind. Many of the proposed changes, redundancies and refiguring of discipline groupings were resisted but most were eventually successful. More may have slipped into my unconscious as I currently face yet another, this time a more drastic downsizing. To date, in my current position as the Foundation Professor of Social Work, all the redundancies across the broader faculty have been women in middle management positions, while senior positions remain the fortune/destiny of men. Many see the NPM as heralding and now responsible for the morally conservative and repressive social, political and cultural forces that plague the higher education sector currently. The NPM has been attributed to the return to a masculinist workplace and the reinstating of masculine subjectivity in the workplace culture. Neo-liberalism has been linked with re-invigorating 'white patriarchy ' and counteracting the social and political gains attributed to feminist activism. Why am I still shocked by the violence of neoliberalism and the return to patriarchy? In many ways, there was a perfect storm

---

[9] See K-A Walsh, *The Stalking of Julia Gillard* (Allen & Unwin, 2013).

in the making. On the one hand, NPM resulted in a repackaging of normative conservatism and economic austerity and micro-management; and with global capital posing a threat to environmental sustainability and world peace, many women are wondering how we can even think about women's transformation now. Add in this mix a general pessimism as feminists ask what exactly has been achieved in the last four decades of activism, we get some glimpses as to why being a feminist has lost its edge. In retrospect, the diversity of women's issues meant a clear 'end point' was always going to be difficult. Despite the diversity, though, what was clear was that women's discrimination and subordination to male power and control was unacceptable. Men's violence was not to be tolerated and unpunished and gender egalitarian politics was to be fought for at every opportunity. And, that the 'personal is the political' must inform each and every women's politics. In this sense, this rallying cry remains true today as it did when I first heard it as young university student in late 1960s and should inform current and future activism.

Conclusion

I have in this chapter given examples of attempts to challenge and change institutional politics and gender relations in the higher education sector, and where some successes in social welfare policies outcomes were achieved and provided examples of how feminist pedagogy was a site of educational transformation. These changes can be directly attributed to feminist activism. But what about the current backlash and conservative male power plays evident in the current politics of the West? Where will we find a strong feminist voice to counteract this backlash? Certainly, there is strong online presence of young women speaking out about the rise of the new patriarchy. I can find feminist voices and activism on Facebook and other forms of social media sites where gender

equality, social justice for women and girls and where anti bullying and shaming sites are quite effective in protecting women
from men's violence. The growing influence of profeminist voice
is heartening as men really do need to interrogate their power and
privilege. So, as retirement looms, I am happy to be able to hand
over to the young feminists to define what the future might entail
for them and I hope they take heart and direction from the limited
success outlined in this chapter and other chapters in this book. I
will also have more time to explore what a strong feminist voice
might entail for older women.

10

CRITICAL REFLECTION AND ACTION:

A Feminist Woman's Journey through Social Work

Wendy Weeks[1]

What has brought me to celebrate the tradition of woman-hood and to grapple with the daily demands of trying to 'live generously' in a world of patriarchal practices and ideas which belittle and harm many women each day? I felt uneasy at the thought of writing about mentoring. But 'so often I don't' shrieked the girl inside me who never feels she has 'done or been enough'. Subsequently, in the year of turning 50, it seemed to be a good opportunity to reflect on and write about the people and experiences which have enriched my life, and to contemplate the lessons learned. In particular, it allows me to celebrate being 'born woman', and the sea of generosity and support which women, and some men provide.

I was a war-time baby born to Edith Philipson and Clem Davenport who had married in 1942. Clem was a navigator in the Royal Australian Airforce (RAAF) and Edith had served several years as an apprentice school teacher. Like many women of her time, she did not complete her evening studies (taken while working), but

---

[1] As noted in the afterword to this chapter, Wendy Weeks died on the 31st July, 2004. However, any anthology on radical social work in Australia during the turbulent period described in this book would be inadequate without a contribution from her. Consequently, we are pleased to be able to reprint this earlier publication. The chapter was originally published under the title 'Critical Reflection and Action: A Mutual Sharing'. In J. Scutt (ed.) *Living Generously: Women Mentoring Women* (Artemis, 1996). Permission to reprint the chapter is gratefully acknowledged.

went to live near the airforce camp. Later she lived with her parents and young baby when her husband went to New Guinea. My mother, Edith, has been a powerful influence in my life in her valuing of women as wonderful and capable people. Loyalty and generosity of spirit are two of her outstanding characteristics. She has known one of her best friends, Margaret (to whom I owe my first name) since she was six years old. Some of my mother's edicts have become part of my social philosophy. 'There is good in everybody.' Do your best in any situation.' 'Look on the positive side.'. Others have proven more difficult to implement: 'Wendy, you should not argue with men.'. Or: 'You can do anything you try.'. Alas, wealth redistribution and abolishing violence require more than individual effort!

Atypical of women in the eastern suburbs of her time, Entered the paid labour force as a teacher when each of her children went to school. A legacy of her juggling act of her generation was a model of 'super mum' – always busy, vacuuming, and tidying before she went to work; cooking casseroles for sick neighbours; playing the piano or doing the flowers for the Church; listening to women at her kitchen table; and being a good wife and mother. She was the first pre-school teacher for physically disabled children in Victoria at what was then called the Victorian Society for Crippled Children. She taught a remedial class at the Salvation Army Boys Home, taught at Travencore and later at Alkira. At the age of 54 she went back to school herself and qualified as a special education teacher. Since her retirement from paid work, she has enjoyed devoting more time to community work and to her crafts and music.

My father is a shy man, who has been a quiet rock of Gibraltar in our family, and has a good sense of humour and fun. Originally, a country boy from Dunolly, my father was employed in a bank and in addition has a range of practical talents. While earning a steady income in a job which I think he often found boring, it seemed he gained his greatest pleasure from being a handyman at home; from his family; from sport; and his lovely pottery in the last 20 years. In my childhood, when I was something of a 'tomboy', he taught me to fish and shoot holes in tins lined up on a tree. I drew a line at learning to shoot rabbits. Clem has always been well liked and I remember once when he was approached to stand for the local council. The decision was not to do so. My mother explained: 'We're little people.'. 'We do not have the money to buy the sort of clothes and do the entertaining' that such positions were seen to require. Of course, neither did they have much spare time – families with two adults in the paid labour force faced even more constraints than now. Their community involvement was through the Church and neighbourhood.

My brother Christopher was born in 1953. Having a loving and loved father and brother provided the ground for my views that women and men could be different but equal.

In the lower middle-class suburbs of the 1950s, of the adult women's lives seemed thoroughly boring. My mother's life made more sense, but it seemed pretty hard work and she had a terrible struggle getting me to help with the housework. I recall being impressed by two independent women who were family friends. Besse Ridgeway, a 'war widow' and neighbour who taught art, and Gwen Outhred, a hospital matron. Both seemed to be pretty happy and to laugh more than most women I knew. I began to search for adventurous women's lives through reading. Along with many others, Louisa M. Alcott's character Jo (in *Little Women*) was an early heroine – in retrospect a model of vicarious social contribution: supposedly 'doing good' through adopting children and marrying a non-conformist professor. There was 'Wendy at Winterton' and 'Nora of Billabong' who were later replaced by the novels and other writings of Simone de Beauvior and Doris Lessing.

My parents made considerable sacrifice to give me an education at Methodist Ladies College (MLC), though a scholarship helped in part. At an all-girls school, it was possible to stretch myself academically, without fear of the conflict between femininity and competence. But when I did well it was a secret not to be shared at the youth club, in case the boys were threatened and rejected me. I also learned the mixed blessings of formal leadership positions through being form captain, a prefect, house captain and leader of the debating team. This education resourced me well for academic life, and I enjoyed it. We students knew nothing then of the personal struggles of our women teachers. They were 'spinisters' and were seen as 'maiden aunts' to be pitied, as apparently they had been 'left on the shelf' (as the saying was) and not chosen to marry. It did not occur to me then that they might have chosen independence. Dorothea Cerutty, with her sensuous love of literature, and smartly dressed, fun-loving Betty Jackson, inspired some hope in youthful souls seeking to combine womanhood with competence.

I studied social work at the University of Melbourne in the early 1960s. As the first member of our extended family to enter a university, this was new territory. I recall an interview at enrolment, when a young man in the registrar's office told me that with my matriculation results I really should do honours. But, as it was, four years seemed a long time to perpetuate being a student (women were meant to be married, not have careers) and so I felt affirmed, but nevertheless enrolled for a BA and diploma of social studies.

The course thoroughly engaged me, and a lifelong friendship with Helen Friday and Frank Pavlin began. I edited *Electra,* the social work student newsletter (the year after David Green and the year before David Hall) and I was active in university and social work student affairs. My final two placements were at Winlaton Girls Training Centre in the youth welfare division of the Social Welfare Department, Victoria. This sparked a commitment to women whose lives had been damaging and hurtful to them – the form of 'sisterhood' which Dorothy Smith describes as an identification with other women in their oppression. Kathleen Crisp, from the Commonwealth Department of Social Services, recruited me – I received a Commonwealth cadetship. On graduation, I began to serve it out, but when I married I received what I often call the one benefit I obtained from sexism. At that time (1965) there was a marriage bar in place. When I married, they had to resign me from the permanent to the temporary service, and I was free of my bond. I still felt morally bound, but, gradually disgusted by the trivial role social workers had in the department of social services at that time, I took my freedom and joined the non-government sector.

In retrospect, I realise how fortunate it was that no one could help me find a 'career' in that department, or that I did not have the confidence or know-how to forge one. No one talked about the difficulties of women having careers and traditional marriages; or took any steps to help me think long term – rather than simply having a desperate feeling that I had to make my social contribution before I had children, which in my era could be postponed for a few years with contraception. Lyra Talyor, Kathleen Crisp, Francis Donovan and Joan Scratton were models in that they were 'mothers' of Australian social work – but were all single women. Without advice and help on how to manage dual careers, children's needs and domestic management, or a wider social understanding of democratic work and family life, neither I nor many other women of my generation could envisage emulating them. Our 'lot' was to be the 'juggling act' of home, family and career. Connie Benn was significant for many women social workers in my generation precisely for this reason. Although she set us high standards and challenges, she modelled a democratic marriage. She also passed out helpful hints, such as: 'You need a good childcare arrangement and two lines of back-up childcare as well.

When I try to identify a few key women who helped me along the way, I recall instead literally hundreds of individuals in groups and networks, studying or working together on common life issues, supporting each other's solutions and efforts to change things for women – and for children and men. The tradition of women's lives – doing caring work, supporting the personal and social processes of family and community life – was 'collectivity'. Actively trying to make sense of our lives as women – in relation to the political economy, our children, men and each other – we talked and shared, read, wrote and acted together. We rejected male-dominated hierarchical structures of power and decision-making. We wanted to learn and act in more democratic groups, where we had our won voices, where leadership was shared. We wanted to define the issues and problems of life through our own eyes and experiences.

At Citizens Welfare Services (CWS) in Melbourne in the mid 1960s, I was involved in developing one of Connie Benn's 'brain child' projects: the first secular hostel for young women who were wards of the state or in conflict with their families and/or the law. The couple-based assessment categories used in marriage counselling at CWS did not, we found, explain or address women's experience. When Betty Friedan's book, *The Feminine Mystique* [2] was published, Joan Walters, our intake worker, began to use 'feminine mystique problem' ('the problem which has no name') as in informal intake category. Women whose lives were unfulfilled, deeply unhappy, and sometimes endangered by domestic violence, came to the agency. We tried to support them in fulfilling their dreams that they might have meaningful lives. We made some bad mistakes in supporting young pregnant women to relinquish, rather than fight to keep, their babies in those years before supporting parents' benefits were available. Many years later I learned from people in the Adoption Reform Movement – David, Tricia, Marie, Gillian and others – about the pain and difficulties such professional practices supported.

In 1970, in New Haven, Connecticut, in the United States of

---

[2] B. Friedan, *The Feminine Mystique* (Penguin, 1963).

America, where I had gone with my husband for him to study, I recall going to hear Kate Millet speak. Joining a standing ovation at the end was, in retrospect, a turning point in my life. I knew as I stood there, lonely among the still-sitting group with whom I had come, that I had just heard the naming of my life issues: being a woman in a sexist society. What was to be done? A year later in Canada where my husband had taken a job, I obtained a scholarship to do my MA. There was a lot for women to think through, and I had better set my mind to the task.

My first son Dion, had been born in 1969, just before Ian Weeks and I had left Australia. Karl was born in Canada in 1972. Beautiful, curious and enchanting children, it was easy to love them and celebrate motherhood. At the same time, there was no choice but to grapple with the obligation for which my education had groomed me to make a social contribution – as though high quality child care grew on trees and women had wives to help out in the home! I was arrogantly determined that our generation could work this out, preferably without using other women's labour to free us on the basis of our 'class privilege', as had previously been the case for educated women. There were many times when this vision of full citizenship for women seemed daunting. When I was writing my MA thesis, on the implications of part-time work for women, Dion put a photograph of himself in front of the typewriter and announced: 'This is so you won't forget me!' Later I recall Karl stopping me at the front door and asking: 'Is there really any need for more committee meetings?' So rather than cringe too long with guilt, it all had to be talked out and worked out together.

From 1973 to 1975 I worked part time. Linda Siegal, a neighbour also working part time as a psychologist, and I developed a cooperative child care group for Dion, Laura and some other children. Five families pooled funds and employed a woman with child care qualifications from Belgium. She was the wife of a graduate student, and would otherwise have been unable to engaged in paid work. Car-pools and cooperative lunch arrangements supplemented this. From when Karl was two years until he was six (the age for starting school fulltime), he was in a wonderfully warm and stable family day care arrangement with Millie Selman- either part or full days. Fred, her husband, was a union organiser and worked at Westinghouse. Millie and other union women pioneered a cooperative family day care group around a child care centre in Hamilton.

However, 1975, International Women's Year (IWY), marked by marital separation, with lots of associated guilt and pain for us all. Subsequently, we lived family life very differently, with a carefully worked out and cooperative joint custody arrangement. Doing things differently has a cost. Sole parenthood meant I went to work fulltime, and I was grateful my rent was low enough to manage. Buying a house then was out of the question.

The 1970s at McMaster University in Ontario, Canada – as a graduate student in sociology and then eight and half years working half time, then fulltime in the School of Social Work – were intellectually exhilarating years. A year of reading social theory – Hegel, Marx and many women writers (between the dishes, the diapers, and playing in the park) gave me a way to locate social work practice in an analysis of the state, power and social inequality. Having read Freud, and the neo-Freudians in the 1960s, I at last began to see an intellectual canvas broad and deep enough to refine clearer questions and tentative answers which were less ideological than the popular theoretical explanations of people's lives.

In 1973 at the local women's centre, Ann Duffy and I ran a discussion group on women and social class, while Karl sat in his baby seat. Ann has been a kindred spirit on the journey to transform women' experience ever since. In the same year, Linda Graff, Cathy Coady and I brought together a group of women from the mental health services. All of us thought our mothers' lives had been hard and hurtful. The outcome was Phyllis Chesler, author of *Women and Madness*,[3] Tina Mandell, a feminist therapist from New York, and 800 women from across Ontario spending a weekend discussing women and mental health, from women's points of view. McMaster security service was not pleased that we had exceeded by 300 people the fire regulations limit for the main lecture theatre. The School of Nursing officials were a little amazed at the content of the conference they had helped to fund. Eight hundred and three women went away exhilarated. The videotapes of the weekend flew freely around the country for several years, in spite of Phyllis and her publisher Doubleday trying to make a commercial profit from them.

The School of Social Work at McMaster, under the leadership of Harry Penny, was an unusual place. It had begun in 1968 and people there had a strong commitment to social justice; to social workers, community service workers and service users working together for better social conditions; and staff/student parity in decision-making. Being a junior staff member in a School of experienced, ethical and practical theorists, I was privileged to participate in years of well-formed debate about the School's responsibility in education and research in the wider community. A wonderful apprenticeship! By teaching one night a week, I was able to adamantly refuse to attend late afternoon meetings, and living five minutes away from my work was a great help to parenthood.

Harry Penny taught me a lot about management. He believed himself to be among equals and encouraged staff to follow their social values and to develop their ideas and practice. He always asked first: 'What needs to be done?' and only then considered whether the existing rules could handle it, or whether the rules should be changed. In this climate, it was possible to innovate: to take social work students on field visits to the steel company (the largest

[3] P. Chesler, *Women and Madness* (Doubleday and Company, 1972).

employer in town); to place and work with students in politicians' offices, with the Council of Advocates, the native women's centre, the white women's centre, and so on. Later it was possible to run women's groups at the Red Hill day-care centre, and involve students on placement.

In preparation for International Women's Year, Helen Levine from Ottawa, involved me as a regional representative on the planning committee for the first 'Women in Social Work' conference in 1975. This began a long association with Helen, who has been an inspiration for me as a feminist activist, a who now works as a feminist therapist. Her partner Gil Levine, was the research director at Canadian Union of Public Employees for 30 years. He contributed to making sure that the union movement used my part-time work research, as well as alerting me to support the industrial action of part-time cleaners in the Hamilton-Wentworth Schools.

In 1978, some students and I initiated our first class on women in social work which then became institutionalised as a regular elective. Maureen Orton was also involved with students and me in editing *Connections*, the newsletter of the Women's Caucus of Canadian Schools of Social Work, as well as developing a framework to put feminist content throughout the curriculum. Telling it like this makes it sound too simple. We were pioneering new ideas and practices and that is never easy, even in a relatively supportive environment. During these years, Marylee Stephenson, editor of the first sociology of *Women in Canada*,[4] was denied tenure. She obtained an open hearing for the appeal in which feminist epistemology was on trial.

In the 1970s, feminists of various traditions in Hamilton, Ontario, worked together across our differences. Had we not done so, there would have been no collective analysis or voice. There are many women who could be named, and many wonderful stories

---

[4] M. Stephenson (ed), *Women in Canada* (New Press, 1973).

from that era. There were hard times and sad times. There were 'Persons Campaigns' to encourage women to use their vote; Reclaim the Night marches to bring safety on the streets; women's dinners for building a community of support. Much of this was around the Hamilton Women's Centre. At the Social Planning and Research Council in 1976, we developed proposals on income security for single parents which involved a combination of part-time work and state assistance. This was based on my research into part-time work, and was part of a series of efforts to improve the situation of sole parents in Ontario. At the Elizabeth Fry Society volunteers worked with women on prison and after. I convened a social action committee comprised largely of women who knew the flaws of the system from having 'done time' inside. Nancy Adamson, Linda Brisken and Margaret McPhail much later theorised the practice of the Canadian Women's Movement in 'making change'. It was a privilege as an immigrant woman to have been part of it.

My personal and political 'struggles' (a word used advisedly, because that is how it felt) were sustained bay wonderful friendships and mutual support: Ann, Elena, Shelia and our children, Linda, Anna, Donna, Liz, Mordure and others. Peta Trancred (Sherif) was at McMaster in the 1970s, and her intellectual rigour and personal dignity came to symbolise for me excellent and accountable scholarship. Michael Wheeler proved to be both a loving friend and my toughest intellectual critic. Over subsequent years, I learned much about myself from him, not least of which were lessons about the importance of independence of mind and spirit.

The year 1982 began with the boys and me returning to Australia. The re-entry was very rocky because the other adults in the family network did not join us as soon as we all planned and expected. Moving to a new job on the others side of the world is no fun for either a single parent or her children, in spite of the support of extended family and old friends such as Rae Mathew. My brother Chris and his family were then, and have been since, wonderful friends to the boys and me.

The social backdrop to what could be a much longer personal story of returning to my homeland, was the nature of rather polarised an 'tough' public and organisational politics in Australia. The intellectual and personal freedom and support which I had glimpsed and experienced in Canada, seemed thwarted in a society where citizenship is about mateship and fraternity, and where conceptions of equality contain too little respect for sex, racial and ethnic differences. Whereas in Toronto in 1979, a street poll reported that 54% of women and men were 'feminists', feminists in Australia appeared to be viewed as 'man-hating lesbians', whatever their sexual preference. Australian society is one where too many women are cowed into apologetic manner and polite, angry or frustrate silence. The 'masculinist' 'cut and thrust' culture of public life appears to me to be destructive, unknowing of women's 'lived experience', and unwilling to learn from women's ways of doing things. Rather, women who enter public life are expected to 'toughen up', 'take it like a man', while dressing like a *Vogue* magazine model. There are of course some notable women who have displayed great courage and strength in public life in the 1980s and 1990s in Australia, and have kept close to their communities and 'done it' like women. Carmen Lawrence, Jonan Kirner, Kay Setches and Kate Gilmore, stand out for me. They have my great respect.

I found myself in the 1980s, continuing to most strongly identify with community groups and the 'creatively marginal' possibilities of community cooperation and action and education. The means cannot be sacrificed for the end goals. As a woman, I had to focus first on what this might mean for equality, and restructuring work and family life appear necessary to achieve equality. I had learned 'the personal is political', that 'everyday life' and personal and social practices were as relevant as 'public life'. At best, these are social processes which can contribute to a stronger and more just and equal social fabric, even if indirectly and slowly. If education can survive the assaults of the economic rationalists, it may be possible for us in that location to follow Hugh Stretton's suggestion that its prime purpose is stimulate debate about social values and purposes.

From 1982 to 1991 I was employed as Principal Lecturer in Social Work at Philip Institute of Technology (PIT, now part of RMIT). Building on the strong foundation of Frances Donovan and her staff in the 1970s, a team of people in the 1980s worked together around a commitment to social justice and learning structural, developmental and feminist approaches to social work, welfare and community work theory and practice. My personal educational philosophy is that teaching is not possible, but that education is about resources and opportunities for learning. 'Teachers' can pose only the most relevant social questions they have learned, systematically share their learning, and develop resources, structures and processes to support people learning, working and acting together. Staff and students at PIT in the 1980s worked together to do this in a dynamic and challenging educational community.

This community was no 'ivory tower. People worked hard and were active in community and social issues. Internally, we tried to transform social relationships to be democratic, cooperative and mutually respectful. We not always succeed, and individual 'egos' sometimes thwarted community. In the wider institution, School staff and students were involved in the development of many important workplace and student policies and practices. All staff were union members, and I enjoyed working with and learning much from Jaccie Adie and Faye Gravenall who were active in the staff union, and with Theresa Ewinska, the Equal Opportunity Officer. Time spent as a sexual harassment advisor on Academic Board and PIT Council taught me more than I ever wanted to know about being the 'token' women representatives in a climate of patriarchal practices and economic rationalism. Externally, the staff group were engaged in social criticism, advocacy and community development.

Some of the happiest memories of what felt like 'socially useful work' at PIT were the Social Policy classes I taught with John Wiseman, and our success in offering social work and community development in Northern Victoria. The development of women's studies in both social work and community development was exciting. This was complemented by Bob Pease's work in developing pro-feminist men's studies. New models of community-based field education were developed in the Western Region, involving Sharon Moore, and in Broadmeadows, Marjorie Quinn (who both subsequently joined the staff). Learning together about shared management and leadership with Valerie Gerrand was an unusual and excellent experience in bureaucratic organisation. We all many hours talking and working things out in the staff group, with many others than those who I have named making their contribution. The MA in Social Policy was crafted in many hours of work, and finally offered in 1991.

We developed our theory and practice with a wide range of people outside the institution. The first Social Work Education conference was in Beijing in 1988. Bob Pease and I were proud to be two of the 10 Australians. Subsequently, after Tian An Mien Square, we hosted a moving visit from Hong Kong social work educators committed to social democracy in the future of China. In 1984, when I was a visiting scholar at the University of Queensland, I met and began to learn from Lilla Watson, by her generosity in allowing me to sit in on her classes. In 1988, Lilla came to PIT/RMIT as the first Aboriginal visiting scholar and launched Aboriginal Studies in the Social Work program. Glenn Alderson, from Common ground Cooperative in Seymour, worked with us in expanding the Summer School for the Human Services. Subsequently, several staff developed an on-going association with them. Yoland Wadsworth taught research in the program and concurrently several of us continued to be involved with her in ARIA, the Action Research Issues Association.

Another hindsight, which allowed me to write and theorise, was the collaborative writing about Community Services. First came the book on *Issues Facing Australian Families*,[5] co-edited with Robyn Batten and John Wilson, which includes case studies of Australian programs and practice, and more recently, the collaboration with feminist women's services to write about lessons from their pioneering efforts, *Women Working Together*.[6]

Several of the School's loyal group of administrative staff took up studying Women's Studies and other tertiary subjects, and then moved on to become independent businesswomen. After a long, slow process we introduced a permanent job-sharing position for two administrative staff with family responsibilities. The students who shared in learning became colleagues in the local community services. Working together at the Centre of Sexual Assault (CASA) at the Royal Women's Hospital, where we developed the first feminist field education centre, and at the Victorian Council of Social Services (VCOSS) are two examples.

So, in my experience, learning, mutual support and taking action all seemed to happen concurrently, with people working together. Sometimes one receives from one, and then gives to another, in an individualised 'mentoring' progression based on the model of elder and child. Most what strikes me about social action or practice is its shared, mutual and dynamic process of critical reflection and action. Sometimes the younger ones insist that the elders learn. In 1991, after three years as Head of Department, I stepped 'out and

---

[5] R. Batten, W. Weeks and J. Wilson (eds), *Issues Facing Australian Families* (Longman Cheshire, 1994).

[6] W. Weeks, *Women Working Together* (Longman Cheshire, 1994).

down'. My analysis of organisational gender politics suggests to me that shared and rotating leadership is essential, especially for those who cannot or will not learn to do it 'like a man'. In my experience, 'earth mothers' are particularly prone to being seen and treated as stronger than they feel, and receive their unfair share of cultural 'mother blaming' while getting pretty tired doing the organisational housekeeping.

In 1991 I took up a teaching post at the University of Melbourne, very much enjoying further developing Women's Studies and its potential contribution to women's personal and social liberation. There are many women at the university and in the community working together on this important agenda and again I feel privileged to work among them.

Afterword

Bob Pease

When we were brainstorming potential contributors to this book, we all reflected on how Wendy Weeks would have been on the top of our list, had she still been alive. It again brought back the sadness of her death and we pondered how we could consider such a book without her contribution. It was then that I remembered that in 1996, Wendy had written her story in a book edited by Jocelynne Scutt titled *Living Generously: Women Mentoring Women*. A few days later, I pulled my copy of the book from my bookshelf and read Wendy's contribution. While the theme of Jocelynne's book was different to ours, Wendy's story included her reflections on social work education, community activism, women's services, teaching and scholarship over the time period we were focusing on. Maybe we could add her important voice to the book after all.

I immediately set about exploring how we could get permission to reprint her chapter. The original publisher Artemis Press had since gone out of business. However, I tracked down Joselynne Scutt in the UK and she kindly gave us permission to reprint Wendy's story with acknowledgements. Wendy's son Karl also gave his endorsement of the re-printing. And so, we have been able to bring Wendy's voice back in our anthology.

Everyone who knew her, has a special Wendy memory. For me it was in 2004, just a few weeks before her death on the 31st July. One night in July that year, I heard a knock at the front door. When I opened the door, there was Wendy with a bunch of letters in her hand. She said: 'I was cleaning up and I discovered these letters. I thought you might like to have them'. These were letters I had written to her from Montreal in 1988, when I was on my first sabbatical leave, which Wendy had kept all of these years. Montreal in the late 1980s was an exciting place to be. I had come there to spend time with the French Canadian Social Work educator Maurice Moreau and Peter Leonard, one of the founders of the radical social work movement in the UK, who was then at McGill University. I wrote very long letters to Wendy during my five months in Canada, telling stories about my travels throughout Canada and my encounters with radical social work academics, many of whom knew Wendy from her earlier time there. The letters contained stories of intellectual excitement, political involvements, live theatre and concerts, home sickness and love. Writing to Wendy at that time was like keeping a diary of this period of my life. As I read them again sixteen years after I had written them, the memories came flooding back to me. Wendy knew that the letters would be important to me one day and so she kept them. The timing of her returning them to me, just weeks before her death, gave her gift a special poignancy.

Although Wendy's published story stops in 1996, between then and 2004, she continued to publish, teach, advocate for women's rights, supervise Higher Degree Research students and mentor the many women she came into contact with through her teaching, research collaborations and community activism. Her work lives on and continues to inspire women through her published books, articles and book chapters.[7] At the time of her sudden death from an aneurism, she had just recently 'retired' from her academic position in Social Work at the University of Melbourne. Her latter period there had not been a happy time and she was looking forward, albeit with some anxiety, to more time for writing, research, gardening and spiritual connections with Aboriginal women who had become increasingly important to her in the latter years of her life.

Wendy inspired thousands of women through her teaching and involvements in community activism and women's services. Many women came to feminism through her grounded approach to understanding women's lives. The editorial committee of *Women Against Violence* marked Wendy's founding contribution with a special issue dedicated to her life and work.[8] Jane Dixon, guest editor, asked a cross-section of women who worked with Wendy to write tributes. The journal assembled ten tributes that reflected aspects of Wendy's life as an activist, a colleague, a critical friend, an educator, a writer, a mentor, and as a teacher. She had an enduring influence on the lives of so many women, as the tributes in the special edition of the journal attest.

What is less well known perhaps, though, is her positive impact

---

[7] In addition to the books already cited, she went on to publish four other books with colleagues. W. Weeks and J. Wilson (eds.), *Issues Facing Australian Families* (2nd edition, Longmans, 1995); T. Dalton, M. Draper, W. Weeks and J. Wiseman, *Making Social Policy in Australia* (Allen and Unwin, 1996; W. Weeks and M. Quinn (eds), *Issues Facing Australian Families* (3rd edition, Pearsons Education, 2000); W. Weeks, L. Hoatson and J. Dixon (eds), *Community Practices in Australia* (Pearsons Education, 2003).

[8] See *Women Against Violence: An Australian Feminist Journal*, Issue 17, 2004-2005. See also *New Community*, 12 (3), Issue 47, 2014 for a special commemorative edition celebrating Wendy's contributions to community development, ten years after her death.

on men who, like so many women, were also influenced and challenged by her. When I turned again to her chapter in Jocelynne's book, I was reminded of the dedication she wrote to me, when she gave me the book as a present. In the front page after the subtitle of the book, 'Women mentoring women', she wrote....'know they can't do it without men mentoring men. Looking forward to critical women' studies and critical men's studies....' It was Wendy who encouraged and supported my intellectual engagement with pro-feminist men's writing, teaching and activism. She wrote a foreword to my first book *Men and Sexual Politics* [9] and she believed in the possibility of transforming gender power relations to create a world where men and women lived in harmony with each other and the planet.

I had the pleasure to work alongside Wendy at PIT for eight years during the 'social experiment' with structural, developmental and feminist approaches to social work, which she describes in her chapter. And we maintained our friendship over the years, often meeting in the evenings after work to discuss ideas, books and politics over a glass (or two) of red wine.

I often find myself in political situations and intellectual discussions when I ponder: 'I wonder what Wendy would think' about the political or intellectual matter at hand. I feel that her perspective on the world is still with me, and I'm sure that I'm not alone in experiencing that. However, I continue to miss her physical presence in my life and I surprise myself with how easily my emotions flow when someone mentions her name. She has a lasting influence on my life, as she does on the lives of so many others.

---

[9] W. Weeks, Foreword to B. Pease, *Men and Sexual Politics: Towards a Profeminist Practice* (Dulwich, 1997).

11

Working from the 'Outside':

Reflections on Sexual Assault Prevention and Social Work

Moira Carmody

Much of my working life since 1983 has been focused on challenging the cultural practices and impacts of sexual violence. In this chapter I reflect on this work which took place within a hospital sexual assault service, a state health bureaucracy, the academy and within non-government organisations. Most of these roles were not social work designated positions. Rather I utilised the skills and knowledge of my critical feminist and social work perspective to inform my practice in these diverse settings. Drawing on early writings, reflections on critical moments and activities, I chart my acts of resistance to dominant knowledges and practices. I argue that social work has been a key element in shaping my ethics of practice, research, education and policy.

The personal was indeed political

My early years as a social work student were filled with the possibilities of creating new ways of relating, of working and standing alongside those who were disempowered, silenced and ignored. The global feminist movement was alive, vociferous and there were many struggles within as well as focused on 'the enemies' of the revolution we believed we could achieve. The personal experiences

182

of women's lives were central to political strategy and reflected the wider social and cultural conditions.[1] I was in there fighting for justice for women and others, bemused and at times angered by my sisters' arguments and behaviour. I emerged as a young woman ready to be an active player in creating a new cultural landscape. I needed to understand my own subjectivity and how I was positioned as a white middle-class educated woman and the impact this may have on the work I wanted to do. In this process which we later refined as self-reflexivity, I was changed – the politics were indeed personal and the personal was very political.[2] I wouldn't have missed it for quids. In 1984, I wrote:

For many feminists, myself included, rape is the ultimate expression of patriarchal power. It is the expression of woman hatred, the ultimate statement of women's powerlessness in a male dominated world ... We have long ago put on notice that rape is unacceptable and will be challenged in every way we know how.[3]

There had been much campaigning from the early 1970s for legal reform and police training and to gain better services for victims of sexual assault.[4] The NSW Task Force into the Care of Victims of Sexual Offences was announced by Premier Wran in November 1977. The combined influence of radical feminists pressuring for action from outside and the increasing influence of liberal feminists within government departments was instrumental in gaining this government attention. The Women's Coordination Unit provided key leadership then and for several decades that fol-

---

[1] W. Weeks, 'Women: Developing Feminist Practice in Women's Services' In *Critical Social Work: An Introduction to Theories and Practices* (eds) June Allan, Bob Pease, Linda Briskman, (Allen and Unwin, 2003), 107-123.

[2] J. Fook, 'Critical Reflexivity in Education and Practice'. In *Transforming Social Work Practice* (eds), B. Pease and J. Fook (Allen and Unwin, 1999).

[3] M. Carmody, 'The Fear of Rape', (1984) *Social Alternatives* 4(3), 21-22.

[4] The term 'victim' was contested especially in the early years as feminists wished to focus on women's agency. At the same time, there was a parallel political need to force the community to recognise women were victims of male oppression.

lowed. Radical feminists were very critical of the apparatus of the state and argued hospitals had failed in their duty of care to victims of sexual assault. Punitive and dismissive attitudes by medical staff added to the trauma that victims experienced. The Task Force was composed of the Health Commission's Chief forensic medical officer, police representatives, and the Premier's Department as chair despite Carmel Niland a prominent feminist and Director of the Women's' Coordination Unit being named in NSW parliament as the chair. There was no representation of Sydney Rape Crisis Centre, the only victim support service, no legal representation or members of the Royal Colleges for doctors or consultation with the social work profession.[5]

The major recommendation of the report was the establishment of 24 hour 7 day a week crisis counselling and medical care. As a result, eight services were established in teaching hospitals in Sydney, Wollongong and Newcastle. Funding was allocated to the Health Commission to implement the strategy. At that time, the Health Commission fortunately had two social work advisers, Pam Rutledge and Lindsay Napier. Pam Rutledge had primary responsibility for the implementation of the new services for victims and located the services in social work departments. From this moment, social work played a key role in the delivery of services to survivors of sexual assault which continues three decades later. At the time, it was new work for social workers and many were hostile and resistant. Many reflected victim blaming attitudes to women, something they shared with many community members. This model of service was unique in engaging professionally trained social workers operating within hospitals. In other states, services developed within non-government organisations and in the early years many had no

---

[5] For a detailed discussion of this period, see M. Carmody, 'Midnight Companions: Social Work Involvement in the Development of Sexual Assault Services in NSW' (1990) *Australian Social Work* 43(4), 9-16.

formal qualifications. The influence of the anti-professionalism in this period also played a part in feminists wanting to hold on to woman centred services where women's experience was more important than formal training.

It was against this backdrop that in 1983 I rather hesitantly took a position as a social worker in one of the new hospital-based sexual assault services. Was I selling out by working in a hospital? What did this mean for my feminist politics? These personal questions were reflective of wider political debates within feminism and the tension between radical feminist critique and emerging liberal feminist's engagement in working more closely with government to achieve gender equality.[6]

I had been a passionate advocate for other groups such as adults and children with an intellectual disability and neuro-surgery patients in the first few years of my career. However, very quickly working with the women and children who experienced sexual violence gave me a direct opportunity to combine my feminist politics and my social work skills to try and make what I hoped was a small difference in their lives.

The work was and is hard. It is personally confronting. Having the honour of standing beside someone as they tell you of the harm and lack of respect and degradation they have experienced can challenge your core beliefs about humanity. The hospital police and legal systems were imperfect and often reluctant to consider the impact of their attitudes and procedures and the additional harm it did to women and children. Despite this, I felt that I could draw on a range of knowledge and skills from my training as a social worker and my political activism. I utilised a feminist analysis of rape to understand the structural factors that promoted and condoned attitudes that resulted in some men believing they could rape women

---

[6] V. Bryson, *Feminist Political Theory: An Introduction* (Macmillan, 1992).

and children without consequence. I used woman-centred counselling skills, crisis intervention models around what we saw as 'the medical emergency of rape', group work skills to provide support groups for women, advocacy skills for individual representation of women's needs, and educational group skills to run training to enhance the skills of other social workers and other professions. My critical analysis of issues using a systems model gave me the skills to think about the whole organisation, opportunities for alliances and how to work across disciplines and departments.

These skills I saw as acts of resistance to a community that was reluctant to accept these crimes occurred. Rape was viewed by many in the community as a rare event which only happened to 'certain sorts of women'. The extent and lasting impact of rape on women and children was also not well understood. Collectively, front line workers were helping women and children explore alternative ways of understanding what happened to them and where the responsibility lay. They developed diverse ways of working and the meaning they gave to their work.[7, 8]

There was a lot of energy and passion amongst the women I worked with in this and other services and we utilised our social work skills well most of the time. The field of what is now called trauma counselling was in its infancy. One of the areas that we failed to understand was the impact the work could have on us, the social workers involved. It is now well known that repeated exposure to traumatic material can lead to negative consequences for workers in a range of fields. Workers run the risk of developing rapid burnout, compassion fatigue or vicarious trauma.[9]

[7] M. Carmody, 'Submerged Voices: Coordinators of Sexual Assault Speak of Their Experiences" (1997) *Affilia: Women and Social Work* 12, (4), 452-470.

[8] J. Breckenridge and M. Carmody (eds), *Crimes of Violence: Australian Responses to Rape and Child Sexual Assault* (Allen and Unwin, 1992).

[9] C. Figley, 'Compassion Fatigue as Secondary Traumatic Stress Disorder: An Overview'. In: C. Figley (ed), *Compassion Fatigue: Coping with Secondary Traumatic Stress Disorder in Those Who Treat The Traumatized.* Brunner-Routledge, 1995, 1-20.

While supervision was provided, it tended to focus on client management issues. The need for organisational responsibility to manage work practices and to encourage critical reflection and self-care planning was not something we understood or recognised. It would take many years before this was recognised within the field and strategies for self-care and external supervision were crucial aspects of the duty of care of the workplace. Sadly, there are still workplaces that are failing their staff in this regard.

Over time, I became the coordinator of the sexual assault service. More and more of my role was spent fighting against archaic policies and procedures within the health, police and legal systems. My time was full running training and giving talks to police and other agencies to try and shift their attitudes. In the following I reflect on one of these police talks in 1985.

Mary and I arrived at Police Headquarters early. We were both anxious about the talk we were about to deliver. We were taken to a room with a podium up the front and rows of chairs spread around the grey drab room. There were about 25 men in the room and one woman. They were called to order and we were on. I am thinking 'God what are we doing here – they all look so angry – arms crossed, legs spread'. I talked about the short and long-term impact of sexual assault on victims and the importance of their role in assisting victims to make a good recovery. They sat silently and then we got to questions. And they were off! 'Why should we waste our time bringing victims to you? They seem keen to make a complaint and after they have had a private conversation with you they change their mind'; 'why can't we sit in the room with you while you counsel them so we know what is going on?'; 'why do we have to wait so long for the doctors? It was quicker when we took them to the medical officer at the morgue'. We parried the questions, tried to get across our role was to explain the options to women and help them decide about a formal complaint. It was not to tell them what to do as this would replicate the powerlessness of their rape experience. After an hour, we made a hasty escape.

This kind of training was the most difficult for me and for others – we came hard up against the highly masculine police culture. Many had countless years of service. To them we must have appeared as very young, inexperienced and ignorant of the 'true' nature of rape complaints. The negative attitudes expressed by some officers about survivors of rape reinforced how much more work there was to do. It was exhausting; they were rude, belligerent and had the power to make life hard for the women who were brave enough to report if they wished. We felt worked over and could only imagine how this might feel to a woman trying to make sense of a sexual assault. Despite these attitudes, service coordinators were committed to this work seeing it as essential to challenge poor practices and to build interagency collaboration. This kind of situation was repeated numerous times over the 1980s as the police training gradually began to catch up with a more victim focused form of policing. The perception that social workers convinced women to not make a formal complaint lasted for many years and was only resolved over time and with extensive cross agency work and the building of trust.

Sister in a suit: Working within government

From the early 1970s second wave feminism began to impact on reshaping government responses to women's needs. This had resulted in the appointment in 1973 of Elizabeth Reid as the first women's adviser to Prime Minster Gough Whitlam. Her appointment was not only sensationalised in the press but was also controversial within the women's movement.[10] Over time, women's units were established in key departments across states. The willingness

[10] M. Sawyer, *Sisters in Suits: Women and Public Policy in Australia* (Allen and Unwin, 1990).

of feminists to engage with the state, however difficult and contradictory is one of the hallmarks of Australian feminism which distinguishes it from both American and the British experience.[11] Tensions remained between radical feminists and liberal feminists who were willing to work with the state to try and bring about much needed reforms in key issues impacting women's lives. The femocrat was born:

Depending on your point of view a femocrat was a woman who'd been co-opted into a cushy government job or one who had entered the government arena to fight for equality and redistribution of resources for women.[12]

I was increasingly concerned that providing high quality counselling and support services for women and children who experienced sexual assault was not enough. Social policy changes were needed to challenge the problems survivors were still experiencing in court. Conviction rates remained low and community attitudes to rape remained negative in large sections of the community. Services were hardly adequate in number and most were in metropolitan areas. In 1985 the opportunity to work at a state level occurred. It was against the backdrop of contested feminist politics that I became one of the 'sisters in a suit'.

I was appointed to a new position in the Health Department as Senior Policy Advisor (Sexual Assault) within the Women's Health Unit. I stepped out of direct service provision and took on a complex and wide-ranging role to oversee the roll out of 22 new sexual assault services in rural and outer urban areas. Over the next four years, I travelled extensively across the state working with local health providers to set up new services. This was followed by training of staff, establishing network meetings for the state-wide net-

---

[11] A. Summers, *Damned Whores and God's Police: The Updated Edition of The Classic Study Of Women In Australian Society* (Penguin, 1994).

[12] S. Dowse, 'Dilemmas in Femocracy' (1990) *Australian Society*, 29-30 June.

189

work and the development of policy and procedure standards for sexual assault services to ensure quality and consistency across the network.

In this role, I could draw on my social work skills in working with groups, social policy development, networking, research, fostering interagency collaboration, taking part in key government committees and leading key projects such the training of staff across the state in relation to child sexual assault following the extension of mandatory reporting laws. At the time, I initially would not have identified what I was doing as social work per se. Most of us just get on with the job at hand. Having come from a sexual assault service, I remained committed to ensuring that sector was well informed and supported and that I would work closely with them to advocate for the issue of sexual assault.

In this period in the 1980s we had unprecedented access to government, opportunities to develop new programs and policies and we secured much needed funding for women's projects. However, developing new policy and securing funding for initiatives is only one step in the policy process. Both policy development and implementation are often contested. I had numerous conversations with politicians over the years who failed to understand that just because a new policy has been approved, it may not be implemented in the way it was intended which defeated the purpose of trying to improve women's lives. The following example highlights one situation in relation to trying to establish a new rural sexual assault service.

It is an early winter morning – the sun is just up and I am waiting for the taxi to take me to the airport for a trip out west. It is a moment of quiet before some difficult negotiations with a local health service. They were given funding to establish a service and it appeared they have used most of the money on less staff than allocated and redirected the remaining funds to other program areas.

At that time, head office could control local expenditure. My job was to find out what service was being provided and to advise them that all remaining funds were being withdrawn and that they would not receive any further funding.

Issues like this were extremely frustrating and disappointing. Naively, we believed we could structurally counteract their arguments that they had no money for a sexual assault service by giving them funding. We failed to understand that the issue was not a priority for them and they would decide local expenditure. There were lessons to be learnt from examples like this such as building a local network of support prior to funding and to find senior champions of the issue which could prevent the funds being misdirected. The lack of acceptance by the local health service of sexual assault as a major issue with significant poor health outcomes meant women and children in that area had to wait several years before more funding came their way.

After four hectic and exciting years, I was exhausted and pretty much burnout. I left the Health Commission and took a different direction. I became a welfare teacher in TAFE and worked on my PhD.

Sites of struggle

The volume and speed of policy change I had been part of left little room to critically reflect on what had been achieved and explore ways to understand it. I wanted to think about the many issues my work in sexual assault raised for me personally but also to consider what it could add to our knowledge about feminism, the state, social policy and power. Most importantly, I wanted to explore how these factors may have positively contributed to improving the lives of women and children. I also wondered what we had missed.

The theoretical underpinnings of my work until the mid-1990s had been influenced by both radical and liberal feminist models. These strands of feminism were central to how rape was defined and responded to in the 1970s-1980s. Radical feminists believed the patriarchal state was the cause of rape and other discrimination of women.[13] Only a revolution to overthrow the state would achieve a woman centred society. It seemed unlikely to me that the revolution would happen and result in the overthrow of the state. Maybe revolution could be achieved from within. Liberal feminists recognised that the state is not neutral in its treatment of women, considering the state has been captured by men. Under this model sexism and patriarchy are a case of imperfect citizenship requiring redress.[14] This approach was used to achieve significant success in rape law reform, employment, child care, education and broader social policies focused on reducing violence against women. They reflected significant reworking of the cultural landscape and were in their own way revolutionary.

Despite the gains that had been made, I had often felt a sense of unease. As I began to reflect on these different strands of feminism, this unease began to take a clearer shape. My readings lead me to critically analyse some of my previously held assumptions. Differences between women were often obscured and the women's movement was critiqued as middle class, white, heterosexist and ableist resulting in a need for great intersectional analysis.[15] Radical feminist universalising and determinism concerned me as it suggested a never-ending structure of gender relations in which women were doomed to be passive victims of male power. Despite this, historically and in the contemporary world there were many

---

[13] For example, in the work of A. Dworkin, *Woman Hating* (EP Dutton 1974) and S. Brownmiller, *Against Our Will: Men, Women and Rape* (Penguin,1976).

[14] S. Franzway, D. Court and R.W. Connell, *Staking a Claim: Feminism, Bureaucracy and the State* (Allen and Unwin, 1989).

[15] K. Crenshaw, 'Mapping the Margins: Intersectionality, Identity Politics, and Violence Against Women of Color' (1991) *Stanford Law Review*. 43(6), 1241-1299.

examples of women who developed strategies to resist the excesses of male dominance. Men had also developed critiques of the oppressive nature of gender role prescriptions placed on them.[16] The theory of patriarchy does not necessarily imply all men oppress all women.[17] Another important distinction was to be made between the structures of male domination and the behaviour of individual men.[18]

Liberal feminism also has several limitations. Development of the liberal subject assumed a strong belief in the power of the individual and the importance of securing human and legal rights for women to fully take part in society.[19] There is also an assumption that change will come about from within the existing political structure – that men will willingly give up power and control to ensure women can exercise their rights to full equality. It seemed both radical and liberal feminism conceptually and practically had limited possibilities for understanding the diverse ways in which power could be exercised within the gender order or within the liberal state.

Increasingly, like many others in the early 1990s, I was drawn to alternative ways of thinking about power within intimate relations and questioning a structuralist model of the unitary state. Feminist poststructuralist theory created alternatives to the grand narratives of power. The French philosopher Michel Foucault's argument that power is not always coercive or repressive but rather can be productive changed my thinking.[20] He argued that power is produced in every social relationship rather than being a unitary and coercive concept residing in the state and that where there is power there is

[16] R.W. Connell, *Masculinities* (Allen and Unwin, 1995).

[17] V. Bryson, op. cit., 188.

[18] S. Walby, *Theorising Patriarchy* (Blackwell 1990).

[19] V. Bryson, op. cit., 159.

[20] M. Foucault, *Power/Knowledge: Selected Interviews and Other Writings 1972-1977*, C. Gordon (ed) (Harvester, 1980).

resistance. The state can therefore be understood as a site of competing discourses and practices. This can be summed up as:

The state is a site of struggle over social, political and cultural practices as well as economic ones in which a plurality of interests and movements variously shape its policies.[21, 22]

The emancipatory project of feminism was re-examined within the shifting configurations of power and struggle. Feminist resistance in all its forms created an alternative discursive space in which new and different forms of knowledge became possible about women, men, about rape and working to create a more just society. This insight allowed me to reconsider the work I had done within the bureaucracy from an alternative perspective. The state and its bureaucracies was no longer a unified oppressive force. Understanding that power can be viewed in a capillary fashion also created the possibility of thinking more fully about resistance. New social policy, legal reform, the development of services for survivors of sexual assault for example reflected alternative constructions of gender relations and the challenged the masculinist state to take these demands seriously. Recognising the dynamic and productive model of power created hope of change in ways where earlier models of feminism had stalled. This position however, did not ignore the structural and material reality that directly impacted on women's lives.

Power: Knowledge tango and sexual ethics

Feminist poststructuralism extended beyond Foucault's gender blindness and recognised that social life is indeed a series of sites

---

[21] A. Yeatman, *Bureaucrats, Technocrats, Femocrats* (Allen and Unwin, 1990).

[22] For a detailed discussion of how I applied this concept to the development of sexual assault services in NSW, see Moira Carmody PhD Thesis, Sites of Struggle: The Development of Social Policy Surrounding Rape and Sexual Assault Services in NSW Australia (1995) Sydney, UNSW.

of struggle not only in the public domain of policy but in the private relations of individuals.[23] The insights I gained during this intense period of reflection, reading, writing and debate with others significantly changed my conceptualisations of my work on sexual violence and my subsequent work on wider issues of sexuality, gender and prevention. It called attention to my own entanglements in what McNeil calls the power-knowledge tango:

Awareness of this could make us better dancers; less naïve about the truth making us free, more tentative about our theories and analyses, less prophetic and triumphalist in our pronouncements and more aware of the specific patterns of power in which we are ensnared.[24]

In 1995, I was appointed to my first academic position as lecturer in sociology in a school of health. I developed my research profile building on my years of clinical work with survivors of sexual violence and my policy experience in health. Most importantly, I approached my work as a better 'dancer' which created many possibilities intellectually but also in developing creative solutions to the complex problems of sexual assault prevention. Over the following twenty years, my work developed conceptually and led me to critique many of the assumptions underpinning sexual violence prevention policy including education and intimate relationships.[25] Many government and community approaches to preventing sexual violence were placing responsibility for prevention on women. It wasn't until the early 2000s when community campaigns and wider

---

[23] J. Sawicki, *Disciplining Foucault: Feminism, Power and the Body* (Routledge, 1991).

[24] M. McNeil, 'Dancing with Foucault: Feminism and Power/Knowledge, in C. Ramazanoglu (ed), *Up Against Foucault: Explorations of Some Tensions Between Foucault and Feminism* (Routledge, 1993).

[25] Early examples include M. Carmody and K. Carrington, 'Preventing Sexual Violence?, (2000) *Australian and New Zealand Journal of Criminology* 33(3), 341-361; Moira Carmody, 'Sexual Ethics and Violence Prevention' (2003) *Social and Legal Studies: An International Journal,* 12(2), 199-216.

prevention education began to shift focus to include men and attempt to engage them in education about respectful and ethical relations with women.[26]

My own work had increasingly focused on trying to explore alternative discourses of desire, consent and mutual pleasure between opposite and same gender partners in casual or ongoing sexual relationships.[27] I argued that sexual intimacy had been dominated by discourses of fear and danger and women's pleasure was invisible. I suggested an alternative approach in which violence prevention strategies acknowledge both pleasure and danger. Central to this approach was a focus on sexual ethics based on Foucault's ideas about ethical sexual subjectivity. In this approach, I argued that both women and men had the opportunity to be ethical or not in their intimate relationships. Rarely had they been given these kinds of ideas in their sexuality education at school or home. The aim was to increase mutual negotiated sexual consent for both women and men.[28]

Taking this stance was not always well received. At a violence against women prevention conference in Sydney in the early 2000s, I suggested that men could be ethical and non-violent and that a radical feminist argument that all men were inherently violent was flawed and was not reflected in many women's experiences. I was hissed at loudly by sections of the audience.

Reflecting on an ethics of practice

Social work laid the foundation for my ethics about the work I have

---

[26] K. Albury, M. Carmody, C. Evers and C. Lumby, 'Playing by the Rules: Researching, Teaching and Learning Sexual Ethics with Young Men in the Australian National Rugby League' (2011), *Sex Education*, 11, 339-351.

[27] M. Carmody, "Ethical Erotics: Reconceptualising Anti-Rape Education" (2005) *Sexualities* 8 (4), 465-480.

[28] For a full discussion on these issues and their application, see M. Carmody, *Sex & Ethics: Young People and Ethical Sex* (Palgrave Macmillan, 2009) and M. Carmody, *Sex, Ethics and Young People* (Macmillan Springer, 2015).

done for four decades. The theories and skills I learnt informed counselling with an individual woman who had been raped, supervising staff, advocating for legal and other policy reform, running groups, advising government, teaching, research and publication. I developed an approach to my work as a critical practitioner and academic. However, social work was not the only influence in shaping my reflexive practice. My involvement in feminist politics and theory, postgraduate study and twenty years of academic research and teaching have been key influences in shaping my work.

The tensions and contradictions in critical social work, feminist politics and theories are ones that have enlivened and challenged the approaches I have taken. I have been working as an outsider to social work designated positions for most of my career. Despite this, I have retained connections with social work colleagues, had the pleasure of being mentored by several wonderful women such as Robyn Stevenson, Wendy Weeks and Jane Woodruff and been an AASW member since the early 1980s. As researchers or as social workers, we are never neutral observers or inquirers as Malcolm Payne argues – the point is to help achieve both individual and social change.[29] I hope that I have been able to contribute to the collective struggle to make a small difference to the lives of women who have experienced sexual violence and to suggest alternative ways of conceptualising gender violence prevention. There is much still to be done and I continue to contribute outside of the academy.

---

[29] M. Payne, 'Social Work Theories and Reflective Practice' (2002) in *Social Work: Themes, Issues and Critical Debates* 2nd edition (eds) Robert Adams, Lena Dominelli, Malcolm Payne UK, Palgrave, 123-138.

12

WHY DON'T WE TALK ABOUT PATRIARCHY ANYMORE?

Reflections on Forty Years of Scholarship and Activism Against Men's Sexism and Violence

Bob Pease

It is June 2015 and I am sitting on a panel and getting ready to present a paper at an Ending Family Violence conference on the topic of the limitations of contemporary discourses and practices in relation to the prevention of violence against women. I've been listening to other papers during the previous day and a half and I've been thinking that the conference has failed to address the issues that I'm going to raise in my paper. I have been frustrated by the level of analysis and the conduct of the discussion at the conference. My frustration might have something to do with the fact that it is now 40 years since I went to my first conference on violence against women as a social work student in Tasmania in 1975 and what I am hearing now is almost as if these last 40 years have not happened. Many papers still use gender neutral language in referring to 'family violence'. Many papers which do talk about gender have an individualistic understanding about gender and tend only to gender the victims of family violence (that is, women) and not the perpetrators of violence (that is, men). While there have been some references to gender inequality, there is no mention of patriarchy. I am left wondering what have we learnt since the 1970s?

What impact have we had on the problem of men's violence against women? Why is the language that we currently use so depoliticised after forty years of second-wave feminism in Australia? Why don't we talk about patriarchy anymore?

What I want to do in this chapter is to reflect on one strand of my political and intellectual work over the last 40 years, as it relates to men's sexism and violence against women. This work has paralleled my movement through social work education as a student, my work as a community development practitioner and my return to social work education as an academic, alongside other forms of activism outside the university context.

Engaging with feminism in the 1970s

I first engaged with feminism in the 1970s in response to being challenged by women about my privilege as a man. My partner would come home from women's consciousness-raising meetings and challenge my limited participation in housework and my over-commitment to study, activism and paid work at the expense of our relationship. I had to work out what these challenges would mean not only for my personal relationship, but also for my chosen career of social work and my political activism on issues of social justice.

As a socialist who was involved in community politics on social justice issues, I found it relatively easy at the intellectual level to see the validity of feminist claims and my own complicity in the oppression of women. I understood theoretically how as a man I was implicated in patriarchy and how I had not escaped the socialisation into patriarchal expectations about women. However, at the emotional level, I was deeply threatened by feminism. Listening to the experiences of my then partner and women more generally brought complex reactions from sorrow to outrage to confusion about how to respond. I can still remember trying to explain to my partner that I didn't have time to do my share of the housework in a particular week because I was organising a meeting of men for gender equality. Clearly, I had a lot to learn. I needed to embrace the feminist notion of 'the personal is political' and I needed to go beyond talking the talk to walk the walk on gender issues.

To begin to address these issues, I co-founded a men's consciousness-raising group in Tasmania in 1977. Many of the men were partners of feminist women. The group was comprised of eleven men, with a core of six. We were all 'middle class', Australian born and in our late 20s or early 30s. All but two of us were heterosexual and a small number of us had socialist politics. Most of us knew each other before. So the group was formed out of existing networks.

We developed three major aims: to explore ways in which as men felt stunted by traditional masculinity; to become more aware of our sexist attitudes and practices in relation to women; and to explore alternative ways of relating to each other as men that broke with traditional male bonding. None of us at that time had a clearly defined theoretical perspective on gender issues for men. Many of us had some level of commitment to feminism; however, as we were to discover, we all meant different things by that. Our meetings were focused around set topics each night. We discussed housework, homosexuality, sexual experiences, pornography, rape, violence, masculinity, work, love and many other topics.

As the intimacy level developed within the group, we would set aside planned topics and respond to the immediate issues that some men in the group were facing in their lives at the time. Our relationships with women became the most constant recurring theme and many of us used the group as a supportive forum to explore our experiences of these relationships. This issue was to become source of major difficulties within the group and it opened up a number of contradictions. Most of us were endeavouring to overcome the barriers that separated us and to achieve a closer emotional intimacy. Relating to other men as emotional beings, especially to their pain and distress, and offering comfort was a very new experience for many of us. It meant directly confronting our homophobia. However, as the emotional intimacy developed, it made it difficult at times to address the sexist attitudes and behaviour within the group. Sometimes, supporting men's struggles meant bolstering their egos and reinforcing sexist behaviour and this became an issue of tension within and outside the group.

Feminist women in Tasmania were divided on whether the group should be supported or not. Many feminist women applauded the formation of the group. 'At last, a group of men were getting together to do something about their sexism'. Other feminists, however, were deeply suspicious. 'Now what are they up to? The formation of our group stimulated a debate among feminist women about the potential of such a group to develop an anti-sexist practice.

Meanwhile, a parallel debate was going on inside the group. One group of men wanted to focus primarily on ways in which they felt stunted as men. They didn't want to hear about the privileges we held as men or the social power we exercised over women. So five men broke away and formed a support group for men. Two men concluded that we were hopeless oppressors and that very little could be done about that personally or politically. A third group of which I was a part, thought that there had to be another alternative, although we didn't know what that was at the time. The larger group disbanded, as men went off in one of three directions.

Four of us decided to get a better grasp about what women were saying about men. So we set up a reading group on feminist theory. We started with Mary Wollstonecraft and then read what we saw as the major feminist authors chronologically: Emily Pankhurst, Simone de Beauvior, Betty Friedan, Germaine Greer, Shulamith Firestone, Juliet Mitchell, Jill Johnston and others. [1] We would share our emotional and intellectual responses to these books. Thus they were not purely intellectual discussions. Rather, we were endeavouring to locate our experience as men in the context of women's experiences and feminist theory. Although, we recognised that we read such theory as men.

Meanwhile, a literature on men and masculinity was emerging. The first books on men and masculinity published in the mid-1970s promoted the idea of a men's liberation movement that would run parallel to the women's movement.[2] Proponents of men's liberation argued that men sexism oppresses both men and women by prescribing stereotyped sex-role behaviours which are dehumanising and which cause emotional suffering. These books accentuated the negative aspects for men of traditional masculinity, focusing on what they regarded as the oppressed aspects rather the oppressor dimensions of being a man.[3] In response to the limitations of this literature, in the late 1970s, a second perspective on gender issues for men was articulated through the publication of two books on profeminist and anti-sexist men's politics.[4] These books validated the political direction I had begun to move in at the time and they provided inspiration and practical ideas about what men could do to challenge sexism and men's violence against women.

---

[1] M. Wollstencraft, *The Rights of Women* (Everyman's Library, 1965); E. Pankhurst, *Suffragette: My Own Story* (Hesperus Press, 1914/2015); S. de Beavoir, *The Second Sex* (Four Square, 1965); B. Friedan, *The Feminine Mystique* (Penguin, 1963); G. Greer, *The Female Eunuch* (Bantam Books, 1971); S. Firestone, *The Dialectic of Sex* (Bantam, 1971); J. Mitchell, *Women's Estate* (Penguin, 1971); J. Johnston, *Lesbian Nation* (Simon and Schuster, 1977).

[2] W. Farrell, *The Liberated Man* (Random House, 1975); J. Nichols, *Men's Liberation: A New Definition of Masculinity* (Penguin, 1975); J. Pleck and J. Sawyer (eds.) *Men and Masculinity* (Prentice Hall, 1974).

[3] See B. Pease, *Men and Sexual Politics: Towards a Profeminist Practice* (Dulwich, 1997) for a critique of the men's liberation perspective.

[4] A. Tolson, *The Limits of Masculinity* (Tavistock, 1977; J. Snodrass (ed.), *For Men Against Sexism* (Times Change Press, 1977).

Becoming politically active in profeminist men's politics

After moving to Melbourne in 1983 to further my academic career at Philip Institute of Technology (later RMIT), I attended a public meeting to discuss the future direction of gender politics for men. At that meeting, I found men like myself who were struggling to reconcile the personal and the political and who were interested in exploring the potential of anti-patriarchal practices by men in the public arena. Out of that meeting a group of six men founded Men Against Sexism. We organised monthly forums on issues such as pornography, domestic violence, rape and sexuality. We produced booklets on men's responsibility for contraception, what men can do to challenge rape culture and ways in which men can explore loving and joyful expressions of sexuality. We gave talks in schools to boys about masculinity, bullying and sexism. We facilitated training workshops for health, law enforcement and welfare workers on the causes of men's violence and what to do to challenge it.

However, it was not until 1989 when I co-founded Men Against Sexual Assault (MASA) in Melbourne that I moved into concerted public activism against men's violence against women. The purpose of MASA was to encourage men to take responsibility for action against sexual violence through community education, social action, public media work and anti-sexist workshops. In September of 1990, we organised the first men's march against sexual assault in which over 300 men marched through the streets of Melbourne. While there had been Reclaim the Night marches by women for many years, men were conspicuously absent in public demonstrations against men's violence. Our march attracted significant media publicity, and gained far more media attention than marches organised by women. While the march was generally welcomed by feminist women, some feminist activists were critical of the march because, for them, it undermined the radical feminist view that all men were potential rapists. Thus, there was an understandable distrust of men's motivations. I was starting to learn that profeminist politics by men was fraught and politically controversial. Nevertheless, men's marches against violence were held annually in Melbourne for a number of years and inspired marches and public demonstrations by men against violence in other states.

I remember nervously giving my first rally speech to the men gathered at the beginning of the 1990 march. With the megaphone in one hand and my speech notes fluttering in the wind in the other, I told the men why we were here and what we could do make a difference to the problem of men's violence against women. I was trying to find a voice to talk to other men about men's violence and how we as men were all complicit in the violence perpetrated by other men in patriarchy. While my theoretical understanding was underdeveloped at that time, intuitively, I reacted against the notion that those of us who were challenging men's violence were the 'good' men and that it was only those 'other' men who were the problem. This would be the first of many such speeches that I would give at rallies and public demonstrations against men's violence. Over time, I became more comfortable with this form of public speaking and I was able to dispense with my notes; although, I would always write a prepared speech out before the event to get the nuance of my message clear in my mind.

In 1992, we organised the first White Ribbon Campaign against men's violence in Australia. The campaign was inspired by the Canadian campaign founded by Michael Kaufman in response to the massacre in Montreal on the 6th December 1989 when fourteen women were killed by a gunman at the University of Montreal. Thousands of men across Canada wore white ribbons to show their opposition to men's violence against women. The aim of the campaign was to provide a means for men to make a public statement about men's violence and to encourage men's responsibility for action against it.

In those early days of the campaign, there was no government funding and there were no paid staff. We purchased reams of white ribbon, cut them up, ironed them into a v shape and inserted safety pins them. We then distributed them to supportive venues and encouraged men to wear them through media releases and radio interviews. Now, White Ribbon Australia is a publicly funded foundation with thirty one paid staff, over 3,000 White Ribbon ambassadors in Australia and over 700 events organised Australia wide in the last year. However, as White Ribbon has grown exponentially, as a campaign, it has also become corporatised, as social marketing strategies and public health promotion models take over from social movement politics.

Until early 2017, I was a member of the White Ribbon Policy and Research Committee advising the White Ribbon Australia Board on violence prevention monographs and I've been a White Ribbon Ambassador, giving numerous talks at White Ribbon events throughout Australia. However, I've become increasingly uncomfortable with the corporate focus and what I've seen as deradicalising of feminist analyses of men's violence against women. It's one of the ongoing dilemmas of unfunded community-based activist campaigns losing their radical politics as they become mainstreamed within the state. Consequently, the White Ribbon Campaign has received significant criticism from feminist activists and feminist journalists in recent years. As a social movement activist, I have had a dilemma about how much to work within the campaign to endeavour to bring it back to a more explicit feminist analysis and how much to disassociate myself from the campaign in its current form.

Educating men about sexism and violence

Over the years, I've sought strategies to educate men in the wider community about sexism and men's violence against women. There are very few sites where men can explore gender issues outside of university gender studies courses and ironically men's behaviour change programs where men have used violence against their female partners.

To address this gap, in 1994 I co-designed a two day patriarchy awareness workshop based on Action for World Development anti-racism workshops that I had experienced. The aim of the workshops are to address the problem of patriarchy and its impact on the lives of women, children and men. The workshop uses small group discussions, simulation exercises and videos to explore such issues as men's personal journeys in relation to gender issues, analyses of patriarchal culture, men's experiences of power and domination, alternatives to patriarchal power, the impact of men's domination on women, social and personal blocks to men's ability to listen to women and visions, obstacles and potential for men to change. The workshops provide an opportunity for men to identify ways of moving profeminist politics beyond the arena of personal change to incorporate collectivist and public political action.[5]

Since the 1990s, I have facilitated hundreds of these workshops as both part of gender awareness and gender equality training within workplaces (including local councils, church-based organisations, schools, universitites and the corporate sector) and as interventions in community-based and social movement organisations and political parties. The workshops aim to disrupt men's emotional investments in privilege. If men are to be engaged in challenging men's violence and promorting gender equality, I believe that they need

---

[5] See B. Pease, *Men and Sexual Politics: Towards a Profeminist Practice* (Dulwich, 1997) for a detailed outline of the two day workshop.

to recognise the role that emotions play in sustaining their privilege and address the barriers that inhibit them from experiencing compassion, empathy and sadness in response to the suffering of others.[6]

Even in those early days of my anti-patriarchal activism in the 1990s, my sense was that work done by men with men against men's violence should be accountable to critical reference groups of women who worked in women's services.[7] We thus invited and paid women who were working with the survivors of men's violence to observe the workshops and offer their feedback. It was an attempt to ensure that the work we were doing with the men was accountable to women. This accountability approach was not without controversy. Some critics argued that we were not taking responsibility for our own thinking and behaviour and were putting that responsibility on to women. However, we accepted the notion that women were experts when it came to gender inequality and men's violence against women and that they should have the opportunity to influence the work that we did. The issue of men's accountability to women's services continues to be a contentious issue in the violence prevention sector. To move this discussion along, I have recently written a paper on the principles and practices of accountability for male allies in violence prevention.[8]

Teaching men and masculinities in social work education

My engagement with feminism and profeminist men's politics ran parallel with, and was informed by, my study, practice and teaching

---

[6] See B. Pease, 'The Politics of Gendered Emotions: Disrupting Men's Emotional Investments in Privilege', (2012) *Australian Journal of Social Issues*, 47(1), 125-142 for a discussion of the role of emotions in sustaining and challenging privilege.

[7] B. Pease, 'MASA: Men Against Sexual Assault'. In W. Weeks and J. Wilson (eds.) *Issues Facing Australian Families* (Longman, 1995).

[8] B. Pease, *Men as Allies in the Prevention of Violence Against Women: Principles and Practices for Promoting Accountability.* (White Ribbon Australia, 2017).

in social work. As mentioned earlier, I came to my second academic position at Philip Institute of Technology (PIT), that espoused a radical philosophy of social work that was influenced by critical theory and feminism. The course held as a basic premise that personal problems exist within the context of political and economic distribution of resources and dominant ideologies concerning race, class and gender. Emphasis was given in the course to knowledge and skills for structural and feminist approaches to social work practice that address these structural inequalities.

I was also fortunate in being mentored at PIT and RMIT by a senior feminist social work academic, Wendy Weeks, who suggested that I take responsibility for addressing the negative and defensive responses of many male students to feminist content in the curriculum. Consequently in 1985, I developed and taught an elective subject titled Men, Masculinities and Social Work to social work students. Although the elective course was originally intended primarily for male social work students, it became popular with female students who wanted strategies for dealing with men in their personal lives as well as in their professional roles. The course provided an opportunity for me to bring a feminist-informed scholarship on men and masculinities into the social work curriculum to address such issues as theorising masculinity, men's sexuality, men and intimacy, fatherhood and men in families, homophobia and men's friendships, men and work, men's health, men and ageing, men's violence, men's movement politics and men and gender equality. [9]

Initially, I was disappointed at the relatively small numbers of men enrolled in the courses. After all, the aim was to invite men to re-examine their lives through a profeminist lens and to encourage them to develop alternative ways of being in the world that were

---

[9] See B. Pease, 'Teaching Patriarchal Men's Studies in Social Work' (1997), *Issues in Social Work Education* 17(1), 3-17.

not defined by patriarchal manhood. However, the courses proved illuminating for the women students, who relished the opportunity to expose and demystify men's culture from the inside. Many of the women felt more empowered to challenge men's sexism and learnt new strategies for doing so. I thus came to see the political value of the course in educating women about how men think and how best to engage with them about gender and men's attitudes and behaviour. Many female students in subject evaluations commented very positively about the couse in this regard. However, I also remember the comments of one student who said: 'I wonder if I'm being disempowered in my interactions with men from doing this course. Perhaps, because I understand more about men, I am not quite so intolerant'.[10] Was it a positive development for women to be more understanding about the foundations of men's sexism and abusive behaviour? Was my work softening women's well-founded outrage and anger at men's behaviour? This was one of a number of self doubts I had about my work at the time. However, on balance, I think that the course was successful at demystifying and interrogating men's privilege and power.

Researching profeminist men's politics

The engagement with activist work on men's violence against women and educational work on men and masculinities took me into theorising and research with men about the pathways by which some men become profeminist and how to analyse men's power and resistance to change. My PhD research undertaken between 1990 and 1996 focused on profeminist men's involvement with feminism and the dilemmas they confronted in their personal relationships, their professional lives and their politics. I invited self-defining profeminist men to participate in a collaborative inquiry

[10] B. Pease, op. cit.

group to examine how men who were supportive of feminism were responding to feminist challenges through an exploration of their experiences and dilemmas of trying to live out their profeminist commitment. The aim was to explore the extent to which it was possible for men to reposition themselves in patriarchal discourses and to reformulate their interests in challenging gender domination.[11]

A key methodological approach to this research involved dialogues with allies and opponents of profeminism. These dialogues contributed to the development of new spaces for the collective positioning of profeminist men's work in the ongoing public debates about masculinity politics. Among these dialogues, I arranged for conversations with feminist women and gay men to explore male privilege and heterosexual privilege respectively. Because many heterosexual men are disconnected from the lived experiences of women and gay men, critical dialogue with these groups is essential to bring about changes in the relations of ruling as they pertain to gender relations. To enable such a dialogue to take place, heterosexual men need to understand their internalised sexism and recognise that their knowledge of women's subordination and gay men's oppression will only be partial. They also need to understand that their knowledge and perception of the world is socially situated if they are to avoid oppressive practices in their encounters with women and gay men.

The men in the collaborative inquiry group listened to women's suspicions about their work, their doubts about how men could overcome their dominant subjectivities and why men would want to change. They also heard from the gay men about their reticence to engage in an open dialogue with straight men because of their reluctance to acknowledge their heterosexual privilege

---

[11] The PhD was published as a book in 2000. B. Pease, *Recreating Men: Postmodern Masculinity Politics* (Sage, 2000).

and the concern that straight men's gay affirmative stance may marginalise gay men's voices. Due to the lack of trust and power inequality, these dialogues were difficult to conduct at times, but charting our way through them left me with some hope for the future of such conversations when engaging straight men in violence prevention.

One of the purposes of the research was to produce a praxis of how men can change and the methodological approaches employed in the research became some of the very strategies being sought. That is, the methods used in the research represented pedagogical strategies for profeminist politics for men. Thus, in addition to theorising men's subjectivities and the insights about issues and dilemmas in profeminist men's lives, the research contributed to the development of these methodologies, both as research tools and as strategies for change in gender relations.

What was underdeveloped in my work at the time, however, was addressing the unstated whiteness in most of the men and masculinity literature. My own early writing about men and masculinity also took whiteness and the centrality of Western masculinity as a given. White men need to recognise social difference and inequality in men's lives. In addressing these issues, in my more recent work, I have explored the impact of migration on the subjectivities and practices of men who are marginalised by racism in Australia.[12] Most profeminist allies are white middle-class men. How to engage working-class men and men from culturally diverse backgrounds continues to be a challenge in violence against women prevention campaigns.

---

[12] See, for example, P. Crossley and B. Pease, 'Machismo and the Construction of Immigrant Latin American Masculinities', In M. Donaldson, R. Hibbins, R. Howson and B. Pease (eds.) *Migrant Men: Critical Perspectives on Masculinities and the Migration Experience* (Routledge, 2009), N. wa Mungai and B. Pease, 'Rethinking Masculinities in the African Diaspora'. In ibid. and B. Pease, 'Immigrant Men and Domestic Life: Renegotiating the Patriarchal Bargain'. In ibid.

Writing and story-telling as political practice

Over the years, I have maintained a commitment to political activism in relation to gender issues connected to men's sexism and violence against women. I continue to be involved in campaigns against men's violence and in facilitating workshops engaging men in violence prevention. I also try to make a difference through my writing and publications. I regard writing as a form of activism and political practice. I am interested in writing as a form of resistance, where I can express my political commitments. I have always been concerned that my writing reaches audiences beyond the academy. Hence, I have tried to balance the pressure within universities to publish in prestigious high-ranked journals with publishing in activist newsletters, professional journals and books, as well as writing opinion editorials in newspapers.

For me, this has always involved writing in the first person and situating myself to undermine any claim to universality. However, in articulating my positionality as a straight white, professional man (albeit from a working-class background), and in demonstrating reflexivity about it, I also need to be clear that this does not erase my power and privilege. If reflexive writing is to have progressive potential it must unmask and interrogate that privilege and explore how dominant identities are constructed. There are dangers here as well that we need to engage with.

As men, we must be aware of privileged speaking positions. What does it mean when profeminist men who challenge patriarchy and men's violence are listened to more than feminist women who are involved in the same work? It has been argued that this is a way of using privilege to challenge privilege. Men are likely to be perceived by other men as more credible and thus they will be listened to more. However, such men can carve out an area of expertise for their advantage and this can in fact reinforce those barriers that prevent women from having their own voices heard.

When feminist colleagues and I have presented papers together at conferences on men's responsibility for challenging men's violence, I have been concerned when my voice has been given more credibility than theirs.

Notwithstanding these tensions and dangers, I believe that politically-conscious auto-biographical writing and story-telling has something important to contribute to social justice struggles. Being critical about the structures of privilege and oppression in the world can sit alongside writing and talking in a personal voice. In fact, interrogating privilege from within requires it. The transformation of oppressive structures will mean that privileged individuals will need to be willing to forego and challenge their privileges. Auto-biographical writing and story telling about privilege provides an insight into the extent to which that is possible.[13]

In light of reflections on previous research with immigrant non-white men,[14] I have been refocusing my work in recent years on straight white middle-class men by more self-consciously exploring our privileged position in relation to women and other men. It is important to interrogate privileged social locations and find ways of undoing privilege. I have hence become interested in the construction and reconstruction of privileged subjectivities. Towards this end, I completed a book in 2010 where I explored the construction of Eurocentrism, class elitism, hegemonic masculinity, white supremacy, heteronormativity, and ableism as six intersecting sites of privilege.[15]

The question of why men (or any privilege group member) should challenge their own privilege is a constant question asked

---

[13] I discuss this issue more fully in B. Pease, 'Reflections on Tensions and Dilemmas in Writing Personal Accounts of Privilege'. In M. Livholts (ed), *Emergent Writing Methods in Feminist Studies* (Routledge, 2012).

[14] M. Donaldson, R. Hibbins, R. Howson and B. Pease (eds), *Migrant Men: Critical Studies of Masculinities and the Migration Experience* (Routledge, 2009).

[15] B. Pease, *Undoing Privilege: Unearned Advantage in a Divided World* (Zed, 2010).

about my work. What's in it for men generally or me in particular, to challenge patriarchy? In response, I will often talk about improved physical and emotional well-being, greater intimacy, and more fulfilment with women in relations of equality and mutual respect and even better societal outcomes in terms of living in a sustainable world that is not facing catastrophic climate change and human-induced 'natural disasters'. However, I always emphasise that what men gain should not be the primary motivation for men to be in involved in these projects. I am concerned that if men's interests, needs and concerns in relation to gender equality come too much into the foreground, that women's interests, needs and concerns will be marginalised. Thus, I also talk about men's relational interests with women and the moral and ethical reasons why men should change which are related to women's human rights and social justice.[16]

Reclaiming the language of patriarchy in current and future work on men's violence against women

Within feminist and feminist-informed theories, violence against women is understood as being gendered and interconnected to gender inequalities in the wider society. Radical and socialist feminist theories explicitly name violence against women as violence perpetrated by men in the context of patriarchy.[17] In the context of a backlash against feminism and the naming of patriarchy as the main source of men's violence against women, feminist language has recently been tempered and liberal feminist ideas have gained dominance.

---

[16] For a more extensive discussion about the reasons for men to change and the dangers of focusing on what's in it for men, see B. Pease, '"New Wine in Old Bottles?: A Commentary on "What's in it for Men?": Old Question, New Data'. (2014) *Men and Masculinities*, DOI: 10.1177/1097184X14558238, 1-3.

[17] R. Dobash and R. Dobash, *Violence Against Wives: The Case Against Patriarchy* (Macmillan, 1983); S. Walby, *Theorising Patriarchy* (Blackwell, 1990).

Social movement politics against men's violence against women have been supplanted by public health and professionalised approaches. However, comparative global research demonstrates that those societies which have the strongest autonomous women's movements applying pressure on the state have the most progressive policies on gender equality and violence prevention.[18]

I argue that we cannot understand men's violence against women outside of an understanding of patriarchy. Consequently, we need to address six primary levels of patriarchy: men's structural power over women, the intersections of gender power and other forms of inequality, patriarchal ideology, men's peer support for violence against women, the exercise of coercive control in family life and the patriarchal psyche of individual men.

As I move out of my paid job in academia, (what the university calls 'retirement'), I free up new spaces for writing and activism. One of the writing projects that I am currently embarked on is a book, *Facing Patriarchy: Overcoming a Violent Gender Order,* to explicate the analysis above. This book aims to bring feminist structural and discursive approaches to gender into analysing men's violence against women and to locate that violence within the structures and processes of patriarchy. The book will also explore links between men's violence against women and other forms of violence by men, in relation to boys and other men and men's involvement in wars and military conflict, as well as men's ecologically destructive practices, which I consider a form of slow violence.

The book will challenge some of the current orthodoxies about violence against women, as they are represented in public health paradigms, government discourses about gender equality and rep-

---

[18] M. Htun and S. Weldon, 'The Civic Origins of Progressive Policy Change: Combatting Violence Against Women in Global Perspective'. (2012) *American Political Science Review*, 106(3), 548-569.

resentations of gender in policies on violence against women. I will argue that a nuanced conceptualisation of patriarchy is required to understand the links between gender inequality and men's violence against women. The aim of this analysis is to contribute to an integrated feminist conceptual framework to guide violence prevention policy and practice.

I am doubtful about whether an explicit feminist analysis of patriarchy and men's violence against women will be operationalised into policies and programs within the patriarchal state. Feminist social movement politics in civil society have waned in the last ten years in particular. While there are important developments in feminist social media campaigns and internet organising and major feminist inroads into the state policy machinery, traditional feminist political organising that applies pressure on the state have weakened. Feminist think tanks and activist networks outside of state sponsored academic conferences and state-based policy forums may provide opportunities for civil society organising unencumbered by state policy discourses. In this context, I hope my intellectual work in progress might provide some useful analytical tools for radical political analysis of the violences of men in the future. The pace of change in gender relations in the last forty years has been too slow. It is time to get back to the problem of patriarchy and devise strategies to end it.

13

RE-IMAGINING MORE THAN JUST 'ACCEPTANCE' OF LGBTIQ COMMUNITIES AND PEOPLE

Jude Irwin

Introduction

In Australia over the last four decades we have witnessed a massive transformation in attitudes, practices, policies, laws and legislation towards people who are members of the LGBTIQ (lesbian, gay, bisexual, transgender, intersex, queer) communities. These changes and reforms are the result of activism involving thousands of people, on a broad scale and over a long period of time. This has required commitment, dedication, persistence, creativity and resistance to confront ongoing challenges. In this chapter I explore some aspects of activism from the late 1970s, surrounding the changes in the social and structural positioning of lesbians and gay men.[1] I begin by briefly outlining the context of lesbian and gay men's situation leading up to the 1970s, followed by an overview of activism from the late 1970s which was the beginning of 'gay liberation' and a prolonged struggle for change. In the 1980s and 1990s, as gay and lesbian issues came more into the public sphere, a number of lesbian and gay organisations were formed. One of these was

---

[1] Throughout this chapter, I refer to lesbians and gay men because this was the terminology used in the 1970s, 1980s and early 1990s. In the 1990s the more inclusive LGBT began to be used (inclusive of bisexual and transgender) and this has been more recently become LGBTIQ (inclusive of those who identify as intersex or queer).

the Australian Centre for Lesbian and Gay Research. I outline the emergence of the ACLGR and explore some of the activism and research that was undertaken by members of the Centre. Lastly, I draw on three research projects, I was involved in as a member of the ACLGR, showing how they have contributed to change, but argue that there is more work needed to achieve equality for LGB-TIQ communities.

Background

The context in the 1960s and 1970s in the western world was one of political unrest, civil rights and anti-war movements. Demands for social change and equality from numerous groups and populations (women, immigrants, peace) were rampant. In Australia, as in other parts of the western world, this gave rise to numerous social movements seeking equality, justice and recognition. By the late 1960s a very active and vocal feminist movement had emerged and was followed sometime later by the gay rights movement.

Gay and lesbian subcultures existed from the early colonisation of Australia but fear of abuse, discrimination and arrest kept homosexuality hidden from the public eye.[2] It is only in the last few decades that both the early and more recent history of homosexuality in Australia has been documented, exploring the active social lives of gay men and lesbians and the development of 'camp' subcultures that, although hidden from the mainstream, flourished.[3] Much

---

[2] E.C.Casella, 'Bulldaggers and gentle ladies: archaeological approaches to female homosexuality in convict-era Australia' in R.A. Schmidt and B. L Voss (eds.), *Archaeologies of Sexuality* (Routledge 2000, 143-159); R. Ford, 'Lady Friend and Sexual Deviationists: Lesbians and the Law in Australia, 1920s-1950s' in D. Kirkby (ed.), *Sex, Power. Justice: Historical Perspectives on the Law in Australia 1788-1990*, (Oxford University Press, 1995); G. Willett, *Living Out Loud: A History of Gay and Lesbian Activism* (Allen & Unwin, 2000).

[3] The word *camp* was the preferred term, referring to both homosexual men and women until the early 1970s when the term gay, was picked up from the United States.

218

Stories of Lifelong Activism

of the early history focusses more on the social networks, lives and subcultures of camp men and women, who had hidden, but full lives.[4] It was in the 1960s and 1970s that visibility of gay men and lesbians became an issue.

In Australia, unlike the UK and USA, there was very little gay and lesbian activist history prior to the 1970s. Much of the gay activism in the UK and USA in 1950s and 1960s focussed on law reform and the legalisation of male homosexuality. There was an attempt to organise a homosexual law reform group in Melbourne in the 1950s but it failed because of fear of legal repression. It was not until the late 1960s that public debate began about reform around the decriminalisation of male homosexuality. Liberal minded heterosexual reformers, including clergy, politicians and academics, supported this reform.[5]

The emergence of lesbian and gay activism

In 1969 the first openly homosexual political organisation, the Australasian Lesbian Movement (ALM) was formed in Australia. It began as an arm of the Daughters of Bilitis,[6] with the specific aim of bringing about social change by educating heterosexual society to ensure that lesbians were treated fairly and not discriminated against. ALM survived for about four years and played a critical role in lesbian visibility but for many lesbians this visibility was too radical and created fear of exposure and the consequential discrimination and prejudicial treatment. In the same year, the Homosexual

---

[4] R.Jennings, *Unnamed Desires: a Sydney lesbian history* (Monash University Publishing 2016); G. Wotherspoon, *Gay Sydney*, Newsouth Publishing, 2016). G.Willett, *Living Out Loud: A History of Gay and Lesbian Activism* (Allen & Unwin, 2000).

[5] G. Willett, *Living Out Loud: A History of Gay and Lesbian Activism* (Allen & Unwin, 2000).

[6] The Daughters of Bilitis were the first lesbian and civil rights movement formed in the USA in 1955.

Law Reform Society was founded in the Australian Capital Territory[7]. Its aim was to publicly confront the prejudicial treatment, discrimination and abuse experienced by lesbians and gay men. Both these organisations broadened the base of activism and played an important role in the emergence of gay and lesbian liberation in Australia. However, it has been argued by some that the foundation of CAMP (Campaign Against Moral Persecution) in Sydney in 1970, was the real galvaniser of lesbian and gay activism in Australia.[8] It aimed to challenge stereotypes of lesbians and gay men as 'sick and sinful' and convince society that lesbians and gay men should be accepted and treated in the same way as heterosexuals.[9] In doing so it moved beyond law reform and drew attention to the importance of changing social relationships and social structures. CAMP provided the impetus for the formation of similar organisations in every capital city across Australia, (for example, Society Five in Melbourne) to campaign and fight for LGBT equality. It is important to note that this happened in the time of the Whitlam government (1972-75) with its focus on citizen participation and social change. This was a context that was ripe for activism and over the next several years, numerous gay and lesbian rights organisations formed and participated in fighting for reform in all areas of life for lesbians and gay men.[10]

---

[7] G. Willett, *Living Out Loud: A History of Gay and Lesbian Activism* (Allen & Unwin, 2000); G. Wotherspoon, *Gay Sydney* (Newsouth Publishing, 2016).

[8] G. Wotherspoon, *Gay Sydney* (Newsouth Publishing, 2016).

[9] G. Willett, *Living Out Loud: A History of Gay and Lesbian Activism* (Allen & Unwin, 2000); G. Wotherspoon, *Gay Sydney* (Newsouth Publishing, 2016).

[10] By mid-seventies, South Australia (1975) followed by the ACT (1976) had decriminalised male acts of homosexuality. This was followed in the 1980s and 1990s by other Australian states and territories amending their homosexuality laws.. LGBTIQ activist groups continue to be vocal and have been successful in obtaining broader law reform, in most but not all areas, at state, territory and federal levels. See J. Irwin 'Lesbians and Gay Men: (un) equal before the law?' in P. Swain and S. Rice (ed.s) *In the Shadow of the Law: The legal context of social work practice,* (Federation Press, 2009, 192-207).

Many of these activist groups were coalitions of lesbians and gay men. Although activist coalitions of lesbians and gay men in the 1970s are frequently referred to in the histories, there has been a tendency to homogenise or discount the differences between gay men's and lesbian's experiences and priorities as there were, and are, substantial differences in their contexts, experiences and priorities. Sexual intimacy between women was not criminalised in the same way as male homosexuality; however, lesbians still experienced exclusion, isolation, prejudice in many areas of their lives. From the 1960s, many lesbians were active in the women's movement fighting for gender equality and, because of their commitment to challenge patriarchal beliefs and practices, chose not to participate in organisations and political activist groups that included (gay) men, instead forming their own activist groups.[11] Many lesbians identified as radical feminists and/or separatists. Their priorities and energies were mostly focussed on women's equality and challenging patriarchal systems, values and practices rather than on becoming involved with coalitionist activist groups.

One of the major civil rights milestones for gay and lesbian communities occurred in Sydney in 1978. In what is now referred to as the first NSW Gay and Lesbian Mardi Gras, lesbians and gay men marched through the CBD and along Oxford Street as part of international solidarity celebrations, which grew out of the Stonewall riots in the USA. They were stopped by police and 53 people were arrested, many of whom were beaten up in the police cells.[12] This violent involvement of the police prompted protests and demonstrations over the next several months and arrests continued until the laws around demonstrations, which had allowed the

[11] S. Phelan, *Identity Politics: Lesbian feminism and the limits of community* (Temple University Press, 1989).
[12] G. Willett, *Living Out Loud: A History of Gay and Lesbian Activism* (Allen & Unwin, 2000).

arrests, were changed in April 1979. This was another key catalyst for change and in the 1980s and 1990s a number of gay and lesbian organisations were founded. The Australian Centre of Lesbian and Gay Research (ACLGR) was one of these.

The Australian Centre of Lesbian and Gay Research

Both students and staff at the University of Sydney had actively been promoting gay and lesbian rights since the late 1970s.[13] Some academics from Government, Political Economy and Economic History were particularly active (both within and outside the walls of the University) and 1988 saw the beginning of the Australian Gay History Project. This project involved seminars and the gathering together of a series of papers which were published in the Gay Perspectives series.[14] This was so successful that the group decided to set up a research centre. The idea of an interdisciplinary research centre was the catalyst for a number of lesbian academics and students from different disciplines to become involved. The ACLGR Centre was approved by the university in the early 1990s and officially opened in July 1993 in the Great Hall of the University. What a great celebration that was! The hall of the 'hallowed men' had been creatively, but respectfully, "decorated' by artistic members of the ACLGR. Packed with people of diverse sexualities, in colourful, flamboyant and outlandish styles of dress, it was officially opened by the Governor-General, the Honourable Bill Hayden, in the company of the somewhat ambivalent university leaders. The opening was followed the next day with the Centre's Inaugural Conference, the first of the many successful conferences organised by the ACLGR. Throughout its relatively short existence the ACLGR and its members worked to increase the visibility and

[13] G. Wotherspoon, *Gay Sydney* (Newsouth Publishing, 2016).
[14] R. Aldrich and G. Wotherspoon. *Gay Perspectives: Essays in Australian Gay Culture* (University of Sydney, 1992).

exposure of issues confronting the gay, lesbian, bisexual and trans-gender communities by undertaking and publishing research, focusing on LGBT issues.

The ACLGR did not receive funding or staff from the University but negotiated a space for the centre. It was a small, some would call dilapidated, terrace house, located on the 'margin' of the university. A small group of us had lots of fun week ends, cleaning up the terrace and the small overgrown backyard. This small four roomed house was where our regular meetings and seminars were held, key discussions about gay and lesbian rights took place, conferences, research, lobbying and other political activities were planned and undertaken. The Centre resources were limited but the ACLGR was given some old computers, a printer and an old photocopier. Many people, including community activists, students, academics from other universities throughout Australia as well as academics from the University of Sydney, participated in the range of activities that the Centre and its members initiated. I recall the strong sense of camaraderie as various groups, at different times, spent many hours preparing and collating material for conferences, designing and concocting signs for marches and devising themes for our participation in the Mardi Gras.

About me and my engagement with the ACLGR

I began to engage with the group setting up the Australian Centre for Lesbian and Gay Research in 1991. Initially, I was ambivalent about being involved in a coalition of men and women but I was keen to contribute to the inclusion and visibility of lesbians. I was, and still am, a staunch feminist, having been active in the Women's Movement and other political activities since the latter part of the 1970s. My engagement with left wing politics, through radical social work and the women's liberation, was a turning point in my life. I had grown up in a conservative rural town environment in post war Australia in the 1950s. The strong messages that pervaded my childhood and strongly influenced my positioning in the world were "Do not rock the boat' and 'Do not question, accept what you are told'. In other words there was no question of challenging the status quo! Included in this was the acceptance of male privilege, gendered roles and heterosexuality. For me in the 1950s, difference was not a concept that came into my life in any way. Life was gendered and heterosexed! Boys played cricket, football and marbles and used most of the school playground. I tried to challenge this a few times but comments such as 'It's not a girl's game!' flowed from the boys, some girls and the teaching staff. I was often labelled a tomboy, because I wanted to play cricket and because I went fishing, hunting, and walking in the bush with my father and I loved it but it was not what 'little girls did'!

My parents accepted these differences but still reinforced gendered roles in numerous ways. However, unlike many of my friends' parents, they encouraged and supported education for both the girls and boys in our family. The educational options made available to me were, however, gendered. I can recall from a very young age, I was told I would grow up to be a nurse. It was in the latter years of high school that a teacher mentioned to me that she thought I was more suited to social work (another gendered occupation). In the early 1960s I had considered law but an uncle lawyer, one of the few lefties in my family, told me that there was no future for girls/women in the legal profession. I accepted this and did social work.

I began my social work degree in the mid-1960s and, perhaps predictably, did not engage with the social unrest that was so widespread at that time. The social work program was quite traditional with a couple of exceptions. It was after I graduated and was practicing as a social worker in the public service, I began to feel a general 'dis' ease with what I was doing, particularly related to not being able to find a way to challenge the entrenched inequality of 'my clientele'. Attempting to raise this in my workplace was futile and my dissatisfaction grew. I became more aware of the politics of social work, and this prompted me to leave the public service in 1978 and take a casual position in academia where I began to 'soak up' the literature on radical social work. This literally turned my world 'upside down', challenging my long held conservative values and beliefs. It was like a blindfold had been removed from my eyes so I could see and understand the world more clearly. I had a similar response when, in the early 1980s, I discovered feminism. The political analysis, the activism, the camaraderie and friendships that developed with people who had similar values and commitments reshaped how I saw myself in the world. I was involved in a range of different political movements (feminist, anti-racism, gay and lesbian) that were aimed at social change and equality and increasing opportunities for people to participate in decisions that impacted on their lives. I 'came out' proudly as a lesbian in 1988 and became more actively involved in the struggle for equality for LGBT communities.

At this time, although there was a heightened awareness of LGBT issues and a number of specific LGBT services developing, much of the federal and state legislation discriminated against people who identified as LGBT. Many of us who identified, or were thought to be LGBT, experienced prejudice, harassment and abuse in many areas of our lives. One of my first experiences of this was shortly after I came out. I was, and still am, very open about my sexuality and the mother of two boys. I overheard one of my senior colleagues exclaiming to several other colleagues 'Oh my God. What is going to happen to those two young boys?'

My research trajectory

As an academic, I began to frame my research to be consistent with my changing politics, philosophies and values. My social work practice had been in the area of immigration where I saw the impacts of social inequality and injustice on those people who had recently arrived from different parts of the world. I had worked with men and women who had been injured in their workplaces and struggled to understand the complex legal and social service system. In the early 1980s, as part of a postgraduate degree, I undertook a research project on immigrants and workers compensation.[15] This was a very confronting experience for me on a number of levels. I saw in much more detail the impacts of moving to another country and the struggles families confronted in their daily lives, and how this was magnified by the trauma of an injury and the loss of health and income. On another level, I became aware of the differential pressures on men and women who were injured in the workplace. Men who were injured were constructed as 'patients' and in need of support while women who were injured were expected to carry on with their everyday household and caring tasks. I gained insights into the entrenched and systemic nature of inequalities and some of the silence that surrounded some aspects of 'family life', including domestic violence. This was a motivating factor for me to begin research into domestic violence.[16] Later, as I became more involved in the fight for gay and lesbian rights, I was aware that similar experiences of silence, denial and invisibility were very much part of the lives of many lesbians and gay men. Since then much of my research has been focused on aspects of social change and 'unpicking' the silence around issues such as violence, discrimination and exclusion.

---

[15] J. Petruchenia, *Immigrants and Workers Compensation*, (Clearing House on Migration Issues, 1985).

[16] See for example J. Irwin, *Domestic Violence-Criminal Assault in the Home*, (Barnardos, 1995): J. Irwin and R.Thorpe, 'Women, Violence and Social Change' in R. Thorpe and J. Irwin (eds.), *Women and Violence: Working for Change* (Hale & Iremonger, 1996) and J. Irwin and M. Wilkinson 'Women, Children and Domestic Violence' in *Women against Violence*, 3, 199. *Communities, Children and Families Australia*, 6 (1), 17-25.

Making LGBT oppression visible

One of the key goals of the ACLGR was to increase the visibility and exposure of issues confronting gay, lesbian, bisexual and transgender communities. As an organisation, we were proactive in seeking and gaining funding for conferences and research that could contribute to challenging the invisibility, marginalisation and discrimination of members of lesbian and gay communities. In doing this, we collaborated with members of the community and with some of the newly formed community based organisations. For example, from the early 1980s the HIV/AIDS epidemic had drawn attention to the specific health needs of those who had contracted HIV. However, outside HIV/AIDS, members of LGBT communities experienced obstacles in dealing with health care professionals that needed to be addressed. In 1995/1996 the ACLGR worked in collaboration with a number of non-government and community organisations to plan, organise and run the first *Health In Difference* Conference.[17] These conferences have continued bi-annually and are an important source of knowledge on all aspects of LGBTIQ health and well-being.

Another priority for the ACLGR was the undertaking of interdisciplinary research that could add to existing knowledge about LGBT communities. In the 1990s one of the communities' major concerns was discrimination and violence in its many forms. This melded with my research interests and with the interdisciplinary research priorities of the ACLGR and two research projects were undertaken with community based organisations. One of these projects was partially funded by a gay and lesbian community-based organisation Twenty-Ten and was on homelessness amongst gay and lesbian young people. Another explored LGBT experiences in the workplace and was funded jointly by the Gay and Lesbian

---

[17] J. Richters et al., *Health In Difference* (Australian Centre for Lesbian and Gay Research, 1997).

Rights Lobby and the Australian Research Council. I undertook a third project on violence in intimate lesbian relationships.

Using research for social change

In the mid-1990s, I began my doctorate and decided to explore domestic violence in lesbian relationships. This was a contentious topic as although, from the mid-1980s, there had been some recognition of abuse in lesbian relationships there had been a hesitation in responding to this violence. The reasons for this were complex and shaped by a number of interrelated factors. Keeping men's violence against women high on the political agenda was critical to the feminist movement. For years, feminists had been fighting about the extent, effect and systemic collusion of men's violence against women. In the mid-1980s violence in lesbian relationships began to be talked about and, at the same time, there was a surge of literature arguing that women's violence was as prevalent as men's violence. [18] For me, as a feminist wanting to explore lesbian domestic violence, three questions arose: 'Would the exposure of violence in intimate lesbian relationships, coupled with the surge of literature, arguing that women's violence was as prevalent as men's violence add 'grist to the mill' for those who were disputing both the extent of male violence against women and its gendered explanations? Would this put at risk many of the hard won gains of the women's movement? Were lesbians likely to experience an increased risk of being exposed to homophobic responses? It was with some ambivalence that I began this project. I knew there were political risks in undertaking this research and although I had no wish to take atten-

[18] This research has subsequently been extensively critiqued for its problematic methodologies and lack of contextual analysis. See L. Kelly, 'When does speaking profit us; reflections on the challenges of developing women's perspectives on abuse and violence by women', in M. Hester, L. Kelly and J. Radford (eds), *Women, Violence and Male Power* (Open University Press, 1996, 34-59).

tion away from the scale of male violence against women, nor from feminist activist focus on the prevention of male violence against women I was also aware violence in intimate lesbian relationships was a complex political issue and an important issue to confront.

The research involved interviewing twenty one lesbians who self-identified as being a victim/survivor of violence in an intimate lesbian relationship. Invisibility underpinned many of the stories the women shared. Many had remained silent about their abuse because they saw domestic violence as a heterosexual issue. Some struggled to identify the violence because they believed this did not happen in lesbian relationships. Others could not believe a woman could be violent. As there was little talk about violence in intimate lesbian relationships women were often ambivalent about approaching services and because of the heteronormative assumptions that pervaded much of the service delivery, they feared a negative outcome. Many of the women had negative experiences with service providers and their lack of knowledge about lesbians, deterring them from seeking help. The stories from this study drew attention to the shortcomings of relying on a 'one size fits all' model to explain domestic violence. It reinforced how critical it is to understand the complexities of violence, particularly how the personal, social and political contexts influence the impacts of violence in women's lives. Undertaking this research gave space to lesbians who had lived with violence in their intimate relationships. Talking about the research, giving presentations and publishing, politicised the violence by making it more visible to lesbian communities, policy and law makers, educators and practitioners in legal, health and human services. It extended understandings and knowledge of the complexities of the violence and increased awareness of its existence. This resulted in LGBTIQ communities, practitioners in legal, health and human services organisations, policy makers and educators developing services and programs that are more tailored to the needs of those who live, or have lived, with this violence.

In 1994 Twenty-Ten Association, a community-based organisation that provided medium and long term housing and welfare services for young lesbians and gay males asked the ACLGR to undertake a research project exploring the housing and other related needs of young homeless gay males and lesbians. The research involved interviewing gay and lesbian young people who were homeless (27) and service providers (41). At that time Twenty-Ten was overwhelmed with requests for accommodation, leading them to believe there were very large numbers of homeless gay and lesbian young people. Although the research was not about counting the numbers of lesbian and gay young people, by drawing on literature and available research, we were able to estimate that there could be between 5,000 and 6,259 young lesbians and gay males homeless on any one night in Australia.[19]

Data obtained from the interviews with lesbians and gay males indicated that all the young people interviewed had experienced violence, harassment and/or discrimination based on their homosexuality. For some, this was in their family of origin, for others it was on the streets, from other homeless young people or from workers in accommodation services. Many commented about the lack of services and supports available. Those who used mainstream services, including accommodation services, often felt safer being 'silent' about their homosexuality. Most of the services who participated in the research provided accommodation for lesbian and gay males, but only two had specific responses to dealing with homophobic violence and discrimination.[20] The report was released at NSW Parliament House and received widespread publicity es-

---

[19] J.Irwin, B.Winter, M.Gregoric, & S.Watts *'As Long as I've Got My Doona': A Report on Lesbian and Gay Youth Homelessness.* (Ten-Twenty Association, 1997).
[20] Ibid.

pecially in the gay and lesbian press. A year after the release of the report the NSW Department of Community Services (the funders of most emergency accommodation services) initiated an audit on the recommendations of the report.[21] The audit showed that the major issues highlighted in the 'Doona' research were still evident and that there was a need for staff training focussing on homophobia and non-discriminatory service delivery. Two decades later, there remains concern about the high numbers of young homeless LGBTIQ people. They are now more visible in accommodation services,[22] but while most services have a 'no violence' policy, this is not routinely monitored or enforced leaving LGBTIQ clients unsupported and unsafe.[23] Unfortunately, in 2017, while there is now greater awareness of the extent of homelessness among young lesbians and gay males, services remain poorly resourced, there is little opportunity for training of staff and as a result young homeless lesbians and gay men are often unsupported and exposed to ongoing to violence and discrimination.[24]

In 1996 the ACLGR and the NSW Gay and Lesbian Rights Lobby embarked on a collaborative research project exploring the workplace experiences of lesbians, gay men and transgender people. It was a massive project completed over a very short time frame and was dependent on the labour and support of students,

---

[21] C. Johnston, *Bedding the Issues Down: Provision of Services to Homeless Young Gays and Lesbians* (NSW Department of Community Services, 1995).

[22] In Australia it is estimated 25 percent of young people who access youth homeless service are LGBTIQ. See M. Toms, S .Redshaw, and Twenty-Ten Association Incorporated, "*It may not be fancy ...*" *Exploring the service needs of homeless gay, lesbian, bisexual and transgender young people.* (Commonwealth Department of Families Community Services and Indigenous Affairs, 2007).

[23] M.Toms, S. Redshaw, and Twenty-Ten Association Incorporated, "*It may not be fancy ...*" *Exploring the service needs of homeless gay, lesbian, bisexual and transgender young people.* (Commonwealth Department of Families Community Services and Indigenous Affairs, 2007).

[24] R. McNair, C. Andrews, S. Parkinson and D. Dempsey, *GALFA LGBTI Homelessness Research Project*, (http://www.lgbtihomeless.com, 2017).

research assistants and numerous volunteers.[25] The research involved a self-completion survey (900 participants), individual interviews (52 participants) and focus group interviews (5). The study showed that workplace harassment and prejudicial treatment of lesbians gay men and transgender people was widespread. The discrimination occurred across all industries, occupations and types of organisations. The homophobic behaviour included sexual and physical assault, verbal harassment and abuse, destruction of property, ridicule and belittling. Prejudicial treatment in the workplace included unfair rosters, unreasonable work expectations, sabotaging and undermining of work and the denial of workplace entitlements (eg partner travel, compassionate leave, partner access to superannuation or workers compensation). The impact of this was extensive, effecting both the individual and their workplace performance. It also influenced the workplace culture, often creating a hostile and unsafe environment for 'out' or suspected lesbians, gay men or transgender people. Only a very small percentage of those who were harassed or discriminated against took any action as they thought there was little chance of a positive outcome.

The Gay and Lesbian Rights Lobby used the data obtained to argue for change with unions, employers and governments. In June 1999 the Full Bench of the Industrial Relations Commission NSW ordered an anti-discrimination clause to be inserted in all awards in NSW, paving the way for employers and unions to work collaboratively towards workplaces that are free from discrimination of any kind. In 2007 the Human Rights Commission released their report, *Same Sex: Same Entitlement,* recommending amendments to 84 Commonwealth laws that discriminated against same sex couples and their children. On 24 November 2008 the Australian federal government amended these laws which related to income support,

---

[25] J.Irwin, *'The Pink Ceiling is Too Low': Workplace Experiences of Lesbians, Gay men and Transgender People, (*ACLGR, 1997).

taxation, superannuation, workers compensation, Medicare, veteran's affairs, employment entitlements and family law. Despite these changes some members of LGBTIQ communities still feel unsafe about being open about their sexuality in their workplaces and different forms of discrimination.[26]

These three research projects all added to knowledge about different forms of discrimination, exclusion and violence to which many members of LGBTIQ communities have been exposed. They provided information that was used by various advocacy groups, LGBTIQ organisations and activist groups to lobby for change. Social change and working for equality for members of LGBTIQ communities remains an ongoing struggle. Constant vigilance is required both to fight for, and sustain, positive changes.[27]

In concluding

In this chapter I have drawn on my knowledge and experiences to explore the complex and multilayered causes and processes of inequality and oppression towards LGBTIQ communities. The activism of the 1980s and 1990s increased visibility and transformed laws, practices and professional and public opinion, ensuring LGBTIQ communities are part of the social and political mainstream. Despite the extensive reforms that have taken place there still remain laws and practices that discriminate against non-heterosexual people. At the federal level marriage equality is probably the most obvious and important. In my view, there are many other issues that need to be addressed (such as homophobia around education) but

---

[26] ABC News, http://www.abc.net.au/news/2016-09-28/lgbti-australians-hide-identity-at-work-ethnic-discrimination/7884752 'Workplace discrimination: Half of LGBTI Australians hide sexuality at work, report, 28 September 2016.

[27] For example in 2017 the NSW government abandoned the Safe School Program funded by the federal government in 2014 to make schools more inclusive environments for same sex attracted, intersex and gender diverse students, school staff and families. This was after ongoing advocacy from conservative groups and individuals.

are perhaps being masked by the focus on marriage equality. We need to keep up struggle and fight for more than just acceptance of marginalised groups and individuals.

14

SOCIAL WORK WITH THE FIRST AUSTRALIANS AND DÉJÀVU:

Or in Other Words – Been There, Done That, So Why Are We Here again?

Christine Fejo-King

Introduction

When I first thought about writing this chapter, I was reflecting on the news about the inhuman treatment of Aboriginal youth in the Don Dale Juvenile Detention facility in my home town of Darwin. I wondered why over the almost fifty years, I and many other First Australians and those from other ethnic backgrounds who supported our struggle for human rights in this country, many for even longer than that period, were once again hearing about and seeing the injustice meted out to our families, in this case, to our children.

As I watched this, quite frankly, I was tired of this seemingly endless circle of our children being removed, of the pain, trauma, grief and anguish of our people. It seemed that a foreign "machine" (a western dominated and structured out-of-home care system, an arm of the child protection system), sucked up our children, spat out their long term best interests as human beings and First Nations people. It seemed as if this machine moved across the country, it threw out bales of lost people and demolished families and communities in its wake, in exactly the same way it had done with the Stolen Generations.

This seemingly endless cycle caused me to ask myself, has no one taken any notice of history? The Royal Commissions and national inquiries and the hundreds of recommendations from them? Did the apology delivered by the Australian government to the First Australians with regard to the Stolen Generations, result in nothing than a hick up in the practice of removing our children? Why has this practice revved up rather than slowed down?

As I thought about these questions, I heard the call of my ancestors to "come home". I decided to leave Canberra and return to my homelands in the Northern Territory, never thinking that I would become a part of *the Royal Commission into the Protection and Detention of Children in the Northern Territory* (2017), and yet this is exactly what happened.

When I received the phone call from the lawyers asking me to meet with them, I once again reflected on the extended period that I had been involved in the child protection area of social work. How my whole life up to that point had been spent trying to find answers, to change that system so that it worked in a better way with First Australians.

As an Aboriginal woman and Elder of my clan (the Fejo family) of the Larrakia nation in the Northern Territory, and as an Elder of the social work profession in Australia, I take the time in this chapter to reflect and critique what is happening today, regarding two key issues that impacted on and continue to impact today on the First Australians.[1] I am firstly speaking about the *Royal Commission into Aboriginal Deaths in Custody* (1987-1991) and secondly,

---

[1] United Nations. (1948). *Convention on the Prevention and Punishment of the Crime of Genocide* (Adopted by Resolution 260 (III) A of the U.N. General Assembly on 9 December 1948). Text: U.N.T.S. (United Nations Treaty Series), No. 1021, vol. 78 (1951), 277. Retrieved from www.preventgenocide.org/law/convention/text. htm; United Nations, (2007). *United Nations declaration on the rights of Indigenous peoples*. Adopted by General Assembly Resolution 61/295 on 13 September 2007. Retrieved from www.un.org/esa/socdev/unpfli/en/drip.html

The Bringing Them Home Report: National Inquiry into the Separation of Aboriginal Children from their Families (1997). Both highlighting violations against the United Nations treaties to which Australia was a signatory and more recently supported (2008) the Rights of Indigenous Peoples as outlined by the United Nations.

Both issues struck at the heart of Aboriginal Australia and resulted in a Royal Commission and a National Inquiry, yet today, these issues still plague us and impact on current affairs, including the recent disclosure of extreme abuse of children in the Don Dale juvenile justice facility in Darwin. The majority of the children incarcerated within Don Dale juvenile detention centre were Aboriginal. The uncovering of this abuse resulted in the third inquiry to be introduced in this chapter, *the Royal Commission into the Protection and Detention of Children in the Northern Territory* (2017).

This chapter is divided into three sections, the first being an introduction to the three Inquiries already identified. The second part focusses on common threads and recurring themes or déjàvu, while the third part focuses on answering the questions, "has anyone been listening? have we learned nothing? From this discussion, ways are identified on how we as social workers (including psychologists) and those whose employment interacts with First Australians, might move beyond déjàvu, to actions that bring about positive change and break out of the rut we are currently caught in. This section identifies and challenges several current dominant theories and practices. But there is a codicil connected to this change, that is that there must be a political will to bring about change, without this, nothing will change.

Section one: The inquiries

This section provides some background information into the three Inquiries central to this chapter as identified in the introduction.

While the *Royal Commission into Aboriginal Deaths in Custody* (1987-1991) and the *Bringing Them Home: National Inquiry into the Separation of Aboriginal and Torres Strait Islander Children from their Families* (HREOC, 1997) occurred some time ago. *The Royal Commission into the Protection and Detention of Children in the Northern Territory* is current (2017) and included hearings in Alice Springs and Darwin.

The information provided within this section about the connecting threads between the two Royal Commissions and the National Inquiry are provided through my lived experience from when I was called to act as an expert witness in child protection. More about how I came to be personally involved in the Royal Commission is provided later in the chapter. The chapter introduces and provides information about each of the inquires according to the dates they occurred.

The 'Royal Commission into Aboriginal Deaths in Custody' (1987-1991)

The *Royal Commission into Aboriginal Deaths in Custody* (RCIADC) was commissioned by then Prime Minister Bob Hawke (1987), in response to growing public concern about the increasing number of Aboriginal people dying whilst in custody. There was also concern about the lack of explanation around these deaths. The RCIADC investigated and reported on 99 Aboriginal deaths in custody between 1 January 1980 and 31 May 1989 – handing down the report in 1991.[2] These included deaths found as the result of suicide, natural causes, medical conditions and injuries caused by police. The Terms of Reference of the RCIADC included 'social, cultural and legal factors which may have had a bearing on the deaths under investigation'. At the conclusion of the investigation, 339

---

[2] National Archives of Australia, n.d.

recommendations were made. The major focal points centered on procedures for persons in custody, liaison with Aboriginal groups, police education and improved accessibility to information.

One of the findings of the RCIADIC was that many of the people who died whilst in custody had been part of the Stolen Generations, or were the children of the Stolen Generations (introduced in the next section).[3] With regards to this issue, it recommended that the mental health of Aboriginal and Torres Strait Islander peoples be a priority, as this issue contributed to the high numbers of Aboriginal and Torres Strait Islander peoples within the criminal justice system and who completed suicide whilst in custody. The RCIADIC was also important because it highlighted the impact on generations of Aboriginal peoples when children were removed from their families, their culture, their identity changed and kinship connections were/are damaged. By highlighting the situation of the Stolen Generations who died whilst in custody, the Commission provided the groundwork and support for an investigation into the Stolen Generations.

The First Australians were beginning to mobilise to take action around this issue and pressure groups were being organised around the country. Non-Aboriginal organisations and people who were interested and had a passion for social justice for all Australians were also enlisted and encouraged to take action independently or to join with the First Australians.

One of these pressure groups organised a conference in the Northern Territory about the Stolen Generations, which provided

---

[3] N. Morseu-Diop, *Healing in Justice: Giving a Voice to the Silent and Forgotten People* (Magpie Goose Publishing, 2017). S.R. Zubrick, K. Kelly and R. Walker, R. (2010), 'The Policy Context of Aboriginal and Torres Strait Islander Mental Health'. In N. Purdie, P. Dudgeon and R. Walker (eds), *Working Together: Aboriginal and Torres Strait Islander Mental Health and Wellbeing Principles and Practice* (43-62) (Commonwealth of Australia, 2010).

another impetus to activism.[4] This was the *Going Home Conference*, held in Darwin in 1994. The pressure from the voices of Australian people in calling for a national inquiry into the Stolen Generations issue resulted in the *Bringing Them Home: National Inquiry into the Separation of Aboriginal and Torres Strait Islander Children from their Families.*

The Bringing Them Home Report: National Inquiry into the Separation of Aboriginal Children from their Families (1995-1997)

This landmark report was commissioned by the Australian Attorney-General in 1995, and led by Sir Ronald Wilson, who was then president of the Human Rights and Equal Opportunity Commission; and the then Aboriginal and Torres Strait Islander Social Justice Commissioner, Mick Dodson. The Report was tabled in 1997 and consisted of 680 pages, and 54 recommendations, which clearly and devastatingly identified how past government policies and practices had impacted on the lives of the First Australians in the most insidious way possible, through the removing of children from their families for no reason other than their race. Every family from the First Nations in Australia had been impacted upon while these policies were in place and it is interesting to note that this year 2017 marks the ten-year anniversary of this report.[5] The *Bringing Them Home* report made visible to all Australians, part of the history of Australia to which they were previously unaware, as it concluded that:

Indigenous families and communities have endured gross violations of their human rights. These violations continue

---

[4] J. Katona (ed), *The Long Road Home: The Going Home Conference,* 3-6 October, 1994 (Star; Human Rights and Equal Opportunities Commission, HREOC, 1997). *Bringing Them Home: National Inquiry into the Separation of Aboriginal and Torres Strait Islander Children from their Families.* (Australian Government, 1997).

[5] ATNS – see Agreements, Treaties and Negotiated Settlements Project.

to affect Indigenous people's daily lives. They were an act of genocide, aimed at wiping out Indigenous families, communities and cultures, vital to the precious and inalienable heritage of Australia.[6]

The impacts of the removal policies continue to resound and be felt by generations of First Australian families. It is like the ripples that result when a stone is thrown into a pond.

An example of this can be illustrated through my own family history with three generations having been removed. These were my grandmother (my father's mother), my mother and my older sister and myself. My children being the first not be removed from our family as a direct result of these policies.[7] The overwhelming evidence from the *Bringing Them Home* report was that the impact of the Stolen Generations did not stop with the removed children (as stated above) – the impact was passed on through generations in multiple complex ways. Some of these impacts included the loss of continued connection to land, kinship systems that the children had been born into and which would have provided extensive safety networks, language, ceremony, models of love and care between parents and children and the capacity to be a parent.

A key recommendation (7a) in the *Bringing Them Home* report was that an apology should be offered by the Australian Govern-

[6] M. Adams, *Men's business: A Study into Aboriginal and Torres Strait Islander Men's Sexual and Reproductive Health*. (Magpie Goose Publishing 2014); J. Atkinson, *Trauma Trails Recreating Song Lines: The Transgenerational Effects of Trauma in Indigenous Australia* (Spinifex, 2002); C. Fejo-King, 'The National Apology to the Stolen Generations: The Ripple Effect'. *The Journal of Australian Social Work: Special Issue on Australian Indigenous Social Work and Social Policy, Part 1.* 64(1), 2011, 130-143; C. Fejo-King (2013), *Let's talk kinship: Innovating Australian social work education, theory, research and practice through Aboriginal knowledge.* Canberra, ACT: Christine Fejo-King Consulting; C. Fejo King, *The Fire of Resilience: Insights from an Aboriginal Social Worker*. Canberra, 2015.

[7] Human Rights and Equal Opportunities Commission (HREOC), *Bringing Them Home: National Inquiry into the Separation of Aboriginal and Torres Strait Islander Children from their Families* (222) (Australian Government, 1997).

ment to Aboriginal and Torres Strait Islander peoples for the removal of their children from their families because of past policies. Another key recommendation was that financial repatriation should be paid.[8] There were several other positive outcomes from the *Bringing Them Home* report. These actions included additional funds being made available to the Link Up services to enable family reunions; and funding for mental health counselling to assist with healing, loss and grief resulting from the experience of being forcefully removed as children from family and kin. Parenting programs were also funded. There was a realisation that, when child after child from successive generations were stolen and raised in institutions and missions, rather than in a home with parents to teach and guide them, and to model good parenting behaviour, these children had little opportunity to develop good parenting skills themselves.

The Stolen Generations was and is a social justice issue. However, rather than treat it on this basis, the Australian Government quickly positioned it within a medical model, which then portrayed Aboriginal people as being ill, rather than the system that placed them in institutions as being wrong. This change of emphasis made invisible the responsibility of government and the role of government to deal with it on a social justice basis. It shifted responsibility from governments to the people themselves and focused on the problems the First Australians were struggling with rather than their strengths.[9]

---

[8] J. Atkinson, *Trauma Trails Recreating Song Lines: The Transgenerational Effects of Trauma in Indigenous Australia.* (Spinifex, 2002).

[9] R. Manne, 'Aboriginal Child Removal and the Question of Genocide, 1900-1940'. In A. D. Moses (ed.), *Genocide and Settler Society: Frontier Violence and Stolen Indigenous Children in Australian History* (218-243) (10), 2004: B. Cummings, (1990). *Take this child ... from Kahlin Compound to the Retta Dixon Children's Home.* (Aboriginal Studies, 1990); S. Zubrick, K. Kelly and R. Walker, 'The Policy Context of Aboriginal and Torres Strait Islander Mental Health'. In N. Purdie, P. Dudgeon and R. Walker (eds.), *Working Together: Aboriginal and Torres Strait Islander) Mental Health and Wellbeing Principles and Practice* (pp. 43-62). (Commonwealth of Australia, 1990).

So how was the *Bringing Them Home Report* received? '...
the genocide conclusion of the *Bringing Them Home* report was
treated by the Australian Government, by the popular media, and
by the right-wing intelligentsia with levity and derisive contempt'.
However, when the broader Australian population became aware of
the fact that genocide, murder, ethnic cleansing and slavery were
part of Australia's history and that their ancestors were involved,
there was what became labelled as 'perpetrator trauma'. This was
described as trauma experienced by the wider Australian population, and defined by Moses as being 'the shock of realisation at
the crimes committed by one's compatriots'. A national day of remembrance, Sorry Day, was instigated as a symbolic response and
celebrated on 26 May, the date that the report was handed down.

The *Bringing Them Home* report and the RCIADIC had major
impacts on the broader Australian community. As everyday Australians heard of the ripping apart of families, and of the trauma,
grief and anguish experienced by their fellow Australians due to the
dehumanising practices of the stealing of Aboriginal children from
their families, they reflected on how they would react if people
walked into their homes and perpetrated these crimes against them.
They contemplated how they would feel and what it would take to
enable healing and forgiveness, and they took action.

This action was visible in a furthering of a people's movement
toward reconciliation, independent of government, and, for many,
a desire to bring about change to the existing way of doing things.
These feelings provided the impetus for the bridge walks nationally in 2000, where over a million-people walked across bridges,
including Sydney Harbour Bridge, to show their support for the
Stolen Generations and to say, *"Sorry"* for the actions of past governments. These walks occurred on Sorry Day on 26 May 2000
and later strengthened the support base for the Apology in 2008
delivered by then Prime Minister Kevin Rudd.

My family was heavily involved in the work around enabling the National Apology to the Stolen Generations to occur. I was at the time the Co-chair of the Stolen Generations Alliance and worked closely with then Minister for Aboriginal Affairs, Jenny Macklin and her staff to enable Prime Minister Kevin Rudd to meet my mother, Nana Lorna Nungula Fejo, to sit down and talk about Nungula's experience of being stolen from her family. This meeting was pivotal in the Apology as then Prime Minister Rudd sought to hear the firsthand experience of someone who lived through and understood the impact of the Stolen Generations. This meeting and the story shared was used to inform the National Apology (2008) and Nana Nungula Fejo is mentioned within the information shared by Prime Minister Rudd.

With regard to the second key recommendation, that financial repatriation should be paid to the Stolen Generations, this has been an ongoing battle since the recommendation was made.[10] Supporting the national inquiry was the book written by Kidd (2007), about the stolen wages owed to the First Australians as a result of the trust funds that were set up by the government and paid into by every Aboriginal Australian employed over the decades they existed. It was only later, when the people who had contributed and/or their families requested that the monies be returned to them that it was found that all the records supposedly kept by the administrators of these funds did not exist and that the funds themselves did not have one cent remaining in them. As stated, this theft was only uncovered when the government was asked to pay what was owned to the people who had contributed their whole working lives to pay into these funds. This also included the interest that should have been paid into these accounts over decades, as the people involved

---

[10] K. Rudd, *Apology to Australia's Indigenous Peoples*. House of Representatives, Australian Parliament (Australian Government, 2008); R. Kidd, *Trustees on trial: Recovering the Stolen wages*, (AboriginalStudies, 2007).

wanted to use the monies and to share what was there with their children as their inheritance. In fact, it was difficult to locate any substantial records that should have been kept by those responsible for oversighting those accounts. As of today, no one has ever been charged, only a small number of people have been refunded minuscule amounts and Aboriginal people remain in poverty, where is the justice in this? How would you respond if this happened to your grandparents, parents and you?

The Royal Commission into the Protection and Detention of Children in the Northern Territory (2017)

In 2016, Australia and the world heard allegations of unnecessary force being used against juveniles detained in the Don Dale juvenile detention centre in Darwin, Northern Territory and their possible abuse, deprivation, torture and tear gassing through the Four Corners,[11] Australian television program (2016). The majority of the children involved in these instances were First Australians. At the time of the report, the Northern Territory Commissioner for Corrections, Ken Middlebrook strongly refuted what was being reported.[12] An investigation into these allegations led by then Northern Territory Children's Commissioner, Dr. Howard Bath was announced in 2015 and completed by the current Northern Territory Children's Commissioner Colleen Gwynne. The investigation focussed on an alleged riot by six juvenile detainees and the alleged excessive force used to control them. Key points emerging from the report were:

---

[11] *Four Corners* Report, Gassing of Juveniles in Don Dale Detention Centre, 2016. http://www.abc.net.au/4corners/stories/2016/07/25/4504895.htm; K. Middlebrook, (2017). Middlebrook refutes findings. http://www.smh.com.au/national/former-nt-prison-boss-ken-middlebrook-decries-militarised-regime-at-don-dale-20170426-gvstfz.html

[12] H. Bath, Investigation announced. http://www.abc.net.au/news/2014-10-29/nt-childrens-commissioner-investigating-inapropriate-force/5852208, 2014.

- Tear gas and spit masks used on juveniles as young as fourteen
- Juveniles in solitary confinement without windows or fans for extended periods,
- No drinking water was provided for more than seventy-two hours.[13]

This investigation resulted in the Bath Report or the Review of the Northern Territory Youth Detention System Report. The Northern Territory Commissioner for Corrections, Ken Middlebrook's response to the Bath Report was that it was, "inaccurate, shallow and one-sided".

Because of all that occurred within the Don Dale Juvenile Detention Centre, and the findings of the investigation and resulting Bath Report, a Royal Commission was convened. In June 2017, i.e., *The Royal Commission into the Protection and Detention of Children in the Northern Territory* which completed taking evidence June 2017. It was expected the report would be released in September 2017.

Within this Royal Commission, there was a focus on child protection and the out-of-home care and placement of First Australian children outside of the Aboriginal Child Placement Principle (Proceedings of the Royal Commission transcript of Wednesday, 21st June 2017).

As indicated earlier in the chapter, what is being shared at this point is taken from my personal experience as I was called upon to act as an expert witness for the Royal Commission based on my extensive personal and professional experience in the child protection area (almost 50 years).

---

[13] M. Vita, The Bath Report or the Review of the Northern Territory Youth Detention System Report, 2015.

The specific knowledge and experience I brought to the Royal Commission was also the fact that I had been involved in the activism that occurred in the 1970s and 1980s. Specifically, that I had sat around the table when discussions with regard to the development of the Aboriginal Child Placement were in process and knew that it had been based on the extensive Aboriginal kinship system, rather than the more narrow western perspectives of family which resulted in genograms, a tool of western anthropologists being brought across to child protection and currently used extensively within that system.

Other factors were that in the 1970s-1980s I had attended the South Australian Institute of Technology, received an Associate Diploma in social work and had gone back to Darwin and practiced as a welfare officer for the Northern Territory Government. This included working at the coal face of child protection. Later, I studied at the Northern Territory University (NTU) in Darwin and completed a social work degree. I returned to my work in child protection, again at the coal face, and extended the work I undertook to juvenile justice.[14] In 1997, whilst still a student I wrote and presented a paper entitled, "The mental health of the Stolen Generations" based on my lived experience of three generations of my family being part of the stolen generations and what I had learned about mental health as a result of my studies.

In 2011, I completed a PhD which focussed on the Aboriginal Kinship systems of the Larrakia and Warumungu peoples of the Northern Territory. In 2013, I published my PhD as a book entitled, *Let's Talk Kinship: Innovating Australian Social Work Education, Theory, Research and Practice through Aboriginal Knowledge,*

---

[14] C. King, 'Mental Health of the Stolen Generation'. *Northern Radius* 4(3), 1997, pp. 7-10. Retrieved from http://trove.nla.gov.au/work/39263988?q=Northern+Radius+%281997%2C+710%29&c=article&versionId=5203397,

and in 2015, I published my second book entitled, *The Fire of Resilience: Insights from an Aboriginal Social Worker.*[15]

At the time that I published my paper on the "mental health of the Stolen Generation", and later when I published my two books, I had no idea that in 2017 I would be called as an expert witness in a Royal Commission based on the work that I had done, and that the two books would be used to inform the lawyers involved.

The information below is based on the questions posed to me on Wednesday, 23 June 2017, and the resulting transcript. The answers to some of these questions will be shared in the final section of this chapter.

Questions were raised around the following and are not in order, if you wish to see the order or to find more information about the answers to the questions posed, you are referred to the transcript for the day:

- The lack of practice aligning to the Aboriginal Child Placement Principle which is legislation in every state and territory of Australia, which by definition means that it is Australian Law. Evidence supporting this lack of accountability to Australian Law was reported by the Central Australian Aboriginal Legal Aid Service, whose lawyer stated that only 32 percent of case workers in the Northern Territory applied this legislation in their practice.

- The child protection system within the Northern Territory, used as its reason for placing less than three hundred of the seven hundred First Nations children in out-of-home care with non-First Nations individuals and fami-

[15] C. King, *Let's Talk Kinship: Innovating Australian Social work Education, Theory, Research and Practice Through Aboriginal Knowledge*, (Magpie Goose Publishing, 2013) and C. King, *The Fire of Resilience: Insights from an Aboriginal Social Worker.* (New Millennium Publishers, 2015).

lies as being, that they could not find sufficient families through kinship care and genograms, which guided their practice.

- Evidence was provided by a First Nations grandmother from the Alice Springs region that she had applied to be a carer for her grandchildren and was found not suitable to do so. This was despite the fact that this grandmother did not drink alcohol or take drugs, had strict rules about who could enter her home and the behaviour of those visiting her home. The grandmother stated that she had informed the case worker that ten years prior to applying to care for her grandchildren she had been in a violent domestic situation, but that this relationship had ceased many years before her application to care for her grandchildren and she did not understand why she had been found unsuitable as a carer.

- The issue of absolute poverty being misunderstood as neglect was raised, as was the fact that when First Nations families agreed to care for the children of their extended family they were not paid to support the family to do this without feeling further the impact of poverty.

- The practice of required two weeks cultural awareness training and a later short electronic course was raised, the question being whether this training was sufficient to inform and guide child protection case workers in their dealings with the First Australians to achieve culturally safe practice within the Northern Territory. An associated question was whether this training could possibly give the case worker an inflated idea of their capacity to work culturally congruently and safely with the First Australians.

Answers provided to the Royal Commission as well as other possible answers to these questions will be shared in section three of this chapter.

Section two: Some common threads and recurring themes or déjà vu

This section of the chapter will focus on identifying some common threads and recurring themes throughout the two Royal Commissions and the National Inquiry and the way that they continue to appear over time, making one think that they are experiencing déjà vu and wondering why this is the case.

The Bringing Them Home Report (BTHR) clearly illustrated the issues experienced by the children being removed from their families as a result of government policy – initially through the stolen generations and currently through the child protection system with the mantra running through the years remaining "in the best interests of the child".

Once the BTHR had been released the practice of those working with First Nations children and families should have changed and the ACPP should have been strictly applied in every case to ensure the legislation was being followed and that Australian law was not being broken. The lack of application of the ACPP by child protection workers when responsible for First Australian children despite it being legislated in every state and territory of Australia is a clear link between the BTHR and *The Royal Commission into the Protection and Detention of Children in the Northern Territory* (2017).

In the evidence provided to the *Royal Commission into the Protection and Detention of Children in the Northern Territory (2017),* council for the Central Australian Legal Aid Service stated that the ACPP had only been applied to thirty two percent of the over seven hundred Aboriginal children currently in out of home care – less than three hundred children being placed within this legislative responsibility by child protection.

This lack of accountability to Australian law (legislation) raises the question as to whether family services and child protection officers realise they are in fact breaking the law each time they choose not to apply the ACPP and to incorporate the extensive Aboriginal kinship system. It also raises the question as to whether they realise that they are breaking international treaties that Australia is a signatory to or has supported (and it is quite likely that their nations of origin are signatories to) and indeed whether they are aware that they are in contravention of these laws. If they are not aware that they are breaking Australian law, why is this the case and why has it not been addressed?

The high numbers of First Australian children in the child protection and out-of-home care systems throughout Australia (not just within the Northern Territory) also begs the question as to why these staggering numbers exist as reflected within the child protection practices raised within *the Royal Commission into the Protection and Detention of Children in the Northern Territory (2017).* This must raise the question of whether the same lack of responsibility to act within Australian legislation (laws within the various states and territories) is being replicated throughout the country.[16] This raises the question of the role of the judiciary with regard to the First Australians, the ideology which guides their decisions and why there has been no penalty against child protection workers, systems and practices that contravene Australian legislation i.e. the ACPP.

Another clear link between the two Royal Commissions and the national inquiry that resulted in the BTHR is the numbers of Australia's First Nations children being placed outside their own families and kinship networks.

Section three: Breaking out of the cycle we seem to be stuck in

The focus of this section is on answering the questions, "has anyone been listening? have we learned nothing? From this discussion,

---

[16] S. Hagan, *The Rise and Rise of Judicial Bigotry* (Magpie Goose Publishing, 2017).

ways are identified through which we as social workers, psychologists and others whose employment interacts with First Australians (lawyers, magistrates), might move beyond déjà vu to actions that bring about positive change or, breaking the cycle we seem to be stuck in. This section identifies and challenges a number of current dominant western theories and practices.

As noted earlier in the chapter, I played what could be seen as an important role in assisting the National Apology to be delivered. On the morning of the Apology, as I made my way up to Parliament House, I was interviewed by the Sunrise television program and asked, "What does the Apology mean to you?" In answer, I held up my grandchild through Aboriginal law (my sister's daughter's child) and said, "hopefully that this child and all the other Aboriginal children like her will never know that it means to be taken from their families".

There was hope on that day that practices that brought about profound grief and loss and all that comes with it might be reviewed and changed. Now looking back at what has happened, or current practice, it appears that all the Apology brought about was a very small pause in the machinery that has now ramped up to full throttle in taking First Nations children away. This has caused me to ponder whether what we are seeing happening could be interpreted as being "in the best interests of the workers and the system, including those from outside the First Nations who accept these children as they are being paid to take them?" rather than in the "long term interests of the child?

This question of possible profiteering by some in Australia because of the removal of First Nations children was raised during the Royal Commission when the example was given of a loaf of bread being shared between perhaps four children and their parents now having to spread to feed the initial six people to eight or nine people if an additional two or three children were taken to be cared for by a family already near to already in poverty. The question of "where is the equity in this" was raised, given that when First Nation's children are cared for by anyone from outside of the kinship system, they are paid hundreds, sometimes thousands of dollars to do so.

Evidence of the astronomical amounts being paid to non-Aboriginal kinship carers emerged later in the enquiry and were reported in national newspapers. The focus being on a non-First Nations out-of-home care service being paid $72,000.00 per month for the care of four First Nations children with no special medical needs. This information caused the Commissioners to raise the question of profiteering in this sector.

Where is the commitment to positive change? Are we going to be back to other Apologies in the future for the practises that are occurring now? Where are the moral compasses of the people who are not fulfilling their legislative responsibilities pointing? When they choose to minimise these checks and balances that are moral, ethical, legislated, responsibilities? When they choose to ignore the ACPP, not apply the extensive Aboriginal kinship networks are they taking the time to think about the possible future ramifications of their actions on the lives of these children as they grow into adulthood, and if not, why not? Surely this is the least we can do for these people!

We should all be very aware that with the Stolen Generations, the aim was to move the children to another culture, out of their culture of origin, in an effort to erase their identity as First Nations people. This fits the description of genocide as defined by the United Nations. The intent of the Aboriginal Child Placement Principle was to prevent this practice and to ensure that genocidal practices did not continue. However, given the extensive practice of placing First Nations children with peoples of other ethnic origins (not just dominant white society which is what happened with the Stolen

Generations), it appears that the impact of this practice needs to be re-assessed to ascertain what impact these placements have on these children in the long term and if this practice is really in the long term best interests of the child and are genocidal practices continuing unabated within Australia?

What should also be reviewed is the often-given reason for these placements occurring, which are amongst others, "we cannot find placements within Aboriginal kinship networks/families". This raises the question of just how much these social workers, psychologists and the child protection departments understand what is meant by "Aboriginal kinship", and how extensive the Aboriginal kinship system is.

What about the other issue of this legislation becoming a quick tick and flick because of the high case load carried by child protection workers? This leads to questions about the effectiveness of cultural awareness training, and whether this is sufficient to inform the case workers about their accountability for violating Australian law when choosing to either enact or not enact legislation.

Another factor for discussion should be the vetting of child protection workers who are making life changing decisions that contribute to the issues identified through both the *Royal Commission into Aboriginal Deaths in Custody* (1987-1991), and the *Bringing Them Home Report: National Inquiry into the Separation of Aboriginal Children from their Families* (1997).

This vetting should include the stereotype around the capacity of Indigenous social workers of other countries of the world and others to make immediate connections with the First Australians simply because they are Indigenous to another country, or are people of colour. Let us be very clear! Being an Indigenous person of colour, does not mean that one is positioned in a place of authority or understanding to work unquestioned and unchallenged with the First Australians. This is a stereotype that must be challenged, as is the idea that foreign social workers as well as Australian social workers who have never worked in any meaningful way with First Australians and with no greater knowledge than cultural awareness, with a gap of knowledge of the Aboriginal kinship networks and system are within a position to work culturally congruently, safely and ethically in this field of practice.

One of the major points of evidence provided to the Royal Commission was the fact that three separate lots of evidence all stated that genograms should be replaced by Kinship Mapping. This occurred without any of the people giving evidence talking to one another before providing their evidence. The evidence provided by First Nations people in Central Australia was that Elders are using Kinship Mapping to ensure the continuation of culture, law, language and kinship networking through painting Kinship Maps.

The evidence from the Tiwi Islands also provided information about the use of Kinship Mapping around the right people to work with children and their families. This information does not fit within a genogram. The evidence I provided in Darwin was that not only should Kinship Maps be used in place of genograms, they would need to be individual for each child, as not all children had the same parents and the people responsible within the extended kinship networks and systems would not necessarily be the same for each child.

The Commissioners then made the comment that there would need to be a repository for these Kinship Maps that could be accessed by the children when they needed or wanted to access this information and that they also be available when the child was released from the child protection and out-of-home care systems.

Conclusion

Taking the time to review The *Royal Commission into Aboriginal Deaths in Custody*, the *Bringing Them Home Report* and the current *Royal Commission into the Protection and Detention of Children in the Northern Territory* (focus of Child protection and the Aboriginal Child Placement Principle) provided a unique opportunity to examine the questions, "has anyone been listening? have we learned nothing through a Royal Commission into Aboriginal Deaths in Custody and the Bringing Them Home Report? From my perspective, it appears that the answer is "no".

My challenge to you is to take the time to personally go through a similar process and see if you come up with a different answer. If you do not agree with anything that I have said, gather your evidence, research the topic and bring forth your findings.

With regards to answering the question as to why nothing has changed over so many years in the child protection and out-of-home systems? I believe the answer relates to political will and to the continuing domination of the First Australians for the best interests of others.

15

RESPECTING AND HONORING AUSTRALIAN ABORIGINAL AND TORRES STRAIT ISLANDER ELDERS IN SOCIAL WORK PRACTICE

Mick Adams and Jean Boladeras

Introduction

We begin by clarifying that "Elders" and "elderly" family members are not necessarily one and the same, consequently the distinction is focused on life stages and relative degrees of maturity, rather than on chronological age, and Elders can be comparatively young in a biological sense. We would also like to inform readers that we incorporate an interchange between "Aboriginal" and "Aboriginal and Torres Strait Islander" people and the use of "Indigenous" when we refer to First Nation peoples of Canada, Native Americans in USA and Maori from New Zealand

Respecting or honoring our Elders is a sign of compassion – a trait that is valued in many cultures. This is common throughout the world and many of us Indigenous peoples believe it is a natural human impulse that has become enshrined in collective wisdom. In Australian Aboriginal societies, Elders are often addressed as "Uncle" or "Aunty" which in this context are terms of respect. This form of address is used for people who are held in high esteem, generally older people (but not restricted to) who have earned that respect.

Canadian Social Workers Raven Sinclair, Michael Hart and Gord Bruyere[1] confirm that our Elders encourage us to know where we come from in order to know where we are going. It is important, they say, for social workers to initiate and act upon an understanding of the world, of their particular society, and of historical, cultural, social and political context in which they work. It is also crucial for social workers to situate themselves in terms of the implications of their personal and professional values, beliefs and practices. Too often, they unwittingly misunderstand and unknowingly hurt rather than help Indigenous families, communities and peoples.

We would like to point out that there are many Aboriginal Elders who have not had the opportunity to discover all layers of their culture, storylines or songlines. This has sometimes put those Elders in a difficult position. Because of recognition of their Elder "status", they are often under pressure to pass on their knowledge to younger generations. They may not always be able to provide the required knowledge. It is important for non-Indigenous people and Social Workers to recognise this, as Aboriginal and Torres Strait Islander peoples in common with other Indigenous peoples around the globe are invariably seen as all-knowing repositories of culture. Non-Indigenous professionals can sometimes adopt an accusatory tone if an Elder is not completely knowledgeable about the matter in hand.

As Aboriginal Elders, we have had first-hand experience of the welfare system and have seen our families and communities traumatised by its assimilationist and segregationist policies. As a result, we have concerns that social work theories and practices are based on the principles of Western non-Indigenous principles and ideas. We have both been caught up in the Stolen Generation sys-

---

[1] R. Sinclair, M. Hart and G. Bruyere, G. *Wicihitowin: Aboriginal Social Work in Canada.* (Fernwood Publishing, 2009).

tem – Aunty Jean is a mentor and Uncle Mick is a descendant – yet Aboriginal children are still being placed in the out-of-home care system. We are concerned that social work theories impose professional ideas in ways that are prejudicial to the interests of clients or lack synchronicity with their concerns. Indigenous peoples around the globe continue to confront disadvantage and inequity and often find themselves at the front-end of service delivery.

We believe that if Social Workers are going to engage and consult with Aboriginal and Torres Strait Islander peoples (and peoples of other cultures) their methodology needs to incorporate the specific cultural understandings and priorities of Aboriginal and Torres Strait Islander peoples.[2] For example, while Uncle Mick was undertaking his social work degree he had noted and questioned as to why the university did not have a core subject on Australian Aboriginal and Torres Strait Islander affairs. Sue Green and Eileen Baldry[3] agreed with him that Aboriginal and Torres Strait Islander peoples would have more than likely made up a significant proportion of Social Workers' clients.

As Aboriginal Elders, we are respected for our narrative historical value of Aboriginal daily community life. We write this chapter with the intention of helping white social workers and others to understand the practical aspects of Aboriginal life along with customs, beliefs, and society. We intend to provide an opportunity for white social workers to discuss, formulate and develop appropriate methodologies when conversing with Aboriginal and Torres Strait Islander Elders and peoples.

As we know it, the assimilation policy was a policy of absorbing

[2] M. Adams (2015). 'Utilising Appropriate Methodology and Social Work Practices: Consulting with Aboriginal and Torres Strait Islander Males'. In C. Fejo-King and J. Poona (ed.), *Emerging from the Margins, First Australians' Perspectives of Social Work* (Magpie Goose Publishing) 81-116.
[3] S. Green and E. Baldry. 'Building an Australian Indigenous Social Work' (2008) *Australian Social Work* 61(4), 389-402.

Aboriginal people (particularly those of mixed descent) into white society through the process of removing children from their families. Prior to the 'Yes' Vote referendum in 1967(celebrating its 50th anniversary in 2017) Aboriginal peoples were not recognised as citizens. They could have been counted as citizens if they applied for a certificate. To have a certificate meant they had to give up all ties with their families, communities and culture.

Elders' stories

As authors, we provide a short biography that gives credit of our standings within the Australian Aboriginal and Torres Strait Islander communities, and our expertise that formulates the content of this chapter. We write from our lived experience of being caught up in the welfare system and having journeyed through academia to learn, challenge and inform an Aboriginal perspective to provide an alternative continuum to social work studies, principles and practices.

Aunty Jean Boladeras: I am a Balardong woman from the York/ Northam region of Western Australia. My great-grandmother was Yindolan (Nyoongar name). My grandmother was Mary Shehan and my mother was Pansy Dennis. At the instigation of the local priest, I was sent to be raised by the nuns at a convent school. This was to separate me from the stigma of living in a home with an Aboriginal grandmother. Although this sounds incredible now, more than seventy years later, it is a matter of great concern to authorities that my "whiteness" be protected.

I endured many confronting moments with authorities (Administrators, Social Workers, Welfare Officers) throughout my life, but I was determined to reconnect to my Nyoongar roots. I was fortunate indeed in my young adulthood to connect with members of my Balardong family; to be accepted by them, to be taught by them, and to be recognised as a Nyoongar woman.

I had been lucky enough to have the connection with my great-grandmother, Yindolan of the Balardong people; many other Aboriginal people caught up in the stolen generation system have not had the same privilege. My Nyoongar brother Uncle Ralph Winmar taught me the Nyoongar protocols about respect, relationships and obligations. I stood on country, in the shadow of Walwalinj (The Hill That Cries); where my spirit connected to where our Old People had walked for thousands of generations. I was blessed and very fortunate to find my Nyoongar brother and his wife (both have recently passed away). They reconnected me to the Nyoongar culture, kinship and law that had been denied to me in my childhood. His family became my family; his moort was my moort. My family reconnected me to special places, gnamma (water holes), caves, and paintings. We would sit around the campfire exchanging yarns, listening to the Dreaming stories. This is all about kinship, about support, about connection, about recognition and identity. This is not taught in social work courses or written in social work principles and practices.

For many of us Aboriginal peoples, we do not get the time to grieve, and the grieving process does not seem to finish, with the obligations of attending sorry business (funerals) day after day, week after week. So many of our mob have gone back to be with our Old People. I always think about the ones who have gone before me, and remember the stories they told, and the good and sad times we had shared together.

Every year near the end of November, I wait for the moodjar (West Australian Christmas tree) tree to bloom. My spirit connects with my dear Nyoongar brother I can hear him telling us the wonderful story of the beautiful golden-haired woman who comes back every year to keep the promise that she made. According to legends she promised that she would never leave her Nyoongar moort; she never did and never will.

I had been privileged enough to gain (Katitjin) knowledge of which I share and pass onto others. I am spending my old age in my own Boodja (country). I would not like to be far away from my own Boodja. There are so many stories to think about too. Every day I see something that sets me off thinking; all the lovely memories come flooding back. We can't help but think of those ancestors who walked before us so many years ago. Everywhere I look, there is another story and another scene that overlays the present view. As we get older, we get closer to our Old People who waits for us to be re-united.

As an Elder, I am recognised and treated with respect and dignity; someone is always looking out for me (even Wadjalas – non-Indigenous people). I often wonder what the people 'of authority' (Missionaries, Welfare Officers and Social Workers) thought when they removed us from our families and lands, and what are they thinking now? Our grieving process is not only associated with people dying but of the unwarranted and harsh treatment we received at the hands of so-called protectors of Native children. As a sign of respect and because of my Elder's status people will often ask me to tell them a story, a story about the old days. The stories I tell are not about the harsh old days suffered at the hands of White authority, but of the old ways of Nyoongar culture and storylines connected to the Dreamtime.

Uncle Mick Adams: I am of the Yadhiagana/Wuthathi people of Cape York in Northern Queensland on my father's side and the Gurindji people in Central Northern Territory on my mother's side. I grew up in a place called Parap Camp; a unique multi-cultural community in Darwin situated in Northern Australia. I come from a poor working class family who lived in a struggling environment on the borderline of poverty. I had experienced racism from a number of fronts (police, sporting field, work).

As a school drop-out who had no intention of obtaining a formal education I took the opportunity, gamble and challenge to undertake an associate diploma in social work offered by the Aboriginal Task Force within the South Australian Institute of Technology (SAIT) School of Social Studies. Some fifteen years later, following my attendance at the Aboriginal Task Force, I went on to complete a social work degree through James Cook University in Townsville and later graduated with a PhD.

To learn about social work was the remotest thing on my mind because I knew that the welfare system had done nothing for us Aboriginal peoples, but to harass our families and apply White man standards on how to raise their children – their application of assimilation. My experience with welfare (i.e. social workers) was taking children away from their families and placing them onto missions and reserves or having them adopted into White families[4]. I remember seeing Welfare Officers prowling around our houses in white government cars; my only thoughts were that they are here to take us kids away. My grandmother was not only taken away from her family but from her homeland as well. Families were separated; my grandmother was taken to Darwin and her sister was sent to Alice Springs, some thousand kilometers apart.

I believe the uncertainty of my safety as an Aboriginal child placed an enormous burden on my upbringing. This might explain my early years of growing up hard, angry and bitter with years of self-destruction and abuse. My attempt to cope with the anger and frustrations through excessive alcohol and abusive unsociable behaviour, which made me more destructive and often got me into trouble with the authorities.

The relocation to take up studies changed the whole landscape around me, transferring from a safe environment to a new and in-

---

[4] M. Adams, *My Journey Through the Academic Mist*. (Magpie Goose Publishing, 2016).

tensive environment with new people, new rules and new language that took time for me to get used to. I had to confront and deal with many obstacles along the way, and at times had many run-ins with lecturers, tutors and students. The conception of self-doubt and the frustration of learning and trying to apply theories that were foreign did not make sense to me. The text books contained ideas that did not include or recognise the Aboriginal ways of working, knowing and doing but informed the processes that harassed Aboriginal people, rather than helping them.

This I thought was an opportunity to learn how to assist and counsel people professionally. For many years, we Aboriginal peoples have practiced and 'volunteered' to assist, counsel and comfort our peers in many situations, associated with poverty, grief, sorrow and uncertainty. So, therefore, as I set out to learn from social work texts, in turn I was determined to ensure social work lecturers were informed from my perspective about the Aboriginal ways of being, working and doing. This also got me into trouble; changing White academic structures was not allowed or heard of.

It is important to note that as we Aboriginal peoples age and get older and become identified as knowledge keepers of stories, songs and ceremonies, we do not automatically gain the position of community Elders. It differs from the First Nation Canadian and Native American Chief systems where they are elected for a certain term. Also, as mentioned previously, age is not restricted or the prerequisite for Eldership. Indigenous Elder status around the globe is community acquiesced by positive leadership and high standing performed throughout the duration of your life. As we pointed out earlier, there are many Aboriginal peoples who have not had the opportunity to discover all layers of their culture, storylines or songlines. They, will nevertheless, over time gain recognition of their Elder "status" through community submission.

Talking about family

We believe that it is important for social workers, and other allied health professionals, to understand the concept of *'family' and the kinship system* within Aboriginal and Torres Strait Islander societies. Even though the majority of Aboriginal and Torres Strait Islander people reside in rural and urban regions they still participate in the *'kinship'* system similar to those living in remote communities. As Aboriginal peoples, we place great value on belonging to a group and conforming to the obligations and responsibilities of our other group members. A sense of belonging, to us, is integral to Aboriginal culture, as it enables us to connect to our land and our people. We Aboriginal people incorporate a strong sense of *family'* and *'kinship'* that identifies us through our familial relationships.[5]

The traditional Indigenous family and kinship structures globally are an integral part of one's life that teaches the person how to live, how to treat other people and how to interact with the land. This allows our cultural heritage to be passed on from one generation to the next. We identify ourselves through our land areas, our relationship to others and their language and stories which lead by Elders and expressed through ceremonies, storylines, songlines and art.

Even when we, Aboriginal peoples, were caught up in the welfare system (Stolen Generation, Residential School) we embraced all phenomena and life as part of a vast and complex system of relationships which can be traced directly back to our ancestral totemic spirits. The kinship system establishes the structures of our societies, rules for social behaviour, and the ceremonies performed to ensure our continuity of life and land. The kinship system gov-

[5] C. Bourke and B. Edwards, *Family and Kinship in Aboriginal Australia, An Introductory Reader in Aboriginal Studies,* Second Edition (University of Queensland Press, 2004).

erns the laws of community, cultural lore and how we are required to behave in our communities.[6, 7]

David Suzuki[8] and Kerry Arabena[9] inform us that throughout history Indigenous people globally have always understood, are deeply embedded in and utterly dependent on the natural world – a world where everything is connected to everything else. They have celebrated storylines, songlines, dances and culture as being part of their surroundings.

We proudly assert that Aboriginal families had an ideal lifestyle. The roles of family members were set according to individual positions in the tribe, and families would live together in a communal environment with responsibilities being shared throughout the family. These included child rearing, cooking, hunting and the teaching of knowledge by tribal Elders. Failure to carry out our responsibilities meant that the rest of the family suffered. The men were the hunters, usually tracking down larger animals like kangaroo or emu, while women as gatherers supplied the family with berries, nuts and roots.[10] For example, Aunty Jean would honour her obligations and responsibilities to teach her nieces women skills and to guide them through to maturity. Conversely Uncle Mick would honour his obligation and responsibilities by teaching his nephews hunting skills and guiding them through to adulthood. .

[6] C. Fejo-King, *Let's Talk Kinship: Innovating Australian Social Work Education, Theory, Research and Practice through Aboriginal Knowledge.* (Christine Fejo-King Consulting, 2013).

[7] M. Adams, 'Aboriginal Life Set, Mental Health and Suicide'. In C. Fejo-King and J. Poona (ed), *Reconciliation and Australian Social Work Past and Current Experiences Informing Future Practice* (Magpie Goose Publishing, 2015) (33-74).

[8] D. Suzuki, *A David Suzuki Collection: A Lifetime of Ideas* (Allen & Unwin, 2003).

[9] K. Arabena, *Indigenous Epistemology and Wellbeing: Universe Referent Citizenship* (AIATSIS Research Discussion Paper 22, 2008).

[10] M. Adams, op. cit.; M. Adams and B. McCoy, 'Lives of Indigenous Australian Men.' In R. Thackrah and K. Scott, K (eds), *Indigenous Australian Health and Cultures. An Introduction for Health Professionals* (127-151). (Pearson Australia, 2011), Fejo-King, op. cit.; Maryanne Sam, *Through Black Eyes: A Handbook of Family Violence in Aboriginal and Torres Strait Islander Communities* (SNAICC, 1992).

Australian Indigenous social worker Christine Fejo-King[11] provides an in-depth illustration of the importance of the kinship system. She explains how she, as an Aboriginal woman who has family and cultural affiliations with the Larrakia and Warumungu people in the Northern Territory, having been born into the kinship system, acknowledged and abided by the relationship and connectedness of mother-daughter, aunty-niece (daughter), father-son, father-grandson, uncle-nephew (son). She defines the kinship system through the moiety (skin groups) hierarchy, observed from her standpoint and her Elders' standpoints (Larrakia and Warumungu), as a network of social relationships and a form of governance. She emphasises that this is extensive and includes relationships and inter-relationships of all creation: from the celestial; to mother earth; to all inanimate formations or objects; to living creatures that fly, live on and within the earth, the waterways and seas and even the seasons.[12]

We believe that it is very important for white social workers to understand that the purpose of the kinship system is to enable Aboriginal peoples to work out exactly where we stood in relation to each other within the tribal system. The kinship system provides a mental map of social relationships and behaviours, particularly around how we would greet, address and act towards other members within the tribe. The kinship system controlled potential conflict situations ensured that obligations were fulfilled, and maintained security within the group structure.[13]

---

[11] See Fejo-King, op. cit.

[12] See Adams, op. cit.

[13] Adams, op. cit.; M. Adams, *Men's Business: A Study into Aboriginal and Torres Strait Islander Men's Sexual and Reproductive Health. Canberra* (Magpie Goose Publishing, 2014); M. Adams, 'Establishing a National Framework for Improving the Health and Well-being of Aboriginal and Torres Strait Islander Males' (2002), *Aboriginal and Islander Health Worker Journal* 26(1) 11-12. Adams and McCoy, op. cit.; Fejo-King, op.cit.

Social work practice and theories

Social workers and individuals in social work roles have been a significant presence in the lives of Aboriginal individuals, families and communities. We see that social work theories and practices based on a Judeo-Christian worldview and tradition were developed to address the issues arising from the European industrial revolution and urbanisation. As Sinclair, Hart and Bruyere[14] state, Aboriginal peoples have witnessed that the consequent policies and practices derived from a modern western liberal philosophy have for many generations been of major consequences for the social policies imposed upon Indigenous nations.

Consequently, white social workers do not often recognise or reference Aboriginal and Torres Strait Islander ways of knowing, being and doing within their scope of practice.[15] We observed that during the 1960s to the 1990s the culture, practice, knowledge and awareness of Aboriginal and Torres Strait Islander peoples was not acknowledged or given priority within social work theories and practices. Marie *Connolly* and Louise *Harms*[16] say paying attention to culture and diversity is critically important when thinking about the application of theory in practice. *Connolly* and *Harms* confirm that theories can be used positively to increase understanding and to help people work out difficulties in their lives.

We believe that the social work profession will benefit from continued efforts to explore the intricate interactions of context, discourse and theory. We consider that a discursive approach is required to identify and analyse the key philosophies and ideas that shape social work practices within health and welfare institutions.

---

[14] Sinclair, Hart and Bruyere, op. cit.
[15] Australian Association of Social Workers (2010). Code of Ethics. Australian Association of Social Workers. www.aasw.asn.au
[16] M. Connolly and L. Harms, *Social Work: From Theory to Practice*. (Cambridge University Press, 2015).

In other words, from a poststructural point of view, discourses are the set of language practices that shape social workers' thoughts, action and their identity.

Uncle Mick's 'official introduction' to social work practice and principles was attending the Aboriginal Task Force. The Aboriginal Task Force was formed in 1973 by the Adelaide Aboriginal community Elders who negotiated with the South Australian Department of Community Welfare to partner with the South Australian Institute of Technology (SAIT) School of Social Studies to commission a once-off special study program to train a cadre of Indigenous people to work in the area of social welfare. The Elders and leaders wanted their 'own' people to work as case managers with Aboriginal clients. They wanted to apply cultural perspectives to social work practice in a way it could be more responsive to their community and cultural needs.[17]

The Aboriginal Task Force was perhaps the first of its kind designed that provided a pathway for Indigenous Australians to gain tertiary qualifications in social work from an accredited academic institution. MaryAnn Bin Sallik[18] and Uncle Mick[19] maintain that the Aboriginal Task Force embraced Indigenous histories and cultures from an Indigenous perspective to complement the Western theories and models. The associate diploma in social work gave Aboriginal peoples scope for advancement and to negotiate for a higher level of accreditation. The academic program incorporated Indigenous knowledge systems, cultures and histories as well as social welfare and psychology theories and practices. The program provided a culturally safe supportive environment that had become the blueprint for Indigenous higher education growth in Austra-

---

[17] Connolly and Harms, op. cit.
[18] M. Bin-Sallik (2003), 'Cultural Safety: Let's Name It!', *The Australian Journal of Indigenous Education*, 32, 21-28.
[19] Adams, op. cit.

lia.[20] By 1976 students were enrolling in the host institution's accredited associate diploma in social work, studying alongside their non-Indigenous counterparts.

Wayne Atkinson,[21] one of the first Aboriginal Task Force graduates to obtain a degree in social work along with Bin Sallik[22] and Mick Adams,[23] maintains that the unique thing about the Aboriginal Task Force was that it bought Indigenous students together from across Australia. We came from different geographical and cultural backgrounds, and from a diversity of traditional, regional, and urban settings. For many, this was an enlightening experience; one that enriched us all in our education, self-esteem, and confidence as Indigenous Australians.

Atkinson[24] and Adams[25] clarify that a large number of us had very limited schooling prior to enrolling to attend the Aboriginal Task Force. Most of us left school at an early age taking up jobs as cooks, road maintenance, labourers, painters and hospital domestic staff. The Aboriginal Task Force had offered a great challenge to many of the students which for some became too demanding; they either struggled to cope with the pressure to succeed, or left and moved to an environment where they felt more comfortable.

Many of those Aboriginal peoples who graduated from the Aboriginal Task Force went on to become involved in much of the activist work and lobbing that occurred in the political arena within Australia. They became involved in either setting up various organ-

[20] Adams, op. cit.; Bin Sallik, op. cit.
[21] W. Atkinson (2013), 'Task Force Days: Looking Back and Journeying Forward, 1975-77' 'The Task Force Story: Recalling 40 years of tertiary education for Aboriginal and Torres Strait Islander People', D. Unaipon College of Indigenous Education and Research Division of Education, Arts and Social Sciences University of South Australia, 1-15.
[22] Bib Sallik, op. cit.
[23] Adams, op.cit.
[24] Atkinson, op. cit.
[25] Adams, op. cit.

isations or supporting people who had already begun the push for change. They were able to utilise and at times combine Aboriginal terms of reference with all the knowledge, skills and theories they gained through attending the Aboriginal Task Force program. As an example, many graduates observed that social work in Australia had been firmly focussed on professionalisation and had not taken the opportunity to engage effectively with Aboriginal and Torres Strait Islander peoples. Therefore, in continuing to improve social work practice, graduates went on to become founding members of the National Coalition of Aboriginal and Torres Strait Islander Social Workers Association Inc.

We agree that the Aboriginal ways of working and doing promote and create a better understanding of the Aboriginal and Torres Strait Islander cultures, and improve working relationships with Aboriginal peoples. They increase knowledge, understanding and awareness of Aboriginal history, cultural diversity and cultural issues, past and present; and how current social and political issues impact on the lives of Indigenous Australians. This is not to say that we totally reject Western theory, research or knowledge; it is more about centring our concerns and world views. It's about coming to know and understand theory and practice from our own Indigenous perspectives and for our own Indigenous purposes.

We emphasise that Indigenous experience, knowledge and perspectives needs to be included in social work processes and practices if they are to appropriate engage with Aboriginal and Torres Strait Islander people.

Conclusion

Honouring our Indigenous Elders in social work involves articulating the significant impact that Indigenous educators have made through their personal integrity and dedication to the social work profession. As we witnessed, the role of Elders in Indigenous communities around the globe is supreme. We have noted that even though the Australian Association of Social Workers has adopted a systems approach to facilitate changes to uphold the profession's core values of respect for Aboriginal and Torres Strait Islander peoples, it is concerning to us that the Australian Association of Social Workers' *Code of Ethics* did not acknowledge or mention Aboriginal and Torres Strait Islander peoples until the 1990s.[26]

Indigenous peoples globally are aware that social work has a chequered history among Indigenous populations. Colin Baskin[27] argued that the profession of social work has not tended to be friendly towards Aboriginal peoples. Rather, it has often been intrusive, judgmental, controlling and harmful. We have noted that in recent years, Aboriginal peoples have moved into the area of social work. Baskin says more and more schools of social work are beginning to incorporate anti-oppressive theories and practices into their curricula. This, he says, opens the door for such approaches to include work that is conducive to Aboriginal perspectives.

We emphasise that the importance of understanding Aboriginal and Torres Strait Islander descriptions and perceptions is crucial in making the connections between Aboriginal and Torres Strait Islander communities and western academics and health professionals. We need to diminish the boundaries between Indigenous narratives and constructs of wellness and western biomedical diagnostic labels and treatment pathways for Aboriginal and Torres Strait Islander peoples.

[26] D. McAuliffe, S. Nipperess, K. Daly and F. Hardcastle, 'New Steps in the AASW Reconciliation Journey'. In C. Fejo-King and J. Poona (ed), *Reconciliation and Australian Social Work Past and Current Experiences Informing Future Practice* (157-174). Magpie Goose Publishing, 2015).

[27] C. Baskin, 'Aboriginal World Views as Challenges and Possibilities in Social Work Education' (Aboriginal World Views as Challenges and Possibilities in Social Work Education 2006). *Critical Social Work* 7(2).

We believe that this approach would provide a unique opportunity to develop a 'two-way understandings' between Aboriginal and Torres Strait Islander people and western models of care that will go a long way to realising successful outcomes for Aboriginal and Torres Strait Islander peoples.[28] The involvement of Indigenous social work educators and educational programs are essential. Evidence show that they have had a significant impact on the social work profession. Aboriginal peoples around the globe have been actively involved in changing the way in which social work practice and methodologies are understood.

---

[28] Adams, op. cit., Valmae Ypinazar, Stephen Margolis, Melissa Haswell-Elkins and Komla Tsey (2007), 'Indigenous Australians' understandings regarding mental health and disorders', *Australian and New Zealand Journal of Psychiatry*; 41.

16

THE WISDOM OF HINDSIGHT:

Cumulative Lessons in Activism

Linda Briskman

In my first social work job in a statutory agency, my blundering remains memorable. As was established practice of that time, the 'home visit', I called on an Aboriginal family in the rural Victorian town where I worked. With loads of goodwill but even more ignorance, I arrived in a car that shrieked 'government' by its number-plates. Children happily playing in the front garden disappeared by the time I reached the front door and were replaced by a hostile woman who barred my entry. The more I tried to engage (Social Work Skills 101), the more she glared.

I had studied social work in the 1970s wishing not only to 'help', but to believing I could. This encounter and others that quickly followed revealed to me that I was instead a hinderer. I had been captured by a paradigm of casework about which there had been little critique. Or if it did exist, it was about ways to do casework better.

Fast forward and I have been struck by the contention that we should 'subvert the dominant paradigm'. Upon reflection, that is what I have found myself doing all my working life and once I encountered critical social work and kindred social work activists, I felt affirmed to directly challenge unethical practices; working toward systemic social change is a legitimate collaborative social work pursuit and engaging with 'the political' is a guiding principle.

This chapter is a reflection on almost 40 years of my social work existence. I have dipped in and out of social work during these years over concerns that dominant paradigms were winning. But with the help of people who have inspired my thinking and concern about not only the state of social work but the state of the world, I discovered it's not possible to take the social worker out of the gal. I present my reflections as a career trajectory from the 1980s on, although swerving now and then, as one set of circumstances builds upon another. I believe I can take some liberties after longevity as a social worker.

This chapter is about many social work activists, but I author my story within it. It is testament to the leadership, commitment and passion of many in the critical social work sphere who have influenced and shaped my work. It would take an entire chapter, maybe an entire book, to name and discuss such profound influences so just a few are mentioned. Some of the people who have inspired are no longer in the prime of youth; others have sadly died, often prematurely, but each has a long history of working within what we now name as the critical and radical tradition and one that is activist at its core. A new generation of social workers builds upon the work of those who have gone before. Social work, unlike many professions, does not discard their reflections and insights. The profession develops and recreates but remains systemically challenged by unflinching neoliberalism.

In each section of this chapter, I discuss how I developed my ideas and practice and how recognition and a body of work emerged. I hope that the lessons I learned and the confidence I gained will be useful for social workers intent on following an activist path. Much of my work is collaborative and co-authored, as activism cannot be a lone undertaking. Working with others with similar passions and ideas fosters confidence to act when the odds seem stacked against activist endeavours.

Getting qualified and having doubts: 1970s

The process of being accepted into a social work program should have rung warning bells. All applicants to the nameless social work program were required in those 'olden times' to be interviewed before acceptance. Two questions stand out: 'What are your hang-ups' and 'How do you get on with your mother'? I persevered against the odds, but I have a confession to make. In the two years of my graduate course in social work, I learned little. Both years I was pregnant and by the second year, I was wheeling to lectures a colicky baby and leaving within five minutes of commencement. Now as I look back I think this was an advantage, as I was not indoctrinated into conventional modes of practice and became relatively free to work organically and creatively and to learn the hard way, which was for me the best way. I could be intuitive rather than prescriptive and even apply common sense, something we do not speak much about.

My immediate pre-practice years set the tone for future work. In the mid 1970s, I lived in the remote highlands of Papua New Guinea (PNG). I had moved there with my partner of that time, two small children and my newly acquired social work qualification. In Mt Hagen I became quickly aware that western style social work did not fit and that context matters; something I only became academically cognisant about when I entered the academic realm. What I did become acutely aware of in PNG was the impact of colonisation on the highlanders and the attempts by the Australian government to change those cultural practices that it did not like to practices that were more western. So tribal fighting (which had a relatively minor life/death impact) was replaced by the introduction of alcohol and motor vehicles, which were seriously destructive. Vegetable plots were taken over for the economic gain of coffee plantations, with severe nutritional repercussions. I took the colonialism problematic back with me to Australia in my first social work job.

Questioning practice: 1980s

My first job was located within a rural branch of a Victorian state welfare department where I was ill-equipped to work in a setting where 30% of the people on our books were Aboriginal, with only 2% representation in the population. My schooling had barely touched on Indigenous people. History had been British or European and even studying history at university did not create understandings of the impact of colonisation on the present.

In this first job, I tried to understand through critical questioning, but was responded to in ways that were at best ignorant and at worst racist and stereotypical. I was confronted with an array of forms, procedures and decisions to be made in the absence of an organisational culture that valued consulting with Aboriginal communities. Instead, community members were judged to be failing to conform to western ways of life. And they were told of their 'failings' during case planning meeting, where they were humiliated as reports were read out. There was no recognition of structural barriers, of institutional racism, of strengths or cultural mores from which we might learn; nor was there empathy. Although the state department had a smattering of staff committed to structural change, it did not come fast enough as I witnessed how we inflicted hardship and suppressed Indigenous voice. Much later, I wrote a paper calling on social workers to consider themselves practice ethnographers,[1] to amass stories (data) about their observations and to use these to advocate for change.

My own transformation came from a further error of judgment

---

[1] L. Briskman, 'Nation'. In I. Shaw, B. Briar-Lawson, J. Orme and R. Ruckdeschel (eds.) *Sage Handbook of Social Work Research* (Sage Publications, 2010).

and an inspirational mentor. I was asked to participate in a film about encounters of Aboriginal people with social workers. My memory of this is somewhat hazy but I recall speaking to a camera, while seated behind a desk in my best clothes, making banal statements about how relationships were evolving and improving and good work was being done. I went to the Melbourne conference where the film was launched and was horrified to see that as I was speaking an Aboriginal man was singing in the background: 'And you murdered our people'. And there was worse to come. Aboriginal participants were filmed in relaxed outdoor settings, not holding back about what they truly thought about social workers.

It was at this conference that I was 'rescued' by Mollie Dyer. Mollie was an inspirational, outspoken Yorta Yorta woman who never gave up. She had worked at the Victorian Aboriginal Legal Service where she became aware that most of those entering the criminal justice system had previously been entrapped in the child welfare system. She went on to establish the Victorian Aboriginal Child Care Agency (VACCA), and protocols were set in place for state workers to consult with VACCA about decisions we were making, a huge gain from the arbitrary, uncritical and harmful decision-making that went before. Aboriginal and Torres Strait Islander child welfare organisations burgeoned in other parts of Australia. I was privileged to work over the next few decades with VACCA and with the national umbrella organisation the Secretariat of National Aboriginal and Islander Child Care (SNAICC). My PhD on SNAICC and Aboriginal activism was completed much later in 2001 and published as The Black Grapevine.[2] My research was supported by SNAICC on the proviso that I adopted oral history as my primary methodology. The power of this approach remained with me in future projects where storytelling, narrative and voices were

---

[2] L. Briskman, *The Black Grapevine: Aboriginal Activism and the Stolen Generation* (Federation Press, 2003).

centred. This could be a struggle at times as in the neo-liberal world more conventional evidence was privileged.

Through realising there were wrongs to be righted, I decided to take risks. It was pre-email days. There was somewhat less homogenisation in official practice at that time (or less checking up) and the 'centre' was not particularly interested in the rural periphery. Although we complained about feeling excluded, there were advantages as we could push boundaries. These rural social work encounters led me to my first ever book, *Challenging Rural Practice*,[3] coedited in 1999 with Margaret Lynn and also with Helen La Nauze who sadly died during its formulation.

Although I see myself as a fairly modest person, there are a few actions that fill me with some pride as I reflect. One was a collaboration between the local Aboriginal community, the state office where I was located, and a non-government organisation (NGO) to establish an Indigenous community organisation so that Aboriginal people could take some control over their destinies. This helped counter dominant western paradigms of knowledge by recognising Indigenous wisdom and Indigenous cultures. These principles were behind establishing an extended family foster care approach that defied assumptions of the white system. The NGO responsible for the funded foster care system was supportive and initiated ideas such as devolving funding and responsibility to the Aboriginal organisation. Vernon Knight, the spirited social work founder of Mallee Family Care, was the brains behind this[4] and the social worker with the organisation at that time, the late Lorraine Stark, and I later wrote up the process and the benefits in a chapter titled: 'When the White System Doesn't Fit'.[5]

---

[3] L. Briskman and M. Lynn (eds), *Challenging Rural Practice: Change, Creativity and Diversity in the Australian Context* (Deakin University Press, 1999).
[4] See V. Knight, *Chances Matter* (Yelta, 2016) for a reflection on his work.
[5] L. Briskman and L. Stark, 'When the White System Doesn't Fit'. In W. Weeks and J. Wilson (eds), *Issues Facing Australian Families: Human Services Respond* (Longman, 1995).

A degree of freedom in academia: 1990s

While working as a practitioner I commenced a Master of Social Work degree part-time in the late 1980s. My motives were not academic but I needed to place myself outside rural-thinking and the eight-hour return trip to Melbourne each week allowed me to meet with peers who were also concerned about the status quo. And the pubs in Carlton were more appealing than country ones! My thesis of 1989, Pursuit of Aboriginal Control of Child Welfare, examined the clash between government policy and Aboriginal aspirations, a huge gap that has not been rectified almost 30 years later.

As with most of my opportunities that have been serendipitous, an opportunity arose to coordinate and teach into the extended campus program of La Trobe University. This was another Vernon Knight vision and was supported by government ministers. The idea was to develop and implement a creative means to support recruitment and retention of social workers. Rural campuses have expanded since, as has online learning, but this program was innovative for its time.

La Trobe staff flew to Mildura for weekend intensives and in my first encounter in the academic world I had to learn quickly. Fortunately, help came my way. Sharon Moore from what was then the Phillip Institute of Technology (now RMIT) was developing a similar program in the regional city of Bendigo and invited me there. She showed me books she had ordered; every one of them feminist. Living in a rural community where 'ladies' were expected to bring plates and where at official events women were supplied pink name tags and men blue, this was a revelation.

I met Carolyn Noble at my first Women in Welfare Education meeting. And through the serendipity of a café conversation, we produced research and a volume of writing from 1996 on that problematised social work ethics, particularly for western dominance.[6] Despite critiques, having delved into this area enabled me to look at institutionalised ethics (AASW Code) and adapt these in my later work when I called on the profession to use selective sections of codes for activist purposes such as human rights, social justice and challenging injustice. The theme of western dominance never left and much later I wrote with Aziz Alberaithen[7] on social work ethics in Saudi Arabia. Later, I wrote with Manohar Pawar[8] on social workers and virtue ethics.

In this same decade I worked in the hallowed halls of both Deakin and Monash universities, before entering RMIT University in 2000. It was at RMIT that my academic and activist interests solidified over concern about asylum seeker detention.

Excessively nasty politics: 2000-2010

As critical social work took hold, my reflections grew stronger. At RMIT the first edition of *Critical Social Work* was co-edited with Bob Pease and June Allan, with many contributions from colleagues (2003), later revised in 2009.[9]

At RMIT, my unease about asylum seeker politics influenced my research, writing and advocacy, continuing to the present. It was a time where there was increasing awareness in Australian society about the indefinite detention of asylum seekers. I would

[6] For example: L. Briskman, 'A Moral Crisis for Social Work' (2001) *Critical Social Work* 2(1), 34-38; C. Noble and L. Briskman, 'AASW Code of Ethics: The Impact of Progressive Theory on Moral and Ethical Assumptions' (*Advances in Social Work and Welfare Education*, 2000) 3(1), 89-103.
[7] A. Alberaithen and L. Briskman, 'Social Work Ethics in Saudi Arabia: An Exploration' (*The British Journal of Social Work*, 2015, 45(7) 2192-2209.
[8] M. Pawar and L. Briskman, 'I Cannot Give Up, I Cannot Give Up on the Children: Bernadette McMenamin', in M. Pawar, R. Hugman, A. Alexandra and W. Anscombe (eds), *Empowering Social Workers* (Springer, 2017).
[9] J. Allan, L. Briskman and B. Pease (eds), *Critical Social Work: Theories and Practices for a Socially Just World* (Allen and Unwin, 2009).

wake early each morning in rage and disbelief about the inhumanity that was being meted out in this country. A growing advocacy movement developed and most of us felt powerless to contribute to ending human rights violations against asylum seekers. This sense of powerlessness has never gone away, for as I write now, 17 years on from the time I started in this space, the politics and practices become increasingly malevolent.

Calls for action and opportunities occur in unexpected ways. In 2005 it was revealed that an Australian resident, known as Anna, was detained in the Baxter Immigration Detention Centre in South Australia. Asylum seekers incarcerated there showed a duty of care when the authorities had not, about a supposed German woman who was behaving in an unusual manner. It soon transpired that Anna was Cornelia Rau who had been reported as a missing person. Suffering from a severe mental illness, she was quickly removed from detention to receive medical treatment. Because of the adverse publicity, the Immigration Department instituted an Inquiry into the circumstances of her detention.

Activists and detained asylum seekers pushed for the Inquiry to be widened to include all those detained, but to no avail. As President of the Australian Council of Heads of Schools of Social Work (ACHSSW) at that time, I suggested that the ACHSSW could run an Inquiry; members were enthusiastic as they were deeply concerned at the downward spiral for asylum seekers. Details of what was subsequently termed the 'People's Inquiry' are published in Human Rights Overboard: Seeking asylum in Australia.[10] I spoke earlier about organic processes and the People's Inquiry was indeed organic and learn-as-you-go. After all, none of us had run an Inquiry previously. But we followed our instincts, our hunches and our social justice and human rights lenses.

---

[10] L. Briskman, S. Latham, and C. Goddard, Human Rights Overboard: Seeking asylum in Australia (Scribe Publications, 2008). Winner of AHRC award for literature.

The year 2008 was prodigious as I received recognition from the International Association of Schools of Social Work. I was privileged to deliver the Eileen Younghusband address for the IASSW in Durban South Africa. In that same year, the co-edited *Human Rights Overboard* was not only published but won the Australian Human Rights Award for Literature (non-fiction). The lecture in South Africa provided an opportunity to speak on the world social work stage about the People's Inquiry as an example of how social work might be recast in a time of troubles. This lecture is even more relevant today as we are on the brink of international calamity and a world dominated by danger of Donald Trump and his global supporters. Often when academics publish our work or present at conferences, we lament that our ideas have changed by the next year. But as I look back I don't feel like that and delivering that lecture enabled me to reflect on a social work initiated process that was collective and organic. The way I framed social action then and now is to: recognise human rights abuses, respond through political activism and moral courage, identify guiding principles, and to be a role model for social work students.

Applying these principles to the People's Inquiry, we were impelled by the increasing despair of those who had been detained for many years and whom the courts effectively deemed could remain there for the rest of their lives. As a group of academic social workers we considered it beholden on our knowledge, expertise, values and passion to conduct a national investigation. Social work took the lead but support emerged throughout Australia from various professions, faith groups and community members. Students joined us for social work placements or internships. The Inquiry process confirmed how social work, despite its diversity of practice models and organisational constraints, can garner the support of others to challenge human rights abuses.[11]

---

[11] L. Briskman, S. Latham and C. Goddard, *Human Rights Overboard: Seeking Asylum in Australia* (Scribe Publications, 2008).

From 2007, the role of the professions working in closed environments was very much on my mind. Opportunity knocked. I was invited as a Chief Investigator on an Australian Research Grant with Monash academics Deborah Zion and Bebe Loff about the ethics of working in immigration detention.[12] It was here I first discovered the concept of Dual Loyalty, the question of where the loyalty of the professional lies – funder/employing body or those we are tasked to work with – and wrestled with how this could be applied to social work. At that time, we were focusing on health workers as social workers were rarely employed in immigration detention but now, as I will discuss later, social workers became employed in the excessive human rights violating context of offshore detention in Nauru and Manus Island (Papua New Guinea).

When working in this arena, I had moved to Curtin University in Perth where I followed in the footsteps of human rights social work luminary, Jim Ife, the founding Chair of the Centre for Human Rights Education at Curtin. I worked with fellow social work human rights activist Lucy Fiske in contemplating how human rights education could be implemented in curriculum,[13] a question that remains work in progress. From this West Australian vantage point, I was able to witness the horrors of immigration detention as the locale enabled visits to Christmas Island and to Curtin detention centre in Derby, sites where few advocates could venture. With Caroline Fleay, I wrote of the distress of 'The Hidden Men', as we called them,[14] asylum seekers holed up in remote detention in Derby.

---

[12] See, for example, D. Zion, L. Briskman and B. Loff, 'Psychiatric Ethics and a Politics of Compassion: The Case of Detained Asylum Seekers in Australia' (*Journal of Bioethical Inquiry* (2012), 9 (1) 67-75); D. Zion, L. Briskman and B. Loff, 'Nursing in Asylum Seeker Detention in Australia: Care, Rights and Witnessing' (*Journal of Medical Ethics* (2009), 35 (9) 547-551.

[13] L. Fiske and L. Briskman, 'Teaching Human Rights at University: Critical Pedagogy in Action', in B. Offord and C. Newell (eds), *Activating Human Rights in Education: Exploration, Innovation and Transformation* (Australian College of Educators, 2008).

[14] C. Fleay and L. Briskman, (2013), 'The Hidden Men: Bearing Witness to Mandatory Detention in Australia', (*Refugee Survey Quarterly*, 2013, 32 (3) 112-129).

The year 2010 was distressing, for in December an asylum seeker boat crashed on Christmas Island with fifty people drowning, leaving behind traumatised asylum seekers, many who were relatives of those who died. A PhD student at that time, Michelle Dimasi, was on Christmas Island and was perturbed at how survivor narratives were absent in the public sphere. Together we interviewed some survivors to overcome the silencing.[15] A concerning consequence of the tragedy was the opportunism of government in introducing harsher policies, duping the public into believing these would stop deaths at sea.

In Western Australia I did not forget my interest in the Indigenous sphere but was conscious that I was not as community-connected as I had been in Victoria. Through another social work academic, Fran Crawford, I was fortunate enough to be part of a project that engaged Indigenous practitioners from throughout Western Australia in cooperative inquiry.[16] It was both inspirational and disconcerting to see the work, inevitably unpaid, that communities were doing to support those in their midst who were strugglingfor which they received little recognition and barely any resources. There has been a long-standing problem in Australia where governments seek advice from hand-picked advisors, not always from grass roots, and where Indigenous groups are not trusted in their quest for self-determination.

I saw out this decade and a little more in Perth but then it was time to move back to Melbourne to family, friends, home and a new opportunity.

---

[15] L. Briskman and M. Dimasi, 'Re-living Jenga: Survivor narratives' in L. Mannik (ed), *Migration by Boat: Discourses of Trauma, Exclusion and Survival* (Berghahn Books, 2016).

[16] F. Crawford, P. Dudgeon and L. Briskman, *Developing Therapeutic Communities for Abused Aboriginal Children and their Families: An IndigenousPpractitioner's Cooperative Inquiry* (Ministerial Advisory Council on Child Protection and Curtin University, 2008).

Staying vigilant: 2012 – now

In 2012 I was appointed as Professor of Human Rights at Swinburne University where I continued my work in the Indigenous sphere, publishing the second edition of *Social Work with Indigenous Communities*[17] and continuing in the asylum seeker arena.

At Swinburne I was involved in a special edition of ethics and social welfare on *Outrage,* with Charlotte Williams and Donna McAuliffe.[18] Social workers from a number of countries expressed their outrage in this edition. In producing this volume, we were inspired by Stephane Hessel's 2010 Indignez-vous,[19] which resonated by advocating for the emotion of outrage, calling on civil society members to stand up and speak out against injustice.

I have said little of my international work until now, but I have been fortunate to join in many international conferences and forums including as a keynote speaker. I have had sabbaticals abroad that provide a global context to the localised sphere in which I work, reinforcing the adage 'Think Global, Act Local'.

While at Swinburne, I joined with Lucy Fiske on the challenges facing asylum seekers and refugees in protracted situations in Indonesia. We travelled to Indonesia where the stories of despair were balanced by stories of resilience of people doing it for themselves. It was community development in action, without the benefit of textbooks, financial resources and outside experts. We wrote about survival, community development that was grounded in experience and responsiveness.[20]

---

[17] L. Briskman, *Social Work with Indigenous Communities: A Human Rights Approach* (Federation Press, 2014).

[18] D. Macauliffe, C. Williams and L. Briskman, 'Moral Outrage! Social Work and Social Welfare' (*Ethics and Social Welfare*, 2016, 10(2) 87-93).

[19] S. Hessel, *Time for Outrage* (Quartet Books, 2011).

[20] L. Briskman and L. Fiske, 'Building Community Against the Odds'. In S. Kenny (ed), *Handbook of Community Development* (Routledge, 2017).

I continued my long-standing involvement in Iran. In total, I have visited there ten times including co-organising conferences and events with the Non-Aligned Movement (NAM) Centre for Human Rights and Cultural Diversity[21] and working with Tehran University of Medical Sciences on a project on health ethics and Afghans in Iran.[22] I was impressed by how Iran was able to house 'unauthorised' Afghans in the millions without detaining them, while Australia was excessively punitive to so few. What was of particular interest to me was challenging negative western perceptions of Iran and to see instead a vibrant, intellectual, artistic, internationally focused society. The west fails to see any good in countries that it demonises, and I witnessed the terrible impact of harsh sanctions imposed by many nations including Australia.[23]

I began work at Swinburne on the global phenomenon of Islamophobia that continues to now. I joined fellow social worker Susie Latham in her initiative to co-convene Voices Against Bigotry (www.voicesagainstbigory.org), to write in this sphere[24] and to work with Muslim organisations.

Having partnerships in two Muslim-majority countries, I became increasingly concerned at the inaccurate and unfair portrayal and denigration of Muslims in Australian society. This was not just

[21] L. Briskman and K. Hashemi (eds), Cultures in Support of Humanity, *NAM Yearbook on Human Rights and Cultural Diversity*, 1 (NAMCHRCD, 2012.
[22] L. Bisaillon, E. Shamsi Gooshki and L. Briskman, 'Medico-legal Borders and the Shaping of Health Services for Afghans in Iran: Physical, Social, Bureaucratic, and Public Health Conditions of Care', *International Journal of Migration and Border Studies* (2016), 2(1), 40-58.
[23] L. Briskman, 'Sanctions Against Iran: Violating the Human rights of the Iranian People', *Arena,* 25 (2013), 16-18.
[24] S. Poynting and L. Briskman, 'Black Flags, Plastic Swords and Other Weapons of Mass Disruption in Australia'. In N. Massoumi, T. Mills, H. Aked and D. Miller (eds), *Islamophobia* (Pluto Press, 2017); S. Latham and L. Briskman, 'Refugees, Islamophobia and Ayaan Hirsi Ali: Challenging Social Work Co-option', *Affilia,* (2017), 32(1), 108-111.

the establishment of right-wing groups such as Reclaim Australia, nor just with political parties such as Pauline Hanson's One Nation. Increasingly government and media have joined in criticising Islam and Muslims.

I have given examples of dissemination of academic work but writing for other outlets is also important. Media commentary reaches a wider audience and the tone can be less academic and more accessible. Alternative media outlets such as *Social Alternatives* and Court of Conscience provide more potential to express opinion than many conventional outlets. I mentioned before that social workers have been employed in offshore immigration detention centres. Some social workers of courage have spoken out and, in *Social Alternatives*[25] the problematic of social work employment was discussed. 'Jane Doe' used this pseudonym in fear of repercussions of speaking out, as legislation to bar employees from doing so carried a penalty of up to two years imprisonment.

I briefly step back in time to note that despite trying times, humour can sometimes convey a message more effectively than a serious tome. In 2007, I played the part of the Supreme Bean in the Trial of John Howard at the Melbourne Town Hall, organised by the Fabian Society. In the same year I joined Dave Corlett in a Tramtastic project, where we gave a lecture on refugees to unsuspecting commuters.

It is mid 2017 as I write this piece, a year when I officially become an 'elder' by most definitions. Despite this status I have entered a new career phase as the Margaret Whitlam Chair of Social Work at Western Sydney University. Why am I not retiring? Well, I don't play golf for one thing and I still have much unfinished business. It is also an opportunity to honour two wonderful social workers no longer with us. Natalie Bolzan, the foundation Marga-

---

[25] L. Briskman and J. Doe, 'Social Work in Dark Places' (*Social Alternatives* (2017), 35(4) 73-79.

ret Whitlam Chair and Margaret Whitlam, wife of a former Prime Minister and Australia's best known social worker.

I end where I began by revisiting the Indigenous sphere where I continue to work on Stolen Generations collaborations. Indigenous colleagues and friends have been an inspiration for all my endeavours. I once saw my advocacy fields of interest as separate spheres but Indigenous leader Lowitja O'Donohue changed my thinking when she challenged the way in which both First Peoples and recent arrivals have been treated.

From this, I end where I began by honouring the wisdom of Indigenous Australians who have taught me so much. I dedicate the chapter to the Mollie Dyer, who died in 1998 and left an amazing legacy for us all.

I hope that some of my words will help create a new generation of activist practitioners and scholars. My final word is to urge readers to join up to Social Workers Without Borders (www.social-workerswithoutborders.net.au) to work collaboratively across the globe to achieve social justice and human rights for all.

17

'THINK GLOBALLY, ACT LOCALLY':

Exploring a Catchcry for
Social Change

Mary Lane

*There was another wrong road that led me to six cypress trees
and some shards and blocks of marble that are all that is left
of the oldest temple in Greece, and some prickly pear fruit offered on a fresh-cut vine leaf, and the most profound statement I
have ever heard, from an old man, villainously moustached and
dressed in faded blue, patched and pieced and darned in a way
that Mondrian could never invent. And he said: 'nothing worth
knowing ever happens beyond the distance of a mule ride'.*

(The words of an old man encountered in Greece by Charmian Clift
and included in one of her essays 'Taking the Wrong Road' in *The
World of Charmian Clift*, Flamingo, 1987, 20).

I yearn to hear more from this wise old man, who might draw
out further the meanings behind his words. For my present
purposes though, he draws attention to the local in understanding society and how it works – and by implication how society
might be changed.

In my story about community development during the
1960s through to the 1990s, I'll explore the emphasis on local-
ity which those words, beautifully and rather quaintly, express.
Focus will be on grass roots community work in which I was
involved with people in western and south western Sydney. At

the heart of this work was commitment to the notion of 'starting where people are at'; a slow, participatory, face-to-face process seeking an understanding of local needs and aspirations and the contextual factors affecting the conditions of existence. It was a process of building trust and encouraging people to join with others to take action around common concerns. Listening and gaining an understanding of local concerns was the first step towards tackling injustices and disadvantage; giving people voice and bringing them together was a step towards promoting democracy, learning democracy through local involvement.

Locality-based work was not without its challenges and its critics, as my story will reveal. How does one counter parochialism? Who benefits, who loses from such work? How effective is it in combatting poverty, inequality and other injustices arising from entrenched structural factors in our society? These and other questions about outcomes from the work were the focus for much Marxist critique in the 1970s and 1980s, a critique which troubled my socialist conscience. Was this locality-based community work I was doing just keeping people happy whilst glossing over and doing nothing about the structural factors which led to inequalities?[1] In apparent contradiction, and contributing to the complexity of my reflections, I could point to multiple positive outcomes, articulated by local people, about changes in their lives arising from their involvement in community activity.[2]

The catchcry 'think global, act local', popular at the time, could

[1] L. Bryson and M. Mowbray (1981), ' "Community": the Spray on Solution', *Australian Journal of Social Issues* 16(4), 255-267; and M. Mowbray, 'The medicinal properties of localism: a historical perspective'. In R. Thorpe and J. Petruchenia, *Community Work or Social Change? An Australian Perspective* (Routledge and Kegan Paul, 1985), 44-58.
[2] See for example, M. Lane, 'Community Work, Social Change and Women'. In J. Petruchenia and R. Thorpe, *Social Change and Social Welfare Practice* (Hale and Iremonger, 1990), 166-179.

well describe much of the work. The focus was on neighbourhood work but one which placed that work into a broader theoretical, political, economic, social and environmental context. Whilst starting with people's lived experience, a global mindset promoted critical analysis of the work and led to endeavours to link up local struggles with broader movements for change. The mule ride lends a useful metaphor; those local struggles revealed the bigger picture of what was happening in society and what needed to be done to improve the lives of disadvantaged groups. Perhaps the metaphor can now be extended: can a 'ride' through some happenings of the 1960s – 1990s reveal what is worth knowing in the 21st century? This is an open question for readers.

Learning community organising: Mule rides in local activism

It was no co-incidence that I was attracted to an activist approach in social work. I was an idealistic kid, with an anti-authoritarian streak and forever on the side of the underdog. Added to positive family and school influences was a church allegiance which espoused a radical theology embedded in the pursuit of social justice – a 'Samaritan' and socialistic way of viewing the world and acting in it. After graduating from Sydney University in Social Work and working as a caseworker at a welfare agency, I left to have a baby. In that first paid job, I learned that focussing on family and individual inadequacies (as was the emphasis at the time), was not the direction I wished to take in social work. It wasn't yet clear to me though, where an alternative direction might lie; community work, for example, had not even featured in the social work course I'd completed.

My continuing education took off though, via the 'university of life'. For 18 years, I was out of the paid workforce rearing children, an experience which far from putting me into an isolated space as a mother in a semi-rural area, provided opportunity for a rich life in community activities. My life expanded dramatically from the moment I took our eldest child along to start school at West Pennant Hills Public School, in 1962.[3] I have told a story elsewhere about my involvement in the community use of schools and other local social movements, activities influenced by the global social movements of the 1960s and 1970s, particularly the feminist, civil rights and peace movements.[4] This was a time of challenges to established social relations, including demands for greater citizen participation in government decision making. Suffice here to emphasise that it was through participation in local activism that I learned the processes of community organising, along with the importance of linking local work with wider action and thinking. It was a 'mule ride' which gave me most, if perhaps not all, I would need to know in my later community development work. I borrow words I've used in a longer story about the work to draw out the point:

> The rough and tumble of everyday family and neighbourhood life and the levelling experiences shared with other women – of birthing; of wiping bottoms and noses between the snatched pieces of conversation about the state of the world, or how to set up a local playgroup (the local and global all mixed together!); and of being a one-income family – taught me much about myself, about relationships, about how society works and about how to achieve change.
>
> If I had to single out one significant message from these years it would be this: there is no learning experience better than being involved in such rough and tumble grassroots activities. It was here that I learned the power of col-

[3] M. Lane in P. Smith, *West Pennant Hills Public School Sesquicentenary 1850-2000* (West Pennant Hills Public School P&C Association Inc. 2000), 154-156.
[4] M. Lane, *People Power Participation: Living Community Development* (Borderlands Cooperative, 2013), 23-39.

lectivity and the nuts and bolts of community organising. I learned the value of delegating and sharing power: about how this promotes participation and releases people's skills, how it lessens conflict and leads to positive ways of dealing with conflicts of interest, how it is more efficient in the long-term because more people are involved and are using their knowledge and abilities. It was here, also, that I experienced a freedom as an active citizen about what I did and how, something which was not always possible in later work as a paid employee.[5]

Community health and community development: Taking the mule to Western Sydney

During those years out of the paid workforce, I kept in touch with what was happening in social work through a refresher course at Sydney University in the late 1960s and through reading social work journals. It was the US Journal, *Social Work*, which particularly excited me with its articles about community organisation and the civil rights movement.[6] I knew by then where my future in social work lay – in community work.

Ideas and values associated with the social movements fell on fertile ground for me, prioritising as they did, commitment to social justice, participatory democracy and non-violence. In 1974, inspired by these ideas and values and by my experiences in the area in which I lived, I went off to my first job in paid community work.[7] Mount Druitt Community Health Centre in western Sydney was the base, soon to become the Mt Druitt Polyclinic, the second multi-purpose, multi-disciplinary community health centre set up in Australia. "Come and do in Mount Druitt what you've

---

[5] Ibid., 28-29.

[6] For example, A. J. Vattano (1972), 'Power to the People: Self-help Groups' *Social Work*, 17(4), 7-15.

[7] For a fuller story about the work at Mt Druitt, see M. Lane, op. cit., (2013), 41-53.

been doing in the Hills", said the doctor in charge of the centre. No job description, just faith in activism and development work, a visionary indeed, to whom I am forever grateful! It was the Whitlam years, 'the sky was the limit', and many of us believed that the political context allowed us to achieve anything, so long as it was aimed at lessening disadvantage.

The Mt Druitt area was at that time expanding rapidly, a great deal of the expansion due to the public housing estates being built by the NSW government. Predominantly, it was an area of families with young children, the average age of the population in 1974 being 11 years. Many of these families were struggling financially and were isolated from the family and friendship networks they had left behind in their move to outer western Sydney.[8] In spite of the needs, services were appallingly scarce. There was much to be done.

Officially, my job was titled 'community social worker', a position I held for five and a half years. There was strong support, within and outside the organisation for a community development approach to the work. Not surprisingly, when one considers the influences flowing from the social movements, it was a time in which social and preventive approaches to health were being forcefully articulated within government and within the health professions.[9] The team I was in reflected that context and, as well as myself, included a youth and recreation worker and a health education worker. In writing about the work I have described our approach as follows:

> Ours was a social conceptualisation of health, which linked
> poor health with poverty, unemployment, social isolation,

[8] The social isolation of many families was vividly brought home to me one day when a young mother said to me "Mary, our true poverty is lack of a friend".

[9] Powerful advocates for community health approaches included Dr Gary Andrews, Health Commissioner of NSW, 1976-1979, and Dr Sidney Sax, Head of the Hospitals and Health Services Commission, 1972-1978.

poor access to information and services, lack of educational opportunities and poor urban planning. This social conceptualisation led to a focus on what was labelled 'preventive' community health interventions: tackling the adverse
social and economic factors which we saw as contributing
to poor health outcomes; in positive terms, seeking conditions of existence which would contribute to good health
and life chances.[10]

The locally focussed action we undertook with residents was
linked to a broader 'global' way of thinking which helped to make
sense of the work. Action was conceptualised in a broader framework. We received much support from others involved in developmental and preventive work, notably the generalist community nurses who were based in every primary school and whose
job descriptions included community work. Widespread emphasis
throughout Australia on 'community' and on consumer/citizen
participation also meant that people from other government departments in NSW, particularly those of Housing, Education, and
Youth and Community Services, looked favourably upon community development and worked closely with us on many projects.
The value of alliances with people of like mind was evident – enriching ideas, strengthening actions.

Although there was accountability to the head of the Polyclinic
and ultimately to the hierarchy of the Western Sydney Health Commission, I was allowed much leeway in what I did and the way I
did it. I think the huge support of local people, hundreds of whom
became involved in community activities, was an important factor
contributing to the freedom I had. Certainly, there were times in
which I was 'carpeted' by my boss for being too publicly activist,
particularly when he feared that criticism of government policies
might adversely affect Polyclinic funding. Supporting and empow-

---

[10] M. Lane, op. cit., (2013), 43.

ering local leadership, a crucial aspect of effective community development, was a way of making myself less obvious in the public domain. Although sometimes at the forefront of action, particularly in the initial stages of contacting and drawing people together around an issue, I would describe my primary role in terms classically associated with community development, that is, the enabler. It was a process of promoting opportunities for people to express their needs and aspirations, and of building trust and confidence so that they might join with others to take action around shared concerns.

Encouraging wide participation involved endless contacting and careful listening, keeping an 'ear to the ground', seeking to avoid any tendency to prioritise the loudest voices or push one's own ideas. Informality was a key aspect, as the following emphasises:

> Participation was encouraged when people could meet in homes or other familiar surroundings where they felt comfortable to bring their children and confident enough to voice their concerns. Meetings were frequently held around kitchen tables with children playing, eating and being cuddled. Attending to squabbles and falls, and handing out vegemite sandwiches was part of the planning process. Amidst the noise, and sustained by endless cups of coffee, solidarity was forged and decisions made.[11]

Outcomes associated with this locality-based action included a proliferation of community managed services and mutual interest groups, a strengthening of informal networks of care and friendship, and increases in the organisational and political skills of many residents.[12] The latter highlighted that whilst much of the work was about the gaining of services and facilities, it was more than that. Involvement in community action politicised local people.

---

[11] Ibid., 46.

[12] Ibid., 46-47.

Community development was political work, promoting democracy through citizen participation in decision making about local issues, and building the confidence and ability to dissent when action was required to challenge injustices. Reflecting upon the impact of the work, I could acknowledge these positive outcomes in the lives of local people. But I was also aware of the limitations of locality-based work in reducing the adverse 'global' factors which were associated with material disadvantage and political powerlessness, such as the continuing exclusion of residents from *major* decision making arenas.[13]

Are mule rides enough? Action research and evaluation

It was with these challenging questions in mind that I returned to Sydney University in 1980 to study for a Masters degree. It was a time of great change in the social work course at Sydney, with emphasis now on activism, the pursuit of social justice and 'radical social work'. Community work was an integral part of the curriculum. Fortuitously for me, Ros Thorpe, one of the instigators of the changes, was my supervisor. She introduced me to the latest critiques of community work, many of these arising in the UK from where she came.[14]

At the same time, I was keen to keep my hand in at the 'grassroots'. I applied to job share a community development position in a three-year action research project in the Penrith area in western Sydney. This was another opportunity to evaluate the impact of

[13] M. Lane, 'Community Work in Sydney's Outer Western Suburbs'. In R. Thorpe and J. Petruchenia, *Community Work or Social Change? An Australian Perspective* (Routledge and Kegan Paul, 1985), 61-80.

[14] For example, J. Benington, 'The Flaw in the Pluralist Heaven: Changing Strategies in the Coventry CDP'. In R. Lees and G. Smith, *Action-Research in Community Development* (Routledge and Kegan Paul, 1975) 174-187; and M. Mayo, 'Beyond CDP: Reaction and Community Action'. In M. Brake and R. Bailey (eds), *Radical Social Work and Practice* (Edward Arnold, 1980), 182-196.

locality-based community work and its effectiveness in achieving sustainable change for disadvantaged people. It was to this project that I now moved. Based in St Clair, a new estate in the Penrith Local Government Area, the project was funded by the Federal Office of Child Care and run by Future Lobby, a community organisation concerned with childcare issues. The primary purpose was to undertake, and to evaluate, community development as a means of meeting the childcare needs of families. Whilst the focus was on childcare, this was always placed within a broader context, allowing us to pursue a diverse agenda tackling a range of issues which affected families with young children.

I came with somewhat different expectations than when I had started at Mt Druitt. I was wiser politically and ever more aware that effective local activism called for linkages with activists and policy makers elsewhere. My life experience had been further enriched by membership of the Family Law Council of Australia (1976-1979) where I was able to speak up for western Sydney in a national body.[15] Important though it was to take local and regional concerns to decision makers beyond the area in which I was working day by day, I found that *acting* as well as *thinking* globally was a hard thing to do, time and energy wise – for local people as much as for me. Hard as it was though, St Clair reinforced the need to work on many fronts. When we arrived, the estate was just three years old. It already housed about 3,000 people, with continued and extensive housing development still planned by the State Government. In spite of this rapid growth, the place was completely devoid of services, facilities and community groups. Red roofed isolation; unfortunately, a common picture of the developer-led, politically expedient planning in NSW.

We made a start with the immediate issues, as had been the case

---

[15] Membership of the National Women's Advisory Council (NATWAC) in 1981-1983, provided further opportunity to advocate for western Sydney in a federal sphere.

in Mt Druitt. The early months entailed extensive locality-based work: going out to people, meeting them in their houses (there were no community or child care centres, schools, or other venues in which we might also meet), listening to their concerns, building trust and assessing their interest in joining with others to do something about their conditions of existence. It wasn't long before mutual interest groups, such as playgroups, sporting groups, community arts, a community newsletter and a visiting programme were formed. Work began on more difficult issues including the gaining of 'bricks and mortar' facilities and of community-based workers such as community nurses and youth workers. Whilst focussing on the problems before us, it was always clear, however, that St Clair was just one of many new housing developments in NSW facing this situation. Why then should St Clair be prioritised, singled out as more deserving? Here was a widespread urban planning problem calling for regional, state and federal action. It was in this context that the value of alliances was again underlined, not only as a means of countering parochialism and competition between needy areas, but to increase the power of advocacy aimed at tackling factors associated with that neediness, notably poor planning and the exclusion of citizens from planning processes. In alliance, people from different neighbourhoods were able to recognise that there were similar problems elsewhere. They were then able to work out priorities for action, rather than necessarily putting their own needs first.

Community groups from various neighbourhoods across the Penrith Local Government Area built alliances in their efforts to gain locality-based services, such as childcare and community nurses. In the bigger picture, seeking changes to policies called for alliances beyond local government areas. This could take many forms, and could be forged through everyday relationships with people in government, community and business organisations, as well as through involvement in groups set up for the express purpose of strengthening advocacy. Community workers also formed alliances amongst themselves. The Community Workers Action Group, formed during this time, provides just one example. A small group of five, including myself, all of whom had backgrounds of working in new housing estates in Sydney, provided an opportunity to work collectively on thinking through, and acting upon, broad issues affecting our work – particularly those associated with poor urban planning. Writing papers, lobbying decision makers, presenting ideas at conferences, using the media, were all part of the group's work. An important side effect was the friendship and fun the group offered, sustaining us in the frequently frustrating work of trying to influence public policy.

The return to university proved enriching in 'thinking globally' about my work. The explanatory power of Marxist critiques sharpened my thinking about how society works, but gave little credence to the contribution community development might make to the building of a socially just, participatory society. Democratic socialist[16] and feminist [17] ideas offered more possibilities. Emphasis here was on 'bottom up' cultural change as a means of achieving a fair society. The 'grass-roots' was where meaningful participatory democracy could be learned, where co-operation and respect for diversity could be encouraged. Focussing on the potential of community development to effect change for women, feminists saw that joining up with others in mutual interest and action groups was often the first step out of the home; a means of building confidence, solidarity, and organisational skills. They argued that starting with lived experience, turning personal concerns into public

[16] Particularly helpful were ideas expounded by Dennis Altman and Raewyn Connell. See, for example, D. Altman, *Rehearsals for Change: Politics and Culture in Australia*, (Fontana, 1980); and R. Connell, *Socialism and Labor: an Australian Strategy* (Labor Praxis Publications, 1978).
[17] C. Cockburn, 'When Women Get Involved in Community Action'. In M. Mayo (ed), *Women in the Community* (Routledge and Kegan Paul, 1977), 61-70.

issues, was political work; 'the personal is political' notion. Ideas such as these, renewed my belief in the potential of neighbourhood community development.

It was in the early 1980s that the influences of the green movement were coming to the fore in my thinking and practices. Here, perhaps even more than with any other issue, was realisation that 'thinking global acting local' needed to be expanded to include *acting global*. Fostering a healthy planet called for action at local, national and international levels! A challenge indeed for locality-based community development, but one which once again underlined the value of linking local efforts, theoretically and practically, with broader movements. I began to explore the rich field of environmentalist thought. As had happened with other issues, such as childcare, my life experience beyond the places of my community development work, contributed to my understandings. Involvement with the Hills Environment Forum in the area in which I lived, provided a wealth of ideas about environmentalism and urban planning. Once again, various aspects of my life were all linked together.

Academia: Mule rides and linkages

In 1983, I joined the staff of the Social Work Department at Sydney University. I adopted a 'learning through doing' approach to teaching community work, often partnering with practitioners to directly involve students in field projects. We took up our own project in the class of '85, seeking the promotion of peace studies at Sydney University. Our efforts developed into a local (university-based) social movement which soon, however, saw us thinking and acting in broader arenas as we delved into peace theories and made contact with peace activists beyond the university. The outcome was the setting up in 1988 of the Centre for Peace and Conflict Studies, a local outcome with 'global' ramifications.

My job in the Department allowed me to continue connections with front-line work through various projects the University forged with community-based organisations. Part of the job during 1984-1986 was to run a community work student unit in western Sydney, based within the Western Sydney Area Assistance Scheme (WSAAS) at Parramatta; and in 1987-1992, my position included that of community work consultant at Fairfield Community Resource Centre (FCRC). Both projects arose through belief in the value of alliance between organisations with mutual purposes, in this case, the teaching of students, the continuing education of field workers, and the pursuit of research. Focus of the work at both WSAAS and FCRC was again on locality-based community development. At Fairfield particularly, this involved a good deal of research and evaluation, much of which was documented for wider distribution.[18] At that time, the Fairfield Local Government Area was labelled 'the most multicultural LGA in Australia'. The population was extremely diverse – 98 language groups being identified whilst I was there – and many people were immigrants and refugees from war-torn areas. The pressing needs called for intensive developmental work aimed at gaining appropriate and accessible services and facilities, and at building trust and respect for difference, that is, at building what Eva Cox has called 'a truly civil society'.[19] I witnessed some very skilful community work, mostly focussed around particular neighbourhoods and their particular needs, but also concerned with a bigger picture; for example, working across neighbourhoods to tackle widespread employment and environmental problems.

I mention just a few examples of the work to further explore the

---

[18] For example, M. Lane (1990), 'Community Work with Immigrant Groups', *Australian Social Work* 43(3), 33-38; and K. Henry and M. Lane, *Once Upon a Time ... Stories about Community Work* (Local Community Services Association, Sydney 1993).
[19] E. Cox, *A Truly Civil Society*, 1995 Boyer Lectures (ABC Books, 1995).

global/local theme. I think immediately of Deb Roach's work at Wetherill Park, classic neighbourhood work which acknowledged differences amongst people whilst also bringing them together around shared concerns and interests;[20] Linda Livingstone's work tackling racism at Greenfield Park;[21] Jon Christley and the crime and violence project at Villawood, where an empowering, social development approach was taken rather than a punitive one;[22] and Daphne Cazalet's ground-breaking community arts work which saw women from non-English speaking backgrounds coming out of their homes to take part in collective arts projects.[23] Daphne's work was particularly significant in broadening my understanding of the power of grass-roots arts work to achieve cultural change. These and many other neighbourhood-based community workers with whom I worked at FCRC were thinking (and often acting) globally whilst they acted locally. It's uplifting to remember that they achieved so much in spite of the broader, global influences of economic rationalism and managerialism which Australian governments of all persuasions were embracing – a significant threat to the ability of community development to maintain an activist, participatory orientation. Funding of such approaches was being largely replaced by projects which saw community work as an arm of government and community workers as service managers implementing government agendas.

---

[20] M. Lane, *It's a Tightrope Juggling Trick: Community Work*, video and study guide, (Department of Social Work and Social Policy University of Sydney 1989).

[21] L. Livingstone, 'Anti Racist Practice'. In K. Henry and M. Lane, op. cit. (1993) 24-26.

[22] M. Lane and K. Henry (2001), 'Community Development, Crime and Violence'. *Community Development Journal*, 36(3), 212-222.

[23] M. Lane, *Memory and Imagination: Community Arts, Community Development*, video and study guide, (Department of Social Work and Social Policy University of Sydney 1991).

The future: Things worth knowing

What relevance for today are these stories about activist-oriented community development from previous times? Is anything constant? Has anything lasted? The questions arise in the context also, of postmodern interpretations which emphasise the transitory nature of experience. My fascination with postmodern critiques began in the late 1980s.[24] Whilst disturbing, they tuned into my ongoing reflections about the impact of community development. At first it was difficult to reconcile postmodernism with the modernist values, theories and practices which had guided my work over many years. Postmodern perspectives eschewed universal blueprints for action and explanatory theories; everything was uncertain. How then would we act or explain our actions?

Postmodernism could be seen as destructive, but amidst the challenges, I found aspects that sat well with the way I conceptualised community work, particularly in the Fairfield area. I think, for example, of the emphasis in postmodernism on diversity and difference (the complexity of 'community'), on context and the 'local'. Messages I picked up from postmodernism again confirmed for me the importance for community work of tuning into the lived experience of people in their particular contexts, being careful not to translate ideas from one place to another as if 'one size fits all', and listening carefully to different interpretations of need, aspirations and ways of doing things.

As I see it, a postmodern notion is to both act *and* think locally. This seems a limited approach given world-wide problems such as global warming, the devastation of ecosystems, and constant warfare in many parts of the planet, all of which call for urgent global responses involving cooperation between nations. Nevertheless, it is at local level in which global problems are played out, and they

---

[24] M. Lane, op. cit. (2013) 119.

need to be dealt with locally as well as globally. As a way forward, I suggest we still hold to modernist values and principles (social justice, participatory democracy, respect for difference) acknowledging that the meaning of these concepts needs to be negotiated in particular contexts; prioritise local knowledge and experience, acting flexibly and responsively to particular local contexts; and strengthen local work by linking it with broader movements and agendas. At the same time, we can draw hope and enlightenment from stories of locality-based, outward looking, activist-oriented work from previous decades.

My journey has been a long one; community development work has provided me with diverse experiences and taken me to many different spaces. But at the core of the work, what has been worth knowing is what I learned in those multiple, often tiny, 'mule rides' in neighbourhoods. In emphasising the link between those mule rides and global issues, I recall the words of Rosa Luxemburg: "It is in the tiny struggles of individual people that the great movements of history are most truly revealed".[25] These are apt words for my stories of tiny struggles in some Sydney neighbourhoods

---

[25] I wrote down these words when I was reading Rosa Luxemburg many years ago. Unfortunately, I haven't recorded details of the source. Luxemburg is described by the *Encyclopaedia Britannica* as a Polish-born German revolutionary who 'developed a humanitarian theory of Marxism, stressing democracy and revolutionary mass action to achieve international socialism'. (www.britannica.com/biography/Rosa-Luxemburg)

18

WORKING ON THE FRONTIERS OF NEOLIBERAL AND RACIST INDIFFERENCE

John Tomlinson

The mid-1960s was a time when social work seemed to offer the opportunity to be part of a struggle for an extension of the welfare state and to confront racism directed towards Indigenous Australians. After graduating from the University of Queensland, I worked in Brisbane with the Department responsible for Social Security for nine months. My clients were mainly single mothers, unemployed or homeless people. I transferred to the Welfare Branch in Darwin, where many of the people I worked with were of Aboriginal descent. I returned to Social Services in 1968 disillusioned by the bureaucratic obstructionism placed in the way of genuine improvements in the way people were treated. This was the background to a life-long determination to work towards ending poverty, homelessness, violence against vulnerable people, exploitation, war, racism, and alienation. On that journey, I had to learn to listen, overcome as best I could my inner fears, to gain from formal education, to be prepared to put myself on the line, and help others to organise. On the way, I have met many people who may not have had much money or power but who were prepared to contribute what they could to the common good.

Student days

After matriculation at night school and enrolling part-time in science for a year, I gave up working for the Department of Agriculture and Stock and transferred to studying social work full-time. I joined the radical Student Action group and learnt how to organise. Hazel Smith, a socialist committed to social justice, was Head of the Social Work School at the University of Queensland. She introduced me to Kath Walker (Oodgeroo Noonuccal), Secretary of the Queensland Aboriginal Advancement League, and a member of the Federal Executive of what was then called the Federal Council for Aboriginal Advancement and later came to be known as the Federal Council for the Advancement of Aborigines and Torres Strait Islanders.[1] Kath was to become a bestselling poet. She encouraged me in 1963 to visit a number of Indigenous communities on Cape York, including Yarrabah, Hopevale, Mareeba, Kuranda and Bloomfield River in a 5-week sojourn, hitching lifts, jumping on a government ferry to Yarrabah (at the very last minute) and riding trains, to see what ordinary community members understood about the changes the Country Liberal Parties were intending to introduce on Aboriginal communities in Queensland.

The trip was a great eye opener to me, I was just 21 years old. I got to sit with Aboriginal and Torres Strait Islanders and discuss what they knew and what they wanted to happen. They wanted the system of police and superintendents – the "Protector" system discontinued. They wanted the government and the mission to be prevented from forcing their children into dormitories. They wanted the paternalist assimilation regime stopped and they wanted the nutritionally inadequate ration system replaced by something better. Importantly, they wanted to chart their own futures. I returned and duly reported my findings to Kath. In those days the Queensland Department responsible was called the Department of Native Affairs. University of Queensland researcher, Roslyn Kidd[2], esti-

---

[1] S. Taffe, *Black and White Together FCAATSI: The Federal Council for the Advancement of Aborigines and Torres Strait Islanders 1958-72.* (University of Queensland, 2005).
[2] R. Kidd, *The Way We Civilise* (University of Queensland, 1997).

mates that the "Protectors" – police, mission and government superintendents and the Government itself – stole over $500 million from Indigenous people's bank accounts which they held in trust.

In my final year in social work, we had a visit from the state Director of Social Services, who outlined the benefit, allowance and pension system. I specifically remember getting into a heated exchange with him after he told us that Invalid Pensions (now termed Disability Support Pension) were only paid on the basis of *medical* disability and that people had to be 85% "permanently *medically* incapacitated". I argued strongly that people's total incapacity should be taken into account – including psychological conditions, personality disorders, lack of education, lack of bureaucratic or other skills. Eventually, one of the university lecturers told me to shut up.

Professional employment

My first job was with the social work section of the Department of Social Services, where the officer is charge was Ella Webb, an inveterate punter on the horses. In the first interview I had with her she said:

> John you must understand that we can only assist clients of the Department who have an eligibility for a benefit, allowance or a pension. If I hear you have interviewed someone who is in considerable financial need and for whom you can't find an appropriate payment, you'll have to answer to me.

Ella subsequently became the senior social worker for the whole Commonwealth department and I remained in touch with her long after her retirement.

In line with Ella's injunction, I employed two main strategies:

> Firstly, there existed a special benefit which allowed people, without funds, who would qualify for a payment

from the Department, but who had not met a specific eligibility requirement (for example not having been a resident for long enough or having no previous work history) to be paid the special benefit in lieu of the payment for which they would otherwise qualify.

Secondly, if a client was refused payment, I would appeal against that decision often to head office in Canberra.

Both the special benefit and the internal appeals by staff have largely disappeared from current practice. There was one other appeal system which I employed in difficult cases and that was to encourage the client to get their local member of parliament to approach the Minister for Social Services.

Life in the Top End

After nine months, I left for the Darwin office of the Welfare Branch of the Department of the Interior. The year was 1965. TV had not yet arrived in the town. About 20,000 people lived in there; one in eight were Greek and there was a substantial Asian population. Many people of partial Aboriginal descent lived in houses. Some Aboriginal people lived on Bagot Aboriginal Reserve or in the long grass. Some people of total Aboriginal descent were living in housing commission houses. There were also Territorians from many parts of Europe. About a third of the public servants were replaced every three years.

The Branch, itself, was the greatest culture shock for me after the discipline of Social Services. There were no fixed rates of assistance. People living on government settlements (and who worked) were paid a training allowance at a rate lower than they would receive if living in town and being provided with welfare assistance. The rate of assistance provided to those in town was inconsistent, depending on which welfare officer they saw. Aboriginal families fostering the children of family members were seldom paid, and if paid they were paid at a lower rate than white families. The justification given by senior officers at the time was that it cost less to raise an Aboriginal child in an Aboriginal household.

Many of the welfare workers became good friends. Babe Damaso,[3] who was born in Borroloola and had a father from the Philippines and an Aboriginal mother from the area became my mentor. He taught me many things about Indigenous life. He also enhanced my cooking and fishing skills. He even attempted to teach me how to make my way in the Branch. I had many disputes with senior officers in the Branch whilst trying to get them to codify the rates of payments, and modify the circumstances in which the Branch would assist and so forth.

In 1968, I returned to Social Services in Brisbane feeling I had failed to achieve anything in the best part of three years. Once there, I enrolled in Anthropology 3 in order to complete the Arts degree for which I had been studying part-time and externally. The following year I enrolled in Anthropology/Sociology Honours. My thesis attempted to synthesise the democratic conundrum of Alex de Tocqueville's "tyranny of democracy" and Robert Michel's "iron law of oligarchy". I was awarded 2A Honours and was granted a two-year full-time Commonwealth Public Service Scholarship to undertake a research master's degree to see if community work could assist the Aboriginal and Torres Strait Islanders living in South Brisbane to achieve their aims.

Whilst working with the Indigenous community living in a run-down suburb, I saw a community which had been used to being stood over and harassed by racists (who lived in the area) come to achieve a degree of agency they had not previously experienced.

[3] J. Tomlinson, 'Damaso, Basilo Victor (Babe)', *Northern Territory Dictionary of Biography*. Volume 3, (NTU Press, 1996), 67-70.

The community raised funds by holding Barbeques, Kup-Murri, and Hangis for the Born Free Club to provide a headquarters – somewhere to meet and play pool (outside of the hotels) and to shelter many of the homeless people in the area. They confronted racist publicans and police in a non-violent manner using only their community power. By the end of the 20th century, the Born Free Club was running three hostels for the Indigenous community of the area. A short account of the work can be found in a University of Queensland publication edited by Harry Throssell.[4]

Contemporaneously with my work in South Brisbane, I set out to organise clients of the State Department of Children's Services in Inala and Redcliffe to force Children's Services to codify the payments it made to single parents who did not qualify for a Widow's Pension. We came together under the name of "Client Power". As a group, we confronted what we called "the bed sniffers". They were inquiry officers dispatched by the Department to see if any of the women had a man in the house. The women, their children and junior staff of the University of Queensland Social Work Department staged a number of sit-ins in the waiting area of the Department's head office. Details of this struggle can also be found in Harry Throssell's book.[5]

My favourite memory of these sit-ins was when my parents, dressed up for a day in the city, called in to see me. I had told Mum where I'd be if she wanted to catch up. The Senior Sergeant given the mission of guarding the Children's Services staff from such a dan-

---

[4] J. Tomlinson, 'The Blacks in South Brisbane Are Just a Mob of Metho-Drinking No-Hopers.' In H. Throssell (ed), *Radical Social Work in Queensland* (University of Queensland, 1975), 137-153.
[5] J. Tomlinson, 'Client Power: The Process of helping Clients Organise to Gain Their Welfare Rights.' In H. Throssell (ed), *Radical Social Work in Queensland* (University of Queensland, 1975) 'Client Power Manifesto: an open letter to our politicians.' In H. Throssell (ed), *Social Work: Radical Essays* (University of Queensland Press, 1975), 125-136.

gerous crew was, Teddy Dundas, with whom I'd been to school. We had both been studiously ignoring each other. My father had taught him. Mum walked in and announced that the street was full of police and then walked over to Teddy and said "Now Teddy if there is any trouble I want you to look after John." Our secret was out.

Back to the Top End

I returned to Darwin in late 1973 with my first promotion to Class 2 acting 3 in charge of welfare delivery to the Top End of the Northern Territory. The Whitlam Labor Government had finally broken 23 years of conservative rule by Sir Robert Menzies and those more inadequate prime ministers who came after him. Harry Guise, Director of the Welfare Branch since the mid-1950s, brother-in-law of Sir Paul Hasluck, a minister in the Menzies Government, had been removed from line control.

All was going well until one of the young social workers brought a file to my attention. The file dealt with a 7-year-old girl from Cadell River, an outstation 40 kilometres from Maningrida in Arnhem land who was living with a white foster family in Darwin. Her natural parents had been attempting to regain custody and I wrote on the file that I was determined that she would return to her natural parents.

I worked with the superintendent at Maningrida, some social work colleagues and the Director of Aboriginal Legal Aid, Bill Ryan, whose mother was Gurindji and his father a European. Bill had been brought up by white missionaries at Crocker Island. It was agreed that Bill would charter a plane to bring the young girl's father and brother to town, I handed her over to her father and she flew to Maningrida and then travelled home to Cadell River. I was subsequently demoted to social worker class one and a few months later the forces of reaction replaced Bill Ryan as Director of Aboriginal Legal Aid. The full story can be found at Chapter 2 of *Subversive Action: Extralegal Practices for Social Justice*, edited by Nilan Yu and Deena Mandell.[6]

I was relocated to a small office and given no duties, and so after catching up on my backlog of unread social work journals. I began a research project examining the malpractices in welfare administration in the Branch. I communicated these to the responsible minister and to Prime Minister Whitlam.

In late 1974, a group of us, who were concerned about the way police behaved towards poor people in general and Aboriginal people in particular, decided we should establish the Northern Territory Council for Civil Liberties. We circulated leaflets around the town inviting people to come to a meeting at Brown's Mart to discuss the idea of starting a Council for Civil Liberties. We were initially delighted when about 200 well-dressed people turned up. But what we did not know was that Brown's Mart was just across the road from the Police Union headquarters and that there had been a union meeting there earlier in the night.

To our horror, the meeting elected either police or magistrates to every position, with a senior police officer being elected Secretary. The only motion our group got up was that the Interim Committee was to report back at a further public meeting *at Brown's Mart, on a specified date and at an appointed time*. Cyclone Tracy intervened on Christmas Eve, unroofing Browns Mart and collapsing some of the walls. In the *NT News* on the day of the specified date an advertisement appeared declaring the meeting of the Council to have been cancelled. Not deterred our intrepid crew including one progressive magistrate entered the damaged building at the appointed time. I moved a motion thanking the Interim Committee for their

---

[6] J. Tomlinson, 'Challenging State Aggression against Indigenous Australians.' In N. Yu and D. Mandell (eds), *Subversive Action: Extralegal Practices for Social Justice* (Wilfrid Laurier, 2015).

magnificent achievements and setting up a permanent Council for Civil Liberties which would be elected henceforth. This Council attempted for about a decade to improve policing in the Northern Territory.

Several Larrakia, assisted by Bill Day, the Waterside Workers Union and others, had long campaigned for Kulaluk to be given back to the Larrakia. During one demonstration, a firebomb landed in a surveyor's utility which burnt. Fred Fogarty, an Aboriginal man from Central New South Wales, was subsequently imprisoned for throwing the bomb. A few of us paid for black and white bumper stickers saying "Free Fred Fogarty Political Prisoner." The stickers arrived about three weeks before Christmas in 1974.

We distributed the stickers amongst Fred's supporters and I managed to get several posted on the Fannie Bay Jail walls. Cyclone Tracy arrived on Christmas Eve and destroyed many of the houses and other buildings in Darwin including a lot of Fannie Bay Jail. All prisoners with less than six months to serve were released to help with the required clean-up of the town. Getting Fred out of jail, we reckoned, was one of the quickest victories we had.

After the cyclone, I ran the relief centre in the Northern Suburbs, the most devastated part of the town. Under the auspices of the Australian Assistance Plan, a Regional Council for Social Development was established and I became the social planner in 1975. We set up play centres for children to give them and their parents somewhere safe to meet. We established a welfare union which, subsequently was transformed into the Coalition of Low Income Earners (COLIE). After a couple of weeks, I remember mentioning at a meeting that even though we had only been going a short while we already had a dog and a vegetable named after us. COLIE went on to organise a low income housing organisation for many years. We also set up a squatters union, and a homemaker service to assist Aboriginal families whom the Housing Commission had refused to rehouse. We wanted to convince the Commission that whatever had occurred in the past they were ready for public housing. The Welfare Branch eventually took over the running of the Homemaker Service.

The Darwin Reconstruction Commission was headed by Clem Jones, who gave the Regional Council a demountable to operate from in the Northern Suburbs. After the handover, Clem said he had an hour to fill in before his next appointment. I suggested retiring to the Marrarah Hotel which had ice cold beer. Over a couple of beers, I told Clem some of the horror stories about Essington House, a juvenile remand centre just across the road: the cell blocks of which had been unroofed by cyclone Tracy. Clem told everyone to pile back into their cars and we repaired to Essington House. Clem asked me more about the running of the place whilst his chief engineer and architect went to inspect. They came back and announced that the holding cells were structurally sound and only needed reroofing. "Bullshit" exploded Clem, "I can see the cracks in the wall from here." The Centre was demolished within a couple of days only to be replaced by the infamous Don Dale juvenile prisons.

Four hundred miles to the north of Darwin was the Island of Timor divided between Indonesian West Timor and East Timor. Almost a year after cyclone Tracy, the Indonesian military invaded the Portuguese colony of East Timor, controlled as it was by Fretlin, who had declared independence. The Indonesians invaded Dili, the capital, on 7 December 1975. The Timorese fought back but were quickly forced to retreat into the mountains from where they fought a guerrilla war for the next twenty-four years.

In 1976, one of my friends, Robert Wesley-Smith was organising a boat to take mainly medical supplies and food to East Timor. He asked if I could use my Land Rover to cart some of the supplies, but it was being serviced. I borrowed the Regional Council's Combie van. The boat was intercepted by the Navy and the crew arrested as they attempted to leave Darwin Harbour that night. The next day Customs arrested me and I was charged with "Aiding, abetting, counselling and being concerned with the illegal export of goods." David Scott, the then Director of Community Aid Abroad which had supplied much of the medical equipment, said it was about time a social worker was charged with counselling. After about 18 months, the case was settled and I was fined $50 dollars for being on a quarantine station without permission. The other charges were dropped.

In 1977, I moved to Darwin Community College, now Charles Darwin University, where I set up an Associate Diploma course in Community Work. Some of the struggles my students were associated with included helping to set up the Darwin Unemployed Workers Union, working with COLIE, the fight to stop Ludmilla Creek being turned into a Marina, and the struggle to convince the Community College to build a child crèche on campus.

Whilst at the Community College, I started a small magazine called *Farewell to Alms*.[7] In one edition I published an article, including the photo of the Director of Welfare, which argued he was "murdering Aboriginal children" by restricting access to welfare assistance. The Director of the Welfare Branch was able to determine who would and who would not be assisted because, unlike social security where the type and amount of payment were codified, he had total discretion. In 1975, David Griffiths declared "Discretion as it applies to the present provision of emergency relief is a euphemism for discrimination".[8]

I was charged with criminal libel, the first person in Australia

---

[7] *Farewell to Alms*. (Wobbly Press, 1977-1979) catalogue.nla.gov.au/Record/1175225-ISSN0155-6258

[8] D. Griffiths *Emergency Relief*. (Social Welfare Commission, 1975), 27.

after Frank Hardy[9] to be charged with that offence. After receiving legal advice from a Sydney barrister that while my statistical evidence may have meant that *more* Aboriginal children were dying because of being refused assistance, that this did not *in law* amount to murder of a particular child or children by that man. I had to issue a public apology and the Crown dropped the case. I was then sued for civil libel and paid $5,000 damages to the Director. I subsequently published an article in *Farewell to Alms*[10] stating his tightening of welfare assistance rules was leading to increased deaths amongst Aboriginal children. This was an expensive exercise all round.

In December 1985, the Community Work Associate Diploma course was sent to a committee of the College to be reaccredited. On the day of the hearing time ran out due to delays with other courses and I was informed that an executive committee of the College, consisting of the Principal and the Chairperson, would handle the matter. The course was discontinued in early 1986. I was unemployed. The best option was to return to Murdoch University in the hope of completing my PhD which examined "The political obstacles to the introduction of a guaranteed minimum income in Australia". The PhD was finally awarded in 1989.

Joining the ACT Council of Social Services

In 1987, I was appointed Director of the ACT Council of Social Services. Once there I worked with a series of wonderful executive committees[11]. Our first big struggle was to convince the Federal Government to give Havelock House, an ex-police hostel in the

---

[9] F. Hardy, *The Hard Way: The Story Behind Power Without Glory* (Australasian Book Society, 1961).

[10] *Farewell to Alms,* op. cit., 2, 1978.

[11] J. Tomlinson, 'Community Management.' *Paper given at the National Community Legal Centres Conference in Canberra,* 2 May 1992 (available at http://johntomlinsoncollectedworks.com)

centre of town, estimated, at the time, to be worth $3 million, to the community sector so that it could be converted into 108 units to house low income earners and people with disabilities. Somehow we managed to convince the various Federal Departments involved to give the community the deeds to the building.

Within a year of my arriving in Canberra, self-government was granted to the ACT and Rosemary Follett was elected to lead the Labor Government. The senior ACT administration official Bill Harris, was introduced to me as an unreconstructed Whitlamite. I had fallen on my feet. Rosemary appointed me to the Community Budget Committee to advise the incoming ACT Government on spending priorities, I was also appointed to the Board of Canberra Hospitals. The Canberra press corps was interested in poverty, income security, disability, housing of low income earners and I made the most of that. We were involved in social justice issues with the ACT government. They paid for 50 buses to carry huge 'Child Poverty – Canberra's hidden problem' posters.

Kass Hancock, spearheaded our Child Poverty campaign. She convinced the people in charge of Old Parliament House to allow us to set up a Welfare Maze in the old house. We were the first community group given permission to use Old Parliament House. We had actors playing welfare officials and demonstrating just what a mess our welfare system was and is. Endless bus loads of school kids, welfare operatives by the dozens, lots of ACT and Federal politicians, including Brian Howe the Minister of Social Security, the leader of the Democrats, Ian Sinclair from the Coalition, journalists and TV crews were there in abundance. Brian Howe said he did not want to enter the Maze because he did not want me shouting 'There's Brian Howe caught in the Welfare Maze'. It was bedlam. It generated enormous interest, so much so that we brought out a board game version of it along the lines of Monopoly.

Even when Labor lost government to a coalition of Liberals and community activists, it was possible to maintain good relations with the government. The Minister of Community Services, was Bernard Collaery who remains active, to this day, in assisting East Timor to get a just deal on its oil resources in the Timor Sea. My last meeting prior to leaving Canberra involved sharing a couple of bottles of red wine with Bill Harris at our local wine bar.

Coming back to academia: Queensland University of Technology

After six years as the Director of ACTCOSS I took up a senior Lecturer's position teaching Community Work and Social Policy at QUT's Carseldine Campus. I was hoping to be able to help care for my aging mother and had promised to help her suicide when her Parkinson's Disease got too much for her. When in Canberra I had read this poem of mine on ABC radio during one of the euthanasia debates:

When death comes calling

I lie in bed with poop in my panties,
the nurses grow tired of changing my scanties.
The sheets are stained with urine long past.
I'm treated as if I'm vermin or worse.

The Right to Life forbids that I die.
They'd imprison my son if he were to try
to let me escape my bodily prison
and go to their wonderful Right to Life heaven.[12]

But by the time Parkinson's Disease had made her life very difficult I was not able to get clear instructions. Mum's condition deteriorated and my sister who had been looking after her became ill. Mum had been shifted to Brisbane with another sister but after a couple of weeks she became too great a burden and arrangements

---

[12] J. Tomlinson, unpublished.

were underway for her to be transferred into a nursing home. Then, just before the doctor turned up, she had a stoke which killed her. It was a lucky escape but left me with a sense of impotence. Ever since, I have campaigned for people to be allowed to decide when they should be able to die and for others to be allowed to assist them to die with dignity. I believe it should be possible for people to discuss with doctors whilst they have all or most of their faculties under what conditions they wish to be euthanised. I have a living will. I am also a life member of Exit International, which has to be the ultimate contradiction.

QUT was a busy time, too much to do and too little time to reflect. Much had changed since I had first become an academic; the managerial university had arrived. The National Tertiary Education Union (NTEU) Newsletter in 1994 published my reflections upon this state of affairs:

The Contract

Without fear or favour
Who will be the saviour?
Who will be the one
to save us all?

My contract's up for renewal,
my three years are done;
battles partly started
wars never won.

They talk about efficiency
I think about integrity.
Will anyone employ me?
Is there such a thing as
decency?

No golden handshake at the gate,

no gold watch after fifty years

just a sense of bitterness

futility and tears.[13]

I concentrated on trying to help students, working on unemploy-ment and social security income guarantees, supporting the NTEU and trying to find time to go fishing.

The National Conference on Unemployment which our School had set up settled at the Centre of Full Employment and Equity (CoFEE) at the University of Newcastle. There were the annual de-bates between QUT supporting Basic Income and CoFEE promot-ing Job Guarantees which persevered for the best part of a decade. Our most recent publication was the 2016 Palgrave Macmillian book edited by Jenni Mays, Greg Marston and myself.[14]

Our book attempts to suggest an alternative to the tyranny which welfare operatives inflict on their clients when the welfare system is means-tested and categorical. It suggests that there are better ways of delivering income security than imposing the stench of work-fare and poor law charity into every corner of the client/worker interaction. The book is meant to be an antidote to those politicians who worry more about balancing budgets than assisting the most vulnerable in our society. They are the same people who pontificate about "the end of the age of entitlement", about asylum seekers (ar-riving by boat) presuming on our generosity and those who impose sanctions on Indigenous Australians living in remote Australia for failing to find non-existing jobs. Perhaps they should be made to survive a year without their chauffeur driven cars, inflated salaries and the plethora of overly generous parliamentary perks.

---

[13] J. Tomlinson, The National Tertiary Education Union (NTEU, 1994) *Newsletter*, February.

[14] J. Mays, G. Marston and J. Tomlinson (eds), *Basic Income in Australia and New Zealand: Perspectives from the Neoliberal Frontier* (Palgrave Macmillian, 2016).

The attraction of paying a Basic Income to every permanent resident living in Australia, sufficient to sustain them above the poverty line, as an individual in their own right, irrespective of whether they are employed, seeking employment or not, whether they are married, single, living alone or in combination with others and independent of any other social status is an attractive idea. It is particularly enticing to those who wish to promote liberty and freedom and to all who seek justice for the least advantaged in this country. Anyone wishing to research Basic Income in Australia will find a considerable collection of articles at Basic Income Guarantee Australia and at my collected works websites.[15]

Conclusion

What readers take from this chapter will vary. It is after all a description of one person's attempt to change the world for the better. Each of us has an individual conception of the good life. We live at a specific time and in diverse places. The rules and mores we observe vary with time.

Some of us have not had the privilege of getting to know any Aborigines or Torres Strait Islanders. We may not know any asylum seekers being driven mad in the camps on Manus and Nauru. We may have only had unpleasant experiences with unemployed people.

Some of us have been born into advantaged sections of society and privilege has been our constant companion. Others have struggled with poverty, disability or bad luck. For some education is a breeze, whilst others find it a challenge.

Whatever your circumstances I hope there was something you were able to take away from this chapter and may good luck enhance your every step.

---

[15] Basic Income Guarantee Australia: http://www.basicincome.qut.edu.au; john tomlinsoncollectedworks: http://johntomlinsoncollectedworks.com

19

FROM CHARITY TO INDUSTRY
AND BACK AGAIN?

Confessions of a Socialist Feminist Social Worker

Sharon Moore

Developments in Australian social work between the 1970s to the late 1980s are the focus of this chapter. This was a twenty-year period marked by tremendous social upheavals and, arguably, the coming of age of social work. During this time, those of us active in radical social work education and practice saw our project as one of revitalising and developing civil society and challenging the power of the state. Within and against the state was a common catch cry at the time. We advocated social justice and drew upon social movement theory, while working alongside other protest movements inspired by the revolution in critical social science, class theory and gender politics. We embraced social activism and became involved in social change, through social planning, community development, group work and social action. We took a broader systemic view of social work focusing on the impact of the social structure on the individual, in contrast to the therapeutic practice of earlier periods.

Industrially, many of us became more militant and anti-professional by joining alternative professional groups such as the Australian Social Welfare Union, Women in Welfare Education and Inside Welfare – a Marxist group of welfare workers. Feminism was a major intellectual and personal inspiration due to the dramatic impact of second-wave feminism and it became a radical challenge to women's political, professional and personal lives. Conservative social welfare models were critiqued and we became involved in developing innovative social services. Client perspectives were encouraged as part of the challenge to traditional case work. Our practice was influenced by feminism, Aboriginal land rights and anti-racist theory. As a radical social worker, I was an active and willing participant in this heady period. In fact, it formed my professional and political identity and it has shaped my practice to this day.

Origins of a radical social worker

I was a first year university social work student in 1968. The Vietnam War, the Women's Movement, and left-wing politics were part of my training ground. I studied Social Work somewhat reluctantly, being much more interested at the time in social development and internationalism related to left-wing activism. I soon moved from case work to community work after my first position in public welfare, as I was worn out by the pressures of being 'an agent of social control'. I had attempted to transform correctional social work through critical education and innovative welfare programs, as well as long overdue legal reforms.

Despite some success in changing the 'social control' model in correctional social work, I was tempted back to university to what I hoped would be a different kind of social work. Connie Benn, then Head of Social Work at Phillip Institute (later RMIT University) and my Master of Social Work thesis examiner, offered me a part-time academic role as an action researcher and student unit supervisor at the Western Regional Council for Social Development (WRCSD). Under the auspice of the Australian Assistance Plan, the WRCSD was funded by the Whitlam Labor Government to encourage the development of social infrastructure and services for the western region of Melbourne. The West, as it was known, was an area of working-class struggle and activism with undeveloped community services in its nine local government areas. This was the perfect place for a committed radical social worker to practice what she preached and to educate others in the process. Another part of my role at the WRCSD was social planning that was linked to community development and activism. The job seemed perfect.

My view of radical social work was informed by critical social science and its challenge to traditional orthodoxy in sociology, psychology, health science and education. Marxist class theory and feminism were my tools of analysis. I believed then that social work could be a catalyst for social change, as social workers traditionally worked with oppressed and marginalised people. Radical social work texts at the time argued that social work was in a good position to resist capitalism and organise people to transform society into a more democratic or even socialist state.[1] Because I was aware of the fact that we worked both in, and against, the state, community development and social planning, based on local democracy, seemed to offer a way forward. This was particularly so after having spent five years in public welfare trying to administer state-sanctioned social control programs, often with negative results.

Inspiring mentors

As mentioned above, Connie Benn was an early supporter and mentor of mine. Her left-wing politics and passionate activism accorded with my own views of social work and radical politics. Her leadership of the Brotherhood of St Laurence Family Centre

---

[1] J. Galper, *The Politics of Social Services* (Prentice Hall, 1975); R. Bailey and M. Brake (eds.) *Radical Social Work* (Edward Arnold, 1975).

project from 1971, for more than a decade, was a significant Australian anti-poverty experiment which showed that, given the right resources, supports and opportunities, everyone has the capacity to build a good life. This was a direct challenge to professional orthodoxy about welfare families and the undeserving poor, which remains still part of the dominant discourse of community to this day. Between 1975 and 1982, Connie Benn developed an action research project with a strong focus on employment, family support and social inclusion, leading an organisation abuzz with ideas, innovation and energy. Her ideas still resonate many decades later.[2]

Another long-term friend and mentor was Wendy Weeks, a critical thinker who made ground-breaking contributions to social work education, especially in feminist social work theory and practice in Canada and Australia. Like Connie, Wendy's clarity and intellect were strengthened by her energy and activism. I had the opportunity to develop and teach post-graduate feminist community development subjects with Wendy at Phillip Institute, as well as Social Work and Community Development courses in rural Victoria, in an innovative community services access program. We developed social work subjects to analyse and strategise against sexism and racism and promote multiculturalism. Influenced by Canadian colleague Maurice Moreau[3] amongst others, Wendy led the structural approach to social work practice education at Phillip Institute of Technology, which made a significant and lasting contribution to Australia's radical social work tradition.

Phillip Institute of Technology Social Work School colleagues were a lively mix of radical feminists, socialist feminists and a few profeminist men. Jane Dixon, Vivienne McCutcheon, Mandy

[2] C. Benn, *Action Research Centre Reports* (Brotherhood of St Laurence, 1972-75).
[3] M. Moreau, 'Empowerment through Advocacy and Consciousness-Raising: Implications of a Structural Approach to Social Work' (1976), *Journal of Sociology and Social Welfare*, 17(2) 78-94.

Press, Derryn Wilson, John Wisemen, Bob Pease and Gary Hough were comrades and friends from PIT alongside other activists, including Linda Briskman, active in indigenous, refugee and asylum seeker issues and Hurriyet Babacan, a Kurdish social work activist and academic.

Women colleagues struggled in the euphemistically named 'Women's Writing Group' on Fridays to share our early attempts at writing for social work publication and to theorise our activism. We all found 'doing it' was always so much easier than 'writing about it', but it was always fun and incredibly supportive. One of our mottos was 'don't agonise, theorise' and, of course, 'the personal is political'. When I reread some of our early theoretical work now, I am struck by the sisterhood, wit, audacity and flair implicit in the work. We went away several times to Women and Community Development writing weekends at Common Ground, a community retreat north of Melbourne, to explore our feminist praxis, and to work out how to operate effectively in male-dominated universities and other organisations. We even talked about how to analyse our relationships with our mothers, which we believed was a necessary requirement to being strong women. We were wonderfully ambitious and immodest in our feminist social work education collective.

The Western Regional Council for Social Development and Women in Welfare Education

Social work education and practice at this time was increasingly directed towards both personal and social change, and giving people greater power and control over the decisions which affected their lives. Practice initiatives included participation of consumers in the delivery of all human services, the encouragement of self-help groups, the de-professionalisation of social work and the transference of specific skills to others in the community, the regionalisation and localisation of service delivery and support for initiatives which identify local needs and attempt to fulfill those needs by local solutions. Empowerment was our mantra.

This type of social work clearly aimed to increase the control of people over their own lives. The Western Regional Council of Social Development social work student unit projects included supporting community interaction with the Naval Dockyard in the western suburbs. The student unit also organised peace groups, and environmental campaigns long before social sustainability emerged as a fundamental issue. The students also resourced unemployed workers through the Unemployed Workers Union representing former industrial workers who had lost their jobs with the demise of secondary industry in the western suburbs. They also worked in feminist organisations such as the Women of the West, which was then located in local feminist politician Joan Kirner's electoral office. Joan later become Victoria's first woman Premier.

My social work academic colleagues shaped the PIT/ RMIT Social Work program and influenced progressive social work in Victoria, nationally and internationally, an influence lasting to this day. Wendy Weeks' feminist leadership role in Women in Welfare Education (WIWE) typified this, alongside her many other strategic achievements.[4] She worked to establish the first Centre Against Sexual Assault House (CASA House) in 1986. This was the first sexual assault counseling and advocacy service committed to feminist practice principles. Wendy was also instrumental in arranging the first Aboriginal visiting scholar at Phillip in 1988, Lilla Watson, and introducing Indigenous Studies into the Melbourne University social work program in 1995. Hurriyet Babacan developed early courses in anti-racist social work, while I contributed to anti-sexist and feminist curriculum, particularly in community work as well

[4] W. Weeks, 'Feminist Principles for Community Work', *Women in Welfare Education Journal*, 1(1), 19-44.

as developing innovative field education centred on community activism. Personal, political and professional boundaries were unimportant in our vision of the new social work.

Women in Welfare Education (WIWE) explored the ways in which feminists working in social work education in Australian Schools of Social Work transformed their practice and lives through the 1980s and early 1990s. We experienced changes in the policy context, developed theories which informed education and practice, and contributed to feminist theory, such as taking account of gender in social policy, and the impact of the women's movement on service delivery and on women's personal lives. We worked to provide positive, clear strategies to contribute to a reinvigorated feminism and women's movement.

The strength of WIWE lay in its collectivising of women's experiences and emphasiseng that 'the personal is political'. The implications for feminist practice and scholarship were always central. For many of us, it was a safe space to explore feminist scholarship. WIWE led to an awareness of the feminist agenda in social policy and social work and encouraged feminist scholarship and women's leadership. We argued that a women's place was everywhere, and that women as the majority of community sector workers were eminently qualified for leadership roles in social work organisations, as well as the academy. WIWE introduced me to NSW feminist academics, including my friend and colleague Carolyn Noble, who exemplifies feminist leadership both locally and internationally, along with many other wonderful feminist academics and activists around Australia.

Feminist organising in the Australian Carers Movement and People Together

I became actively involved in the Australian Carers Movement in the 1990s. This was arguably a significant example of feminist organising, as it promoted a social and community-based model of care, which led to the development of major continuing initiatives at Federal, State and international levels. An exploratory preliminary study for the Commonwealth Government, *Listen to the Carers* was a Carers 'Speak Out', based on feminist consciousness raising approaches, community development and action research.[5] This initiative was supported by feminists in both government and the community sector. Its significance was that it formally supported family carers (mainly women) doing the majority of unpaid elder and disability care in the community. Drawing on a strategic feminist analysis, the caring issue was portrayed as nonpartisan and attracted support from all sides of the political spectrum, contributing to the establishment of the Carer Association, Carer Program and Carer Pension, among other achievements. The strength of this movement continues and is largely due to its thoughtful social analysis, and organisational and community support, as well as policy and advocacy contribution to what was then a largely hidden social issue.

I was also involved in the early 1990s with the People Together Movement, led by two social work luminaries, Jean McCaughey, wife of the Victorian State Governor of the time and Ben Bodna, former Director General of Social Welfare Department in Victoria. The Movement was an attempt "to keep before the people of Victoria the image of a just, equitable and caring society".[6] It was a nonpartisan coalition of social welfare and faith-based community groups opposed to the conservative privatisation policies introduced by the then Victorian Liberal Premier Jeff Kennett. Jeff Kennett had attempted to cut and reshape social policy and social work

---

[5] D. Bowman, *Listen to the Carers: The Many Voices of Care* (Carers Consultation for the International Year of the Family (Australian Government Publishing Service, 1996).

[6] J. McCaughey, Closing address to People Together Annual General Meeting, Melbourne, 1993.

services in education, health and social care in Victoria, based on the privitisation model first espoused by Margaret Thatcher in the UK and Ronald Reagan in the USA in the 1980s.

The People Together Movement was successful because it appealed to the non-government former charity sector which had been the major service provider in Victoria and other states of Australia. Being led by the Governor's wife and the former head of the State Government welfare department encouraged wide-spread community opposition to the cuts to services. Communities across Victoria, especially in rural areas and regional centres, were particularly affected by hospital and school closures. People Together was also based on the Speak Out model, whereby communities were invited to present submissions and evidence at public or community hearings on the effects of the under-funding and privitisation on services and users. Perhaps it is not surprising, given the strength of the sector and widespread support of communities and the media and press, that this movement achieved its objective and more. Jeff Kennett's conservative state government was voted out in October 1999 and was replaced two more consultative and progressive Labor state governments until 2010.

Social work as an industrial organisation

Another significant organisation reflecting my interest in new left theory and community organising, was the Australian Social Welfare Union which was established in 1976. The Australian Social Welfare Union (ASWU) was formed as a radical alternative to the Australian Association of Social Workers (AASW). Unable to develop sufficient membership to survive on its own, the ASWU amalgamated with the Australian Services Union (ASU) in 1992. The ASU still exists as an activist industrial union representing community sector workers throughout Australia. It is worth pondering whether social work's radical heart would have been better served if the ASWU had continued to represent social workers beyond the early 1990s. However, the ASU continues to critique conservative social policy agendas nationally and globally. It advances the interests of community sector workers and service users, including recent critiques of privatisation and new public private partnerships which currently dominate social policy agendas. The ASU remains engaged in a wide range of social policy debates and community activism, in sharp contrast to their traditional rival the Australian Association of Social Workers which has a more professional focus.

During the period under review, I witnessed the rise of new occupations claiming similar domains of practice to social work. One contested relationship has been between social work and welfare work. Some Australian welfare workers provided a strident critique of this relationship and argued that social work refused to acknowledge welfare workers through membership in the professional association because of a perceived inherent class distinction. Many welfare workers came from working-class backgrounds while social workers were more typically from the middle class, from the 'bourgeoisie'. This indicated the profession was in fact 'elitist' as working-class people could not afford to go to university before the Whitlam government 1972-75 introduced free university education. Welfare workers also tended to be older women with more extensive domestic family responsibilities who often worked whilst studying. Also, many welfare workers had the experience of being a 'client' and this was often their motivation to study. Fortunately, today, social workers are no longer the 'daughters' of the 'well-to-do' 'doing good'. Social workers now come from diverse backgrounds and experiences.

Significantly, social welfare work education was introduced into Australia during the early 1970s when the demand for workers increased and the small social work programs were not able to respond to increased demand. Each state developed strategies to suit their particular circumstances. The common theme was the development of 'quick' training programs to suit the needs of the employer. However, from the 1980s onwards, a number of universities developed programs in welfare studies, and currently there are ten welfare studies programs in Australian Universities. These are mainly three-year degree programs, most located within Social Work Units. This can be explained through the need of universities to market themselves and develop courses with wide appeal. For Universities, welfare studies courses also offer advantages as they have less restricted course requirements, as they are not covered by Australian Association of Social Workers Policy and Procedures. Indeed, the AASW can arguably be seen as having a constraining effect on social work, as it continues to adopt a conservative charity model of social work rather than actively pursuing its historical social justice commitment.

The AASW, which was established in 1946, has had a very complex relationship with the community sector. There have been attempts to bring care professionals together but these have been largely opposed by the AASW. In the early 1970s, at the height of the de-professionalisation drive, the more radical social workers in the AASW sought to have the association opened up to all those working in human services. What was unique at that time was that the AASW was also a union registered with the Commonwealth Arbitration Court in 1955[7] and the de-professionalisation movement wanted to open the union up to include welfare workers and other community sector workers. A referendum was held and, as noted earlier, the AASW split into two separate organisations: the professional association of social

---

[7] J. Lawrence, *Professional Social Work in Australia* (Australian National University, 1965).

workers that kept the name AASW, and the Australian Social Welfare Union (ASWU).

In the late 1980s and early 1990s, the Australian Labor Government embarked on a training agenda for multi-skilling its workforce for a more open economy. Workers were encouraged to undertake further training, employers were offered incentives for training their workforce, and training institutes looked at closer cooperation with industry needs. There was also to be articulation between the various courses so individuals could advance through training programs to gain certificates, diplomas and eventually degrees. Industry Training Boards linked to the Australian Services Union and Health Unions were developed to equip workers for the burgeoning health and community services sector and funding was made available for each industry to undertake projects involved in skill and career development. However, by then, the AASW had changed its focus to campaign for professional registration, which has still not been achieved and has an ever narrower membership base.

The AASW has moved further away from the broader more political and activist view of social policy and social work practice in the community which characterised the period reviewed in this chapter. Social work would be a very different profession today, if the creation of the Australian Social Welfare Union in the mid1970s had survived as a break-away industrial challenge to the AASW because it reflected the deprofessionalisation and activism of the sector, with its growing strength and huge workforce.

The future direction of radical social work education

For social work education in Australia, the period of rapid expansion in social work education in the 1970s, meant that while in 1964 four recognised Departments of Social Work produced an annual total of 100 graduates, within 12 years, in 1976, there were

14 courses which produced 500 graduates. A major factor was the Federal election of the ALP to government in 1972. Federal Labor policies pursued policies of rapid expansion in both tertiary education and social welfare services. Social work education came to be viewed favourably by university administrators seeking to develop their institutions and by social welfare administrators seeking trained staff for a range of new programs. Labour power studies suggested acute shortages of social workers would persist into the future and social work education bore all the hallmarks of a growth industry.

Change occurred, however, with the Federal election of December 1975 and the return of a Liberal Country Party government committed to public expenditure restraint. This change continued with the election of the Hawke and Keating ALP governments in the 1980s with their new commitment to corporatism and economic liberalism. This marked a significant retreat from the development of the welfare state in Australia, which was expanded in the Whitlam era. It also reflects an increasing attachment to economic rationalism and managerialism which continues to reshape and limit social work to this day. Although the number of universities offering social work programs has continued to grow (there are 32 Schools of Social Work in Australia at the time of writing), the educational imperatives have shifted from critical social theory and activism to a more conservative educational agenda. Case work and case management are back in social work education and practice, reflecting the continuing professional dominance of traditional models. Community development and activism are on the wane, at the same time as we struggle to understand the influences of economic globalisation, materialism and capitalism, accompanied by more conservative global and regional politics. While parts of social work education attempt to resist a right-wing global, national and local agenda which is unashamedly racist, sexist, nationalist and anti-intellectual, is it any wonder some of us are nostalgic for the 1970s and yearn for a return to radical social work politics?

One of the great virtues of social workers is that, based on our social justice and human rights value base, many of us think politically, especially in times of crisis and the examples mentioned in this chapter speak to this ongoing need for a political response. Social work's foundational values of equality and justice and taking a political stance in defence of these values is a consistent feature of critical and radical social work. Critical theory which promotes social and economic justice is a committed approach situated within the radical tradition of Australian social work. I have been fortunate to be a small part of this radical tradition. Radical social work locates individual experience within wider social structures and challenges oppression through progressive social policy and practice. However, the absence of organised social movements for radical change in the current neoliberal era is especially challenging for those of us who are continuing to develop a radical political analysis. While certain sectors in mainstream social work continue to view social work as being about adjustment rather than social change, we face the danger or returning to the charity model of welfare. We need to strengthen the new politics and practices of radical social work in the 21st century to respond to the vast inequalities generated by contemporary economic policies. Hopefully, the new breed of radical social workers will be up to the task ahead.

An Afterword:

From Personal Retrospectives to Future Activism

Jim Ife

The chapters in this book represent a broad range of activism and issues. It is not a 'balanced' selection, and represents in part the vagaries of the process of producing a collection such as this. Some potential authors were unable to contribute to the collection, because
of work or personal commitments, and had they been included the
range of topics would have been different. In addition, authors were
given the freedom to choose their topics; some chose to tell the story
of their career, including several different issues for activist engagement, while others chose to concentrate on only one or two aspects
of their work; again, different choices would have led to a different
coverage of topics. This has resulted in a collection where some
issues are perhaps over-represented, while others are less well covered. The selection of topics also reflects the period of which we
are writing, and the topics that were seen as important, engaging
the attention of social workers, at the time. So it is worth a more
detailed reflection on the issues covered in this selection, and more
significantly perhaps on the issues that are absent, as we look back
on the period 1970-2000 with the advantage of hindsight.

Many of the chapters are concerned, in whole or in part, with
gender, and gender receives more coverage in this collection than
other dimensions of disadvantage. Feminism and the women's
movement were particularly important in informing the radical critique of many social workers in the 1970s and 1980s, especially
(though not exclusively) women social workers, and so the empha-

sis on gender in this collection is hardly surprising. These chapters (especially Chapters 2, 5, 9, 10, 11, 13, and 19) give a vivid sense of the excitement and optimism of the social workers at the time who found their lives and practices transformed by becoming actively involved in the women's movement and applying its analysis and commitment to social work scholarship and practice. Feminism has remained a centrally important aspect of radical and critical social work through to the present day.

Although gender is strongly represented in the chapters, it is worth noting that there are some aspects of gender and sex, such as sexuality and men's responses to feminism, that are not so well covered. There is only one chapter (Chapter 12) dealing with masculinities, and one (Chapter 13) dealing with LGBTIQ matters, and this is largely concerned with struggles for gay and lesbian recognition. Thus in this collection, gender is still seen largely in binary terms, and as a matter primarily for women authors/activists, reflecting the narratives of the period in question. More recently, there has been a concern with dismantling the binary, and seeing in bi- trans- and inter- sexualities a blurring of the conventional binary boundaries. There is now a growing understanding in the West that in some other cultural traditions there are more than two recognised genders, and that, as well as affirming the continuing imperative of working to abolish patriarchy, 'gender' must not be reduced to the simple binaries that underpinned much of the feminist writing of the 1970s and 1980s.

It is perhaps surprising that more chapters did not reflect on Marxist perspectives and a class analysis, though it is present in some chapters (particularly Chapter 6) and assumed in others. This is partly a result of author choice; some authors could easily have chosen to write on more class-based struggles from their careers. But two other explanations also suggest themselves. One is that from the 1990s onwards, we became more influenced by 'identity politics' than by class politics in thinking about social work struggles, in line with dominant narratives of the time (is radical social work so 'radical' after all, if we follow such trends so easily?), and this led our retrospectives away from the Marxism that was so influential in radical social work in the 1970s. At the time of writing, this is reflected in the relative lack of interest in poverty/ inequality as a research agenda for social work schools, compared with more popular areas such as gender, domestic violence, race, mental health, and so on, despite the obscenity of increasing inequality both nationally and globally in these days of turbo-charged neoliberalism. Another possible explanation, so clearly articulated in Chapters 5 and 6, is that there is a sense of failure to achieve the goals of Marxist social work. It made a lot of sense in theory, but we discovered that it was simply not possible to overthrow capitalism through social work practice alone; in 2017 such an idea sounds utterly naïve, but it was the tacit assumption behind some aspects of 'radical social work' in the heady times of the 1970s. Perhaps a sense of failure has resulted in the authors choosing not to emphasise class struggle and a Marxist analysis which was so strongly foregrounded in the radical social work of the 1970s, a formative decade for most of the authors represented here. It is easier to recount stories of achievement than stories of failure. In retrospect, gender struggles were relatively more successful than class struggles in achieving actual results, and feminist social workers can recount more tangible successes than Marxist social workers. The recognition of women has changed significantly since the 1970s, while the conditions of workers have, if anything, deteriorated with increased precarity, frozen wages and decreased unionisation – and so it is perhaps not so surprising that the achievements of the women's movement, though far from complete (patriarchy is still alive and well), figure more prominently in the retrospective accounts in this book.

Another important theoretical development which is perhaps not so strongly represented in these chapters is postmodernism, though it is mentioned in several chapters, especially Chapters 11 and 17. Postmodernism was a very important theoretical position for many social workers in the 1990s. Again, one of the problems for social workers excited by postmodernism is the difficulty of translating a powerful theoretical perspective (or more correctly, perspectives) into action. Postmodernism enables one to think in a creative way, but social workers, including radical social workers, are driven by the need for action. Of course the chapters in this book are largely stories of action rather than of theoretical analysis, but it is interesting that such an important perspective from the 1990s is not more strongly represented.

There are two chapters (Chapters 14 and 15) that deal with Indigenous struggles, which of course are of critical importance for Australian social work, and were important during the period this book reflects. Indigenous struggles are also discussed in Chapters 16 and 18. A reflection on more recent times, however, would emphasise not only the political struggles of Indigenous Australians, but also the cultural and particularly the epistemological struggles, as there is more awareness in the wider community of the importance of Indigenous world views in moving to more ecologically sustainable ways of living.

There is, however, no content in this book, other than a brief discussion in Chapter 13, relating to multicultural Australia, and the struggles of immigrant groups against racism and towards meaningful 'inclusion' in Australian society. Radical social work in the 70s 80s and 90s did very little to engage with, or support, these struggles, though there were of course some social workers active in this area. In recent times, with the rise of Islamaphobia and more virulent forms of racism in Australia (dating from the Howard Government's influence from the mid-1990s), this has become more of a concern for radical social workers, especially those who have supported refugees and asylum seekers (see Chapter 16). But racism was alive and well in Australia before this, and many immigrant communities' struggles were of little interest to those of us who wanted radical change in the system. It represents a significant blind spot in the radical social work movement of the time.

In retrospect, we can see that radical social work at that time lacked an analysis of its own whiteness, a lack which largely persists to this day. Social work curricula, including units or electives in critical or radical social work, often do not include an analysis of whiteness, and of how 'radical social work' has operated from a position of unexamined white privilege, with the associated epistemological assumptions unacknowledged. This can be seen in the literature drawn on by critical or radical social workers: most of it is from the Anglosphere (Australia, Aotearoa/New Zealand, Canada, USA, UK) sometimes extended to include French or German philosophers, as if this is the only source of valid critical knowledge. Postcolonial writers have become more important in recent years, though were largely absent from 'radical social work literature' in the 1970s to 1990s. And Southern epistemologies, including the knowledge systems of Indigenous Australians, have only recently begun to be taken seriously in Anglosphere social work; certainly they were invisible in the social work of the period covered by this book. Future 'radical social work' will need to take these cultural and epistemological challenges more seriously.

Another notable omission from the book is the struggles of people with disabilities. This is partly the result of an invited author being unable to contribute a chapter, but it still reflects the marginal status of disability within critical or radical social work. Disability advocates and activists have undertaken very important work, but it is still the case that disability remains a marginal category in social work, compared with more 'centre stage' issues such as child protection, domestic violence and metal health. Its absence from this collection will be no surprise to many readers.

There is only one chapter (Chapter 7) that deals with environmental issues, as these were largely not of concern to social workers in the decades covered here, even though they were high on the agenda of many more broadly-based activists concerned to build a better world. A more contemporary collection of chapters on radical social work practice would surely include more emphasis in this area, given the dramatic social costs of environmental degradation, the role social workers have played in disaster relief and reconstruction, and the impending social, economic and political crises which will surely be the result of ecological irresponsibility as we enter the period of the Anthropocene. These crises will have most impact on the most disadvantaged and vulnerable, so must be of primary concern for social workers.

The chapters in this book represent important and inspiring attempts by social workers to address significant issues of social justice during three decades of major change in Australia. Social workers have played important roles in trying to shape these changes, and in seeking to work against those changes that reduced options for disadvantaged groups in Australian society. But we must ask how successful were radical social workers in achieving their aims? The answers emerging from these chapters are mixed; some are stories of success, and others are stories of failure. But to make such binary judgements is too simplistic. All the chapters in this book describe events where the author, in trying to effect radical change, achieved things that were less dramatic, but perhaps ultimately more long-lasting. As all activists are aware, the little things are important. The social workers who contributed to this book, through countless interactions, conversations, dialogue, teaching, writing or argument, have had their impact on others. Every act we undertake changes the world, and interactions with colleagues, students, teachers, managers, friends and opponents can initiate small changes in world view, in motivation, in understanding and in action, which in turn have further consequences of which we can never be aware. The ripple effects of attempts at radical change – even if the attempts themselves were less than fully successful – can be long-lasting and significant. The authors of these chapters, in their different ways, have had a major impact on the understanding and the work of many social workers and others in Australia, and indeed beyond Australia's borders. Australian social work, wider Australian society, and social work internationally, are the richer because of their work.

What, then, of the future? Despite the frightening uncertainties as we contemplate the future in this second decade of the 21st century, there is one thing of which we can be certain: there will be more need than ever for radical activist social workers who can challenge the structures and discourses of disadvantage. In times of increasing inequality, and increasing instability, there will inevitably open up spaces for creative action and the promotion of meaningful social change in the cause of social justice; these are the spaces where social workers need to be active. But we also see at the time of writing a resurgence of conservatism within social work; ground down by relentless neoliberal ideology and managerial practice both in social agencies and in universities, it is hard for social workers to retain a vision of alternatives and to find the energy for creative activism. Yet activism in other arenas is on the rise – especially activism around impending ecological crises, Indigenous rights, refugees, and the politics of austerity – and social workers have much to contribute to these movements. Radical social work, in a country like Australia, has perhaps never been so challenging and so necessary at the same time.

The future of radical social work will be different from the stories in this book, as Australia is, and will be, a different place from the experience of the 70s, 80s and 90s. We are now so much more aware of the reality of globalisation, which we were only beginning to talk about in the 1990s. Refugees and asylum seekers in unanticipated numbers, with the resultant racism and xenophobia, have posed new challenges for social workers and others concerned with social justice. The crisis of the state, that we liked to analyse in the 1970s, has become a reality with the impacts widely felt by all, but especially the most vulnerable as the welfare state is continually eroded. Precarity has become the norm for many people in the workforce, with the increase in temporary, part-time and insecure working conditions. All these trends seem likely to get worse rather than better, as globalised neo-liberalism enters its inevitable time of crisis.

Social media and the internet have significantly changed the nature of activism and of social work. Not only has social media opened up exciting new forms of activism and connection, which social workers are learning to utilise, it has also made possible greater surveillance and control of activism by the state and by other powerful coercive interests, globally, nationally and locally. It seems certain that, in times of instability and crisis, we will see more draconian measures introduced to control those who dare to challenge the agenda of the powerful.

The rise of computer power and artificial intelligence represents a further challenge that we could afford to ignore prior to 2000, but must now confront. Automation will make many jobs redundant, including some aspects of social work, especially social work that is nothing more than assessment and referral according to some standardised computerised rubric. Whether social work will be able to reinvent itself, based on less mechanistic and more relationship-based forms of practice, which after all represent social work's origins, remains an open question. Certainly an automated social work is hardly likely to be radical, and so radical social work will need to address this new challenge to its on-going viability. This is yet another way in which the context of radical practice has significantly changed from the three decades that are the context of this book.

In addition, the certainties that were taken for granted in the 30 year period that is the main focus of this book (economic stability, continuing growth and prosperity, the certainties of modernity, the importance of expertise, the viability of 'democracy', the value of some form of welfare state and the certainty of some form of viable future for humanity) no longer apply. The threat of ecological catastrophe, with associated economic, political and cultural collapse, provides a different backdrop for any activist work. Despite these differences, there are also continuities both in social work and in radical activism, and it is important for activists to remember their historical roots. There will be important lessons that can be learned from the experiences of the chapters in this book, and individual readers will make of these stories what they will. But social work, activism and radical action will have to be reinvented to be effective in the very different climate of 2020 and beyond. It will be up to new generations of social work activists to take up these challenges.

www.ingramcontent.com/pod-product-compliance
Lightning Source LLC
Chambersburg PA
CBHW060137280326
41932CB00012B/1546